Ho

Po

Homo americanus: Child of the Postmodern Age

Tomislav Sunic

Foreword by Professor Kevin MacDonald

Homo americanus:
Child of the
Postmodern Age

Table of Contents

Preface

A preface to a book may serve as the author's place for justifying his scriptural shortcomings. In some cases it tacitly serves as a place for his ethical and ideological disclaimers. Also, when uncertain of the general direction of his main thesis, the author may resort to excuses in his preface, as if wishing to forestall the reader from passing harsh judgments against him, and also nudge him into showing more comprehension and compassion for his often mediocre prose. Some readers, right at the start of this book, may accuse me of similar shortcomings, that is, of presenting my subject matter clumsily or differently from what they expected. I am aware that the subject discussed in the book is very large. Every subtitle in this book could generate several volumes of deeper analyses and each minor bibliographic note at the end of the book could expand into a load of books able to fill an entire library shelf.

However much the vast topic of America and Americanism has the advantage of offering an author methodological and ideological latitudes, it also has its limits. The fluid and much abused word "Americanism" contains an impressive inventory of concepts, each consisting of dozens of distinctive elements and each requiring its own mode of analysis. I conceived of this book as a short summary of ideas by authors critical of Americanism and its two main facets: belief in progress and egalitarianism.

The reader will notice that I mainly use a descriptive style, translating and quoting European and American authors who write from their own perspectives and within their own fields of study about various aspects of *Homo americanus*, without necessarily ascribing value judgments to my own paragraphs. Toward the end of the book, however, I use a more analytical approach, which to some extent, may be viewed by the reader as colored by my own biased assessments. Having lived in Europe and America, having experienced lengthy spans and spasms of life in communism and capitalism, I am trying to project myself into two diverse geopolitical and socio-historical perspectives — both as a critic of Americanism from within and as a critic of Americanism from without; both as a subject of criticism and as the object of criticism. I am trying, however, to avoid the anti-American clichés that still appear among many cultivated European authors and which are often founded on sketchy, vicarious, second-hand hearsay knowledge of America. In fact, I am also arguing that Americanism, with a different system of values, different people in charge of cultural hegemony, and of course, under a different historical setting, could have become a true motivating force of creativity for a large number of people of European extraction.

This book contains quotations and descriptions by authors who are savants in the fields of sociobiology, philosophy, history and literature. The reason I am using an interdisciplinary approach to such a vast topic lies in the fact that I have always avoided a single approach in the humanities. The manner in which the social sciences has been taught in Europe and America since 1945, both in terms of methods and content, has been heavily determined by the referents of antifascism and democracy. Authors, even when mildly critical of liberalism, parliamentary democracy, or multiculturalism, have had marginal readership, which does not exclude the likelihood of the same fate for the present book and its author.

In understanding the spirit of Americanism, be its good or bad side, it is my view that American novelists or essayists like Sinclair Lewis, Henry Miller, Edgar Allan Poe, or H.L. Mencken, let alone French novelists, L. F. Céline, Henry de Montherlant, Jean Cau, or the German Joachim Fernau, to name only a few, can better bring us the stench or beauty of Americanism than hundreds of sociologists, political scientists, eugenicists, and other experts dealing with the subject matter of Americanism within their own narrow field of specialization. Of course, one could study *Homo americanus*, that is the proverbial American man, from the sociobiological perspective; or for that matter one might describe the American life style from the point of a view of a clinical psychologist or a criminologist. One could also use the field of religious studies in examining American foreign policy. All these approaches are valid, but when taken separately and when disconnected from each other, they lead to a boring area study and they also show signs of academic reductionism. It is the intent of this book to reject a one way specialized approach in studying Americanism and try to encompass instead as many other approaches in social science as possible. For that matter, I hope the book will be a good introduction for the future study of Americanism. I have made an effort to describe American man as observed by a cultivated European, but I also examine the self-perception of American citizens.

When a reader opens up a book dealing with a social phenomenon, it is commendable that he looks first into the author's ethnic, social, racial, and historical pedigree. Do not we all have prejudices, even if we do not wish to admit to the fact? And are not our views, however sophisticated and learned they may be, also colored by our racial origin, our family tree, and our early upbringing? This is in particular true when studying contemporary history which this book also uses as a framework for analyzing *Homo americanus*.

A cautionary word needs to be added. The English historian Edward Carr, once wrote that before studying history a student or a reader must first study the historian. This same principle of positive or negative empathy with any author must be applied in any field of social science. Therefore, a reader of this book is justified to raise the question regarding my motives in writing this book. Also, he should ask me a standard question as to who is this book designed for? Hence the eternal: *Cui bono?*

A reader will note that a large number of authors quoted in this book had or still have a reputation of being on the right side of political spectrum, and are often dubbed in the liberal and socialist vernacular as "right-wingers," "nationalists," or "racists." Being a user but also a victim of the English language and its meta-language, as it is in standard use by the late 20th and early 21st century, this may also apply to the choice of my own words in the present text. Many words used in this book, such as "traditionalists," "racialists," "right-wingers," although having politically negative connotation, once upon a time had a neutral or positive connotation. For instance, the word "democracy," acquired by the late 20th century a sacrosanct meaning; it is viewed as a crowning glory for normative political discourse. However, it cannot be ruled out that a hundred years from now, this word will acquire a pejorative meaning and might be avoided like the plague by future opinion makers or the future ruling class in America. I must admit that in my quotations I largely resort to anti-liberal and so-called "right-wing" authors whose critical vision of Americanism has been ostracized or has not received a due hearing. In my chapter on postmodernity and the English language, I examine in more detail the semantic distortions that many English American words were subjected to in the course of the 20th century.

Had I quoted or referred to authors of the opposite ideological background, who are more in line with the egalitarian, democratized, and Americanized spirit of the time, this book would have taken a different turn. To put it differently, any book, dealing with contemporary ideas, however impartial its author may be, carries a distinct flavor that can be best spotted by looking at the list of quoted and bibliography.

The prime task of this book, however, is to redefine some concepts, provide a different meaning to those concepts, and attempt to bring those concepts closer to the reader. In the conclusion of my book, which deals with the notion of democracy in postmodernity, I am "deconstructing" concepts that have been part of the political and media environment since 1945. Therefore, the book can also be seen as an exercise in linguistic revisionism, in so far as it revises the conventional wisdom linked to the concept of Americanism and the recent history of political ideas. Luckily, the unwritten rules of postmodernity encourage everybody to critically examine all grand narratives, including the American narrative of permanent economic progress.

It is a standard procedure in the author's preface to enumerate persons who helped him finish the book. I must admit that I did most of the homework and most of the footwork myself. The idea to write this book and with this title came to me during the conference organized by the Charles Martel Society, in Washington DC, in October 2005. I was then a guest of honor and a speaker on the topic of Americanism. The editorial board of the *Occidental Quarterly* and the publisher Mr. William Regnery deserve credit for organizing that venue. Later, the idea came to me to expand the topic of my speech into a more academic treatise, yet without resorting to an esoteric and a too academic language. Some smaller parts of the book have already been published in different forms, or in an abridged version, in French and English, notably in the journals, *The World and I*, *The Occidental Quarterly*, and *Catholica*. Some thoughts on Americanism also derive from my book *Americka ideologija* which I wrote in the Croatian language in 1993.

I need to mention the names of colleagues and friends who made valuable suggestions and who helped me with some technical issues, including the direction of my thoughts. Without them I would have never started nor finished this book. Joe Pryce from New York, a man unknown outside literary circles, a man of frail health yet of staggering erudition, helped me much with bibliography, particularly when dealing with American Puritanism. Professor Patrick McNally from Japan helped polish up my text. So did the author and artist Jonathan Bowden from London. Bowden's sense of pedantry was of great help in rendering my prose accessible to the reader of little or no background in the social sciences. I also wish to thank the philosopher Alain de Benoist, who himself wrote much on Americanism. My former American mentor, Professor Paul Gottfried, an erudite scholar and a connoisseur of the liberal system in America, also deserves my thanks. I must mention Flemish-European writer Robert Steuckers, whose proficiency in several languages, as well as his knowledge of Western intellectual heritage, helped him easily follow my own train of thought. Also, many thanks to friends David Yates, Troy Southgate from London, the editor and writer Tord Morsund from Norway, and to other intellectual heavy weights, friends and scholars of diverse temperament. Some of these scholars mentioned herein do not agree with each other on many points regarding the American system, nor would they agree with all of my analyses. I respect, however, their free spirit, their tolerance, their great erudition—and their help.

Lastly, to my close friend David Stennett, a true American rebel who now resides in Europe, I must credit with doing the final proofreading and stylization. I hope these colleagues and friends whose names are mentioned above will not be the only ones to read this book.

Zagreb, Croatia
January 2007

Foreword to Homo americanus:
Child of the Postmodern Age by Tomislav Sunic

Perhaps because of America's role as lone international superpower, Americans live in a rather self-absorbed, egocentric universe in which the opinions of non-Americans really don't matter much. This is unfortunate because, just as in one's personal life, it's wise to at least know how others see you, and especially so if the other is a keen observer.

Tomislav Sunic is such an observer. As someone who has lived under communism and has seen firsthand the workings of state terror, he is in a unique position to describe the current slide of America into what he aptly terms "soft totalitarianism." This regime is maintained less by brute force than by an unrelenting, enormously sophisticated, and massively effective campaign to contain political and cultural activity within very narrow boundaries. Dissenters are not trundled off to jail or beaten with truncheons, but are quietly ignored and marginalized. Or they are held up to public disgrace, and, wherever possible, removed from their livelihoods.

The regime is maintained by a consensus that has become part of the furniture of life, repeated endlessly in the major media and reassuringly affirmed by wise-looking professors at prestigious universities. To dissent from this consensus removes one from the mainstream and stigmatizes one as immoral and quite possibly suffering from a psychiatric disorder. One immediately thinks of attitudes on immigration. Even the most fearless mainstream opponents of immigration restrict their opposition to illegal immigrants and are careful to couch their arguments in economic or cultural (but never ethnic or racial) terms.[1] One simply cannot mention in polite company that the end result of this massive influx of peoples into the traditional homelands of European peoples will be displacement, a decline in their power, and ultimately, perhaps, their disappearance as an identifiable people. But there are a host of other issues that are at least as untouchable as immigration.

Soft totalitarian regimes can only be maintained by a sense of moral and intellectual legitimacy - the willing assent of the vast majority of the people. Without this legitimacy, the entire apparatus of cultural control either disintegrates or transforms into hard totalitarianism - the truncheons and the gulags. But here there is a major difference between communism in Eastern Europe and the current cultural regime in the United States. As Sunic notes, "Behind the communist semantics in Eastern Europe there loomed a make-believe system in which nobody truly believed and where everybody, including former communist party dignitaries made fun of in private." However, "in America, by contrast, many serious people, politicians, and scholars, let alone the masses, believe in...the message of the media." The people who dissent from the American consensus have been successfully relegated to the fringes. The gods are still worshiped.

Sunic sees quite clearly that this moral and intellectual legitimacy is fundamentally the result of the triumph of the left in World War II. This transformation occurred first in Western Europe which has now mostly moved well beyond soft totalitarianism to the beginnings or a gulag system where there are formal legal sanctions for thought crimes. The thought crimes, enforced by liberal and conservative European governments alike, are designed to enforce the dogmas of leftist orthodoxy, most notably everything related to multiculturalism, race, immigration, and the Holocaust. Even in England, the *font et origo* of American democracy, academics are removed for stating their beliefs on scientific evidence on race differences in intelligence or criminality. (For example, in 2006 Frank Ellis of the University of Leeds was suspended for statements supporting race differences in intelligence.)[2] Legal sanctions enforce orthodoxies in the area of multiculturalism and anything having to do with the fascist past.

In searching for the origins of this phenomenon, one must begin, as Sunic does, by describing the forcible imposition of leftist ideology and institutions in Germany and France after World War II. As a psychologist, I am always tempted to see the origins of leftist ideological hegemony solely in psychological terms - to wonder what incredible psychological defect would lead to a whole people to adopt an ideology in which they were cast as having a grave psychiatric defect. But first and foremost, the triumph of the left in Europe was accomplished via a purge and re-education of intellectuals, educators and media figures.

As Sunic notes, the most obvious beneficiaries of this sea change were the major leftist ideologies of the 20th century: Marxism, psychoanalysis, and the Frankfurt School. Since much of my writing deals with Jewish issues, I can't help noting that these ideologies have in common that they are all part of the "Culture of Critique": Intellectual and political movements originated and dominated by Jews and intended by their Jewish participants as advancing Jewish interests, such as ending anti-Semitism.

Any claim that an intellectual or political movement is or was a "Jewish" movement immediately raises all kinds of red flags in most readers. Just as the ethnic interests of Europeans cannot be mentioned in discussing the effects of immigration, the Jewish identifications and commitments of the people who originated and disseminated these ideas has been moved to the fringes of intellectual discourse.

But research in the ethnic motivations of people is perfectly respectable. No one would be surprised if Mexican activists proudly and explicitly advocated the interests of Mexicans in immigration and affirmative action. Nor are we surprised if Jewish activists promoted the interests of Israel. By the same logic, we shouldn't be surprised if Jewish social scientists are motivated by their ethnic interests. It is an empirical question that can be investigated like any other question in the social sciences, and I think that the data confirms the hypothesis that the Jews who were central to the origins and influence of these movements had a strong Jewish identification and were motivated by their ethnic interests.

As usual, there is a double standard here. It is a routine for scientists like Arthur Jensen, J. Philippe Rushton, or Richard Lynn to be called racists when they call attention to the biological roots of race differences in intelligence or criminality. And my writing on how Jews have pursued their ethnic interests in the intellectual and political arena has been termed "anti-Semitism" on more than one occasion.

Implicitly the charge of racism or anti-Semitism assumes that these writers are nothing more than ethnic activists and that their claims of scientific truth are nothing more than a fig leaf covering their ethnic interests - exactly the claim that I am making about the role of Jews in the triumph of Marxism, psychoanalysis, and the Frankfurt School. Unfortunately, the people making these charges of "racism" and "anti-Semitism" typically feel no need to dispute the scientific accuracy of the theories they are trying to discredit or even try to provide evidence of ethnic motivation of the scientists involved. Simply making the charge is sufficient. Such is the power of the left.

The Frankfurt School's Program of Ethnic Warfare

Sunic is quite correct in directing most of his attention to the Frankfurt School. The Frankfurt School developed a devastatingly effective ideology that continues to reverberate in the contemporary world even after the fall from grace of Communism and psychoanalysis.

Fundamentally the Frankfurt School attempted to develop an ideology that pathologized National Socialism. Because National Socialism was first and foremost a movement of ethnic cohesion, it is not surprising that the ideology of the Frankfurt School called into question all of the sources of cohesion of Western societies: Family, religion, culture, and race/ethnicity. From the beginning there was a rejection of value-free social science research ("the fetishism of facts") in favor of the fundamental priority of a moral perspective in which Western societies were to be transformed into utopias of cultural pluralism.

According to the Frankfurt School ideology, Europeans who identify with family, nation or race suffer from a psychiatric disorder. In the ideal Frankfurt School world, Western nations would become therapeutic states. They would be dedicated to rooting out the remnants of adherence to traditional cultural forms of family, nation, religion and race in their citizens. And they would do so in the interests of promoting mental health not to mention moral rectitude.

The basic logic pursued by the Frankfurt School stemmed from the fact that positive attitudes toward church, community, nation and race tend to result in negative attitudes toward people from different religions, communities, nations and races. As a result, successful families that inculcate family pride in their children were seen by the Frankfurt School as sources of pathology. For example, *The Authoritarian Personality* - a major work of the Frankfurt School intended for an American audience - claimed that expressions of family pride were "a setting off of a homogeneous totalitarian family against the rest of the world."

In this upside-down world, families that are proud of their ancestors, concerned with moving up socially, or even having biological heirs are viewed as pathological. In fact, one might conclude that the real agenda of *The Authoritarian Personality* is to pathologize adaptive behavior in general. Those who value highly committed marriages and cohesive families, who are upwardly mobile and seek material resources, who are proud of their families and identify with their parents, who have high self-concepts, who believe that Christianity is a positive moral force (p. 408) and a spiritual consolation (p. 450), who strongly identify as males or females (but not both!), and who are socially successful and wish to emulate paragons of social success (e.g., American heroes) are viewed as having a psychiatric disorder.

On the other hand, those who are socially isolated, who have negative and rebellious attitudes toward their families, who are ambivalent and insecure in their sexual identities, who have low self-esteem and are filled with debilitating insecurities and conflicts (including insecurities about whether their parents loved them), who are moving downward in social status, and who have negative attitudes toward high social status and acquisition of material resources are viewed as the epitome of psychological health.

Psychoanalysis - that other pillar of 20th century leftism and the culture of critique - was obviously an ideal vehicle for creating the upside-down world of Frankfurt School ideology. A central feature of psychoanalysis is the idea that surface appearances can often overlay deep unconscious desires and conflicts. And since psychoanalysis never required any empirical evidence for such claims, it essentially allowed the Frankfurt School authors to make up any story they wanted. If the family relationships of ethnocentric subjects were very positive, Frankfurt School theorists could interpret them as surface affection masking deep, unconscious hostilities toward their parents. Any shred of negative feelings by ethnocentric subjects toward their parents then became a lever they could use to create an imaginary world of suppressed hostility masked by surface affection. Yet when another volume of *Studies in Prejudice* found that anti-Semites had poor relationships with their parents, the results were taken at face value.[3] The result was not science, but it was effective in achieving its political goals.

It is not difficult to suppose that the entire program of research of *The Authoritarian Personality* involved deception from beginning to end. This is suggested by the authors' clear political agenda and the pervasive double standard in which ethnocentrism and involvement in cohesive groups are seen as symptoms of psychopathology among non-Jews whereas Jews are simply viewed as victims of irrational gentile pathologies and no mention is made of Jewish ethnocentrism or allegiance to their own group.

Although it is difficult to assess the effect of works like

The Authoritarian Personality on the culture of the West, there can be little question that the thrust of this work, as well as other works inspired by psychoanalysis and its derivatives, was to pathologize adaptive behavior in general. Good parenting, upward social mobility, pride in family, religion, nation, and race were all suspect. Many of the central attitudes of the 1960s countercultural revolution find expression in *The Authoritarian Personality*, including idealizing rebellion against parents, uncommitted sexual relationships, and scorn for upward social mobility, social status, family pride, Christianity, and patriotism.

Viewed at its most abstract level, the fundamental agenda of the Frankfurt School is to influence European peoples to view concern about their own demographic and cultural eclipse as irrational and as an indication of psychopathology. People who do not identify with the basic social categories of family, religion, nation or race would not be concerned with their demise.

The Jewish Intellectual and Political Infrastructure

The success of the Frankfurt School and other varieties of leftist orthodoxy stem not only from their imposition by the military in parts of post-World War II Europe. After all, this forcible imposition did not happen in the United States or other areas of Europe, despite the fact that the Frankfurt School and other movements of "the culture of critique" have also had a great deal of influence there as well.

In the absence of a conquering army, another important source of influence, at least in America, is what one might term the Jewish intellectual and activist infrastructure of the post-World War II era. Despite its scientific weakness, the ideology that positive attitudes about family, nation, and race resulted from disturbed parent-child relationships was promulgated by the most prestigious institutions throughout the West, and especially by elite universities and the mainstream media, as the essence of scientific objectivity.

One aspect of this effort was the production of a great many other writings that reinforced the basic ideas found in *The Authoritarian Personality* and other works of the Frankfurt School. This general intellectual onslaught is important because it produced a zeitgeist that was far more effective than one or two works by isolated authors.

A good example is *The Politics of Unreason* (1970). This volume was part of the *Patterns of American Prejudice Series* funded by the Anti-Defamation League of B'nai B'rith and written by Seymour Martin Lipset and Earl Raab. (Raab and Lipset also wrote *Prejudice and Society*, published by the Anti-Defamation League in 1959.)

First and foremost, we see here the close relationship between Jewish activist organizations and academic writing on ethnic relations. In the same way, the *Studies in Prejudice Series* that produced *The Authoritarian Personality* was funded by the American Jewish Committee. Obviously there is a link between academic research on ethnic relations and Jewish activist organizations like the AJC and the ADL. Raab's career has combined academic scholarship with deep involvement as a Jewish ethnic activist. Raab was associated with the ADL and is executive director emeritus of the Perlmutter Institute for Jewish Advocacy at Brandeis University. He was also a columnist for the San Francisco *Jewish Bulletin*.

The Politics of Unreason analyses political and ideological expressions of ethnocentrism by European-derived peoples as irrational and as being unrelated to legitimate ethnic interests in retaining political power. Movements aimed at retaining or restoring the power of the European-derived majority of the United States are labeled "right-wing extremism." Their politics is "the politics of despair."[4] For Lipset and Raab, tolerance of cultural and ethnic pluralism is a defining feature of democracy, so that groups that oppose cultural and ethnic pluralism are by definition extremist and anti-democratic.

The Politics of Unreason may therefore be seen as an argument that the European peoples in the United States and other areas of the Western world should not resist declines in their cultural and demographic dominance. (Analogous arguments rarely seem to surface among Jews contemplating whether Israel should remain a Jewish state.) Attempts by majorities to resist the increase in the power and influence of other groups are contrary to "the fixed spiritual center of the democratic political process" (p. 5). "Extremism *is* anti-pluralism.... And the operational heart of extremism is the repression of difference and dissent."[5]

"Right-wing extremism" is also condemned because of its populist tendencies—its distrust of institutions that intervene between the people and their direct exercise of power. Indeed, in the post-World War II era *The Authoritarian Personality* was an important ideological weapon against historical American populist movements, especially McCarthyism.[6] "[T]he people as a whole had little understanding of liberal democracy and ...important questions of public policy would be decided by educated elites, not submitted to popular vote."[7]

The conclusion of this analysis is that democracy is identified not with the power of the people to pursue their perceived interests. Rather, government is to be the province of morally and intellectually superior elites who have no commitment to the ethnic interests of the European majority; and in an Orwellian turn, democracy is defined as guaranteeing that majorities will not resist the expansion of power of minorities even if that means a decline in their own power.

The moral and intellectual elite established by these movements dominated intellectual discourse during a critical period after World War II and leading into the countercultural revolution of the 1960s. As a result, college students during this period were powerfully socialized to adopt liberal-radical cultural and political beliefs. These effects continue into the present era.

The importance of the intellectual infrastructure can also be seen with other intellectual and political movements. Neoconservatism illustrates the common features of this intellectual infrastructure: It has been championed by a well-defined group of mainly Jewish authors writing with shared assumptions, a common institutional base in universities and think tanks, access to major media, and mutual admiration.[8] The power of the movement comes not from the work of a few individuals but from its dissemination in the media, its legitimacy in the universities, its promotion by Jewish activist organizations, and its constant repetition in slightly different forms and for different audiences by like-minded intellectuals and writers.

However, this intellectual infrastructure did not occur in a political vacuum. Also of critical importance was the "intergroup relations movement" which was dedicated to passing legislation and disseminating these ideas in the schools. The Frankfurt School was a critical part of the intellectual justification for the "intergroup relations movement" in its effort to "eliminate prejudice and discrimination against racial, ethnic, and religious minorities" in the period following World War II.[9] The intergroup relations movement was a multi-faceted effort, ranging from legal challenges to racial bias in housing, education, and public employment; legislative proposals and efforts to secure their passage into law in state and national legislative bodies; efforts to shape messages in the media; educational programs for students and teachers; and intellectual efforts to reshape the intellectual discourse of academia.

As with the other movements with strong Jewish involvement, Jewish organizations, particularly the American Jewish Committee, the American Jewish Congress, and the Anti-Defamation League, were the leaders. These organizations provided the major sources of funding, devised the tactics, and defined the objectives of the movement.

As was also the case with the movement to open up the United States to immigration from all areas of the world, a conscious aim of the intergroup relations movement was to prevent the development of a mass anti-Jewish movement in the United States: Jewish activists "saw their commitment to the intergroup relations movement as a preventive measure designed to make sure 'it' - the Nazis' war of extermination against European Jewry - never happened in America."[10] A consistent theme emphasized the benefits to be gained by increased levels of intergroup harmony. But there was no mention that some groups, particularly European-derived, non-Jewish groups, would lose economic and political power and decline in cultural influence.[11]

Based on the writings of the Frankfurt School, the intergroup relations movement disseminated the ideology that ethnocentrism and discrimination against outgroups was a mental disease and thus literally a public health problem. The assault on negative attitudes toward other groups was likened to the medical assault on deadly infectious diseases. People with the disease were described by activists as "infected"[12] and terms like "virulent anti-Semitism" were invented. Negative attitudes toward groups were viewed not as the result of competing group interests but rather as the result of individual psychopathology.[13]

The story of the Frankfurt School and the intergroup relations movement are paradigmatic example of Jews producing formidable, effective groups - groups able to have powerful, transformative effects on the peoples they live among. In the modern world, these traits of Jewish groups have resulted in great influence on the academic world, the political process, and the world of mainstream and elite media. In my book The Culture of Critique and monograph on neo-conservatism, I have identified several very influential Jewish intellectual and political movements: Boasian anthropology and the campaign against the concept of biologically based racial differences; Jewish involvement in the political left; psychoanalysis; the Frankfurt School; the New York Intellectuals; U.S. immigration policy; and neoconservatism.

The end result of the triumph of these movements has been a huge increase in Jewish power and influence, and a concomitant decrease in the political and cultural power of European-derived peoples - ethnic warfare by any other name.

The reality is that Jews have repeatedly become an elite and powerful group in societies in which they reside in sufficient numbers. Despite the fact that Jews constitute less than 3 percent of the U.S. population, the Holocaust has become a cultural icon as a direct result of Jewish activism and influence in the media, Israel has become a sacred cow in American politics, and the role of Jewish organizations in helping unleash massive multiethnic immigration into the U.S. goes unmentioned in public debate. Yuri Slezkine was quite correct to title his book on Jewish involvement with Bolshevism in the USSR *The Jewish Century*: Quite simply, Jews have been central to all of the important upheavals of the 20th century, and there doesn't seem to be any change in this trend as we enter the 21st century.

Responding to Breaches of Decorum

Because the Jewish community has been so intimately involved in creating the therapeutic state, it is noteworthy to examine how the Jewish community responds to breaches of decorum - that is, to challenges to its hegemony. Here the methods are quite similar to those used in post World War II Germany, as described by Sunic: "When silencing their critics the German authorities do not need to resort to violent means. They usually create a cultural smearing campaign whereby a cultural heretic is portrayed as a funny, pseudo-scientific crank that does not merit a place in mainstream publishing houses. Moreover, the heretic is often induced into a self-muzzling behavior making impossible any portrayal of himself as a martyr."

A good example is the response to the unflattering portrayal of the Israel Lobby, by John Mearsheimer and Stephen Walt. The power of the Israel Lobby is legendary and has had a major effect on U.S. foreign policy, including the recent war in Iraq. The typical response has included an argument or two aimed at small pieces of the edifice erected by Mearsheimer and Walt, but the real common denominators are intimidation, guilt by association, and charges of anti-Semitism. The guilt by association tactic appeared in the very earliest media accounts of the article and has continued to be invoked regularly. For example, David Duke has been repeatedly cited as supporting Mearsheimer and Walt. Alan Dershowitz's 46-page rebuttal of Mearsheimer and Walt contains no less than 14 references to David Duke and 5 references comparing Mearsheimer and Walt's article to the Protocols of the Elders of Zion. Charges of anti-Semitism abound. This occurs despite the fact that David Duke is never cited as a source on foreign policy issues or anything else in the mainstream media. However, since Duke is an activist on behalf of European-Americans who is regularly linked in the media with the Ku Klux Klan, Nazism, and "White supremacy," the technique works to marginalize the work of Mearsheimer and Walt - even though Mearsheimer and Walt have performed the ritual denunciation of Duke.

The sad reality is that discussing a whole host of issues related to Jews, even in a rational, informed manner, brings charges of anti-Semitism and incompetent scholarship ringing down from the highest reaches of academia and the elite media. One can easily see that this is a recipe for paranoia, frustration and ultimately anti-Semitism.

But the tactics of the Jewish intellectual and political infrastructure are effective because even if they create dark suspicions about the behavior of the organized Jewish community among a few and vague twinges of anxiety among many, these attitudes are forced to remain underground. They occur in the privacy of one's thoughts or in guarded conversations and coded emails. And because there is more than a grain of truth to these attitudes, for some they readily give rise to apocalyptic, impossible conspiracy theories. After all, if the reality of Jewish power on issues such as Israel is as plain as the nose on your face and you know that its power is ultimately maintained by intimidation, smear tactics, and endlessly repeated propaganda emanating from the mainstream media and elite academic institutions, at some point informed people start thinking that there's probably a whole lot else they aren't telling you.

There is an old saying that "sticks and stones can break my

bones, but words can never hurt me." However, the sad reality is that the vast majority of Americans in politics, the media, and the academic world are terrified of being labeled an anti-Semite or of having their work compared to the Protocols of the Elders of Zion. This is at least ironic, because there is an image of academicians as fearless seekers of truth. Unlike politicians who must continue to curry favor with the public in order to be reelected and unlike media figures who have no job protection, academics with tenure have no excuse for not being willing to endure labels such as "anti-Semite" or "racist" in order to pursue the truth. Part of the job - and a large part of the rationale for tenure in the first place - is that they are supposed to be willing to take unpopular positions - to forge ahead using all that brain power and expertise to chart new territories that challenge the popular wisdom.

But that image of academia is simply not based in reality, as shown by an article appearing almost two months after the publication of Mearsheimer and Walt's essay and appropriately titled "A hot paper muzzles academia."[14] "Instead of a roiling debate, most professors not only agreed to disagree but agreed to pretend publicly that there was no disagreement at all. At Harvard and other schools, the Mearsheimer-Walt paper proved simply too hot to handle —and it revealed an academia deeply split yet lamentably afraid to engage itself on one of the hottest political issues of our time. Call it the academic Cold War: distrustful factions rendered timid by the prospect of mutually assured career destruction." Professors refused to take a stand on the paper, either in favor or against. As one Ivy League professor noted, "A lot of [my colleagues] were more concerned about the academic politics of it, and where they should come down, in that sense."

Bear in mind that the vast majority of the professors unwilling to take a stand on this issue have tenure and can't literally be fired. They are afraid not of starvation but of having their career ruined by being associated with the wrong side in this debate. The downside is that they won't be invited to deliver papers at other universities or important conferences. They will not be able to publish their work at prestigious academic or commercial presses, or they may even have difficulty having their work published at all. They won't be invited to the good parties, or get nice summer fellowships, or get asked to serve as dean, or in a future administration in Washington. Or maybe their sources of funding will dry up.

And it's pretty clear that the "wrong side" of this debate is to publicly approve of a paper that has been denounced in the elite media as anti-Semitic, as endorsing conspiracy theories at the same level as the Protocols, and as being on the same side of an issue as David Duke. Can anyone believe that the Alan Dershowitzes of the world are not taking names and will not hold people accountable for supporting a paper that they have publicly denounced as spreading the most vicious lies about Israel and the American Jewish community?

It's not that professors don't want to sound off on public policy issues. When there is an opportunity to spout righteous leftism, professors leap to the front of the line. A good example is a recent case where three white men from the Duke University lacrosse team allegedly gang-raped, sodomized, and choked a black woman who had been hired as a stripper for a party.[15] Despite considerable evidence that the charges are spurious, three academic departments, 13 programs, and 88 professors at Duke bought an ad in the campus newspaper in which they assumed the guilt of the men, and stated that "what happened to this young woman" resulted from "racism and sexism."[16]

But of course in this case, the professors who went public with their indignation knew they were part of a like-minded community and that there would be much to gain by being on the politically correct side. Indeed, a university committee charged with looking into the response of the Duke administration to this incident recommended more hiring of minorities in order to increase the diversity of the Duke administration.

Sadly, there is now a great deal of evidence that academics in general are careful to avoid controversy or do much of anything that will create hostility. In fact, some researchers are pointing to this fact to call into question whether tenure is justified. A recent survey of the attitudes of 1004 professors at elite universities illustrates this quite clearly.[17] Regardless of their rank, professors rated their colleagues as reluctant to engage in activities that ran counter to the wishes of colleagues. Even tenured full professors believed [other full professors] would invoke academic freedom only "sometimes" rather than "usually" or "always"; they chose confrontational options "rarely", albeit more often than did lower ranked colleagues, and appeared more conciliatory ...than one might have anticipated in light of the principles governing academic freedom. Their willingness to self-limit may be due to a desire for harmony and/or respect for the criticisms of colleagues whose opinions they value. Thus, the data did not support the depiction of *Professorus americanus* as unleashed renegades. Seen in this context, the reaction to Mearsheimer and Walt makes a lot of sense. As one professor noted, "People might debate it if you gave everyone a get-out-of-jail-free card and promised that afterwards everyone would be friends."[18]

This intense desire to be accepted and liked by one's colleagues is certainly understandable. It is probably part of human nature. There have been times when I have had to endure charges of anti-Semitism, most recently in an article by Jacob Laksin titled "Cal State's Professor of Anti-Semitism" published by David Horowitz's FrontPageMagazine.com.[19] It's perhaps worth nothing that FrontPageMagazine.com also published perhaps the most vitriolic anti-Mearsheimer and Walt piece to date, Abraham H. Miller's The New Protocols. (Miller begins by stating "Professors Stephen Walt and John Mearsheimer's recently disseminated anti-Semitic screed has been ripped apart by both prominent scholars and literary figures showing it to be an intellectual fraud being passed off as serious scholarship." The essay ends with "Anti-Semites have now found the new Protocols of the Elders of Zion.")

It didn't really bother me much that such an article was published if the discussion was confined to the impersonal world of the internet. I would write a detailed reply and circulate it among the people who read my stuff, and I knew that people who support my writing would rally to my defense and say nice things about me and my reply to Laksin. And I knew that I would get a few pieces of hate mail and maybe a couple of death threats, but that is to be expected. And it's all rather abstract, since I basically sit in solitude at my computer and read it all, and it pretty much ends there. Frankly, there is a part of me that feels good about it because visits to my website are up and more people are buying my books. I fantasize that the word is getting out, even if only a little bit.

The point is that when this article came out, almost all my anxiety stemmed from worries that the article would be picked up by people on my campus or in professional organizations that I am involved in. I wasn't worried that I would lose my job, although Laksin was clearly upset about California State University's "ignoring altogether the question of why it considers the manufacture of stylized bigotry an appropriate avocation for a tenured scholar." What I dreaded was coming into my office and being greeted by cold shoulders and hostile stares, by colleagues not wanting to go to lunch or nervously looking away when I passed in the hall. I worried about reading sensationalistic articles in the campus newspaper.

I imagined going to academic conferences and receiving the same sort of reception. I worried that people wouldn't invite me to write academic papers or wouldn't cite my writing in other areas not related to Jewish issues.

This little bit of personal experience is doubtless typical of the forces of self-censorship that maintain the political order of the post-World War II West. It's the concern about the face-to-face consequences of being a non-conformist in the deeply sensitive areas related to race or to Jewish influence.

Consider the response of Anne Morrow Lindbergh to the torrent of abuse heaped upon her husband, Charles Lindbergh, for stating that Jews were one force promoting war against Germany in 1941. The speech threw her into "dark gloom." "Will I be able to shop in New York at all now? I am always stared at –but now to be stared at with hate, to walk through aisles of hate!"[20] Again, what is most feared is the personal, face-to-face hatred.

As an evolutionary psychologist, it's tempting to speculate that our evolved psychological mechanisms are triggered far more by the close and personal context of day to day interactions, not in the cold and impersonal world of communicating on the internet.

And it's not just that it is in the face-to-face world of everyday life. It is that the areas of non-conformity we are talking about here have huge moral overtones. If one dissents from the reigning theory of macro-economics or the main influences on 19th century French Romanticism, one may be viewed as a bit eccentric or perhaps none too smart. But one is not likely to be viewed as a moral reprobate. One is not likely to be subjected to torrents of moral outrage.

Evolutionary theorist Robert Trivers has proposed that the emotion of guilt is a sign to the group that a person will mend his ways and behave in the future, whereas shame functions as a display of submission to people higher in the dominance hierarchy. From that perspective, a person who is incapable of shame or guilt even for obvious transgressions is literally a sociopath - someone who has no desire to fit into group norms. Such sociopathy would usually be a death sentence in the small groups that we humans evolved in. Only the most dominant individuals would be able to resist the moral outrage of the group, and even they must be concerned about coalitions rising against them.

What is striking and perhaps counterintuitive is that the guilt and shame remain even when we are completely satisfied at an intellectual level that our beliefs are based on good evidence and reasonable inferences. Anne Morrow Lindbergh writes, "I cannot explain my revulsion of feeling by logic. Is it my lack of courage to face the problem? Is it my lack of vision and seeing the thing through? Or is my intuition founded on something profound and valid? I do not know and am only very disturbed, which is upsetting for him. I have the greatest faith in him as a person - in his integrity, his courage, and his essential goodness, fairness, and kindness - his nobility really ...How then explain my profound feeling of grief about what he is doing? If what he said is the truth (and I am inclined to think it is), why was it wrong to state it?"[21]

Her reaction is involuntary and irrational - beyond the reach of logical analysis. Charles Lindbergh was exactly right in what he said, but a rational understanding of the correctness of his analysis cannot lessen the psychological trauma to his wife who must face the hostile stares of others. In psychological terms, the trauma is the result of implicit, unconscious processes stemming from our evolved psychology and a long history of successful socialization.

Puritan Moralism and Christian Universalism

The preceding discusses the "push" of movements that have attempted to alter American and other European-derived societies into defenseless entities with no ethnic or cultural identity. But the other side of the equation must also be examined –the traits that predispose Westerners to willingly accept their own oblivion as a moral necessity. Here Sunic emphasizes the heritage of Christian universalism and, especially in the case of America, the heritage of Puritan moralism.

Several writers have noted the Puritan spirit of egalitarianism and democracy combined with violent crusades against immorality.[22] In the 17th century, Puritan areas had low levels of personal violence but the highest levels of public violence directed at heretics and those suspected of witchcraft. I have suggested that this emphasis on relative egalitarianism and consensual, democratic government are tendencies characteristic of Northern European peoples as a result of a prolonged evolutionary history as hunter-gatherers in the north of Europe.[23] But the Puritans added a high degree of cohesion within the group made possible by a powerful emphasis on cultural conformity (e.g., punishment of religious heresy) and public regulation of personal behavior related to sex (fornication, adultery), public drunkenness, etc. One might say that Puritans tried to square the circle by combining egalitarianism and democracy - both strongly associated with individualism - with high levels of cultural control - a collectivist trait.

But, as Sunic emphasizes, it is the Puritan tendency to pursue utopian causes framed as moral issues that stands out the most - their susceptibility to utopian appeals to a 'higher law' and the belief that the principal purpose of government is moral. New England was the most fertile ground for "the perfectibility of man creed," and the "father of a dozen 'isms.' "[24] There was a tendency to paint political alternatives as starkly contrasting moral imperatives, with one side portrayed as evil incarnate - inspired by the devil. Puritan moral intensity can also be seen in their "profound personal piety"[25] - their intensity of commitment to live not only a holy life, but also a sober and industrious life.

Puritans waged holy war on behalf of moral righteousness even against their own cousins. Whatever the political and economic complexities that led to the Civil War, it was the Yankee moral condemnation of slavery that inspired the rhetoric and rendered the massive carnage of closely related Anglo-Americans on behalf of slaves from Africa justifiable in the minds of Puritans. Militarily, the war with the Confederacy rendered the heaviest sacrifice in lives and property ever made by Americans.[26] Puritan moral fervor and its tendency to justify draconian punishment of evil doers can also be seen in the comments of "the Congregationalist minister at Henry Ward Beecher's Old Plymouth Church in New York [who] went so far as to call for 'exterminating the German people ...the sterilization of 10,000,000 German soldiers and the segregation of the woman.'"[27]

This Puritan moralism and its deep roots in America account for the importance of moral legitimacy in maintaining the current cultural regime. It's interesting that Anne Morrow Lindbergh commented in her thoughts on her husband's speech that "I would prefer to see this country at war than shaken by violent anti-Semitism. (Because it seems to me that the kind of person the human being is turned into when the instinct of Jew-baiting is let loose is worse than the kind of person he becomes on the battlefield.)" In other words, the thought that even a disastrous war that might kill hundreds of thousands of Americans (and, as her husband believed, might result in the destruction of European culture and the white race) is preferable to the possibility of an outbreak of violent anti-Semitism. For Puritans-at-heart like Mrs. Lindbergh, the moral demeanor of Americans is more important than their survival as a nation or people.

Elsewhere I have argued that this tendency toward moralistic punishment is a form of "altruistic punishment" described recently by research on group behavior in individualistic cultures.[28] Because Europeans are individualists at heart, they readily rise up in moral anger against their own people once they are seen as morally blameworthy - a manifestation of their much stronger tendency toward altruistic punishment deriving from their evolutionary past as hunter gatherers.

Thus the current moralistic crusade of the left so characteristic of contemporary Western civilization: Once Europeans were convinced that their own people were morally bankrupt, any and all means of punishment should be used against their own people. A major theme of *The Culture of Critique* is that the most influential intellectual and political movements of the 20th century presented European civilization as morally bankrupt and the proper target of moralistic punishment. Western culture had become the culture of guilt whose central icon had become the Holocaust and the slavery of Africans.

Conclusion

The forces maintaining the current cultural regime are multi-layered. Because this culture of guilt has seized control of the pinnacles of moral and intellectual authority, resistance carries huge costs that go far beyond practical considerations like keeping one's job. The costs are also psychological and deeply personal.

But resistance does serve a function. As Sunic notes, there

is a real prospect of social breakdown given the increasing ethnic divisions in the U.S. In *The Culture of Critique* I predicted that the current regime would lead to increased ethnic strife and an increased sense of group consciousness among the European peoples of the United States. As an evolutionist, it is difficult for me to believe that a racial group would be unconcerned with its own eclipse and domination.

I believe that in the United States we are presently heading down a volatile path - a path that leads to ethnic warfare and to the development of collectivist, authoritarian, and racialist enclaves. Although ethnocentric beliefs and behavior are viewed as morally and intellectually legitimate only among ethnic minorities in the United States ... the development of greater ethnocentrism among European-derived peoples is a likely result of present trends....

Ethnocentrism on the part of the European-derived majority in the United States is a likely outcome of the increasingly group-structured contemporary social and political landscape - likely because evolved psychological mechanisms in humans appear to function by making ingroup and outgroup membership more salient in situations of group-based resource competition .... The effort to overcome these inclinations thus necessitates applying to Western societies a massive "therapeutic" intervention in which manifestations of majoritarian ethnocentrism are combated at several levels, but first and foremost by promoting the ideology that such manifestations are an indication of psychopathology and a cause for ostracism, shame, psychiatric intervention, and counseling. One may expect that as ethnic conflict continues to escalate in the United States, increasingly desperate attempts will be made to prop up the ideology of multiculturalism with sophisticated theories of the psychopathology of majority group ethnocentrism, as well as with the erection of police state controls on nonconforming thought and behavior.

At some point the negative consequences to the European population of the U.S. of multicultural ideology and massive influx of other peoples will become so obvious that current levels of control will be ineffective. We will be like the Soviet Union when it became, in Sunic's words, "a make-believe system in which nobody truly believed and where everybody, including former communist party dignitaries made fun of in private."

And if at this point, Europeans stare into the abyss and voluntarily cede political and cultural power, they will have no one to blame but themselves. But they will be cursed by their descendants. Perhaps they will one day read Tomislav Sunic's excellent book and think about what might have been.

Kevin MacDonald
Department of Psychology
California State University-Long Beach

Chapter I

Americanism and Anti-Americanism

With its Latin etymology, the neologism "*Homo americanus*" may stand in a derogatory fashion for American man and his life style. The American system, the American Puritan ethos, and, particularly, American foreign policy, form the subject matter of critical studies in Europe. The word "Americanism" has a slightly pejorative meaning and is more often used in Europe than in North America. Usually the term "Americanism" stands for a set of daily beliefs, life styles, and the American language - all of which could be described as elements of American ideology.

Social behavior that might be viewed by American citizens as un-American or even anti-American is often considered normal and natural in Europe. There are numerous books in Europe dealing with the American mindset. Some of them possess a predominantly polemical and pamphleteering character; some fall into the category of social and political satire, and some attempt to scientifically demonstrate the flaws of American foreign policy.[29] Most Americans would be offended by the label *Homo americanus* and would likely argue, in view of the fact that America is such a large country, that there cannot be any common denominator for so many different American citizens of such diverse social, ethnic, and racial backgrounds. Admittedly, America is the least homogeneous country in the Western hemisphere in terms of the background of its citizens, their life styles, and their different dreams. But there is one common feature which is characteristic for all Americans, regardless of their social and racial background or status; namely their rejection of their previous roots, however much this rejection may be expressed as a hidden desire for the re-projection of oneself into one's former being or embellished roots. The rejection of these roots, be they of racial, ethnic, or cultural origin, by no means implies, as many European critics wrongly assume, that America is an outcast of Europe, although it often appears in its cultural endeavors as a travesty of Europe. In many instances, however, Americans have proven that they can safeguard Europe cultural heritage better than Europeans themselves. But this European heritage, projected by Americans, has a different meaning in postmodern America. Jean Baudrillard, a French theoretician of postmodernity, sees in the American a constant reenactment of all cultural things from Europe; a certain form of anachronism that lends itself through its mimicry of the social and political grotesque, and which often causes among Europeans irrational outbursts of anti-Americanism.

However, Baudrillard is no less critical of the false mannerism of Europeans and their social gesticulation, which is absent among Americans and which gives Americans a unique trait of historical detachment, not to be seen in Europe. Europeans seem to be more concerned with the appearances of their good manners than with good manners themselves that, in the eyes of Americans, often makes Europeans look like theatrical creatures. "Europeans are free in sprit; Americans are free in action," writes Baudrillard."[30] This only reiterates the assumption that American society can function without cumbersome layers of social pathos, so typical of traditional Europe.

One could very well argue that the foundation of America was the result of the supreme will to power on the part of European genius, i.e. an ultimate form of European Prometheism— something unheard of in any other civilization and something unparalleled in the whole of Western history. That this experiment ended in the early 21st century in secularized Bible-inspired fundamentalism and the theocratic system resented by much of the outside world, is a matter for value judgment. Not a single American politician will ever admit that America is a theocratic system with a peculiar political theology. Clearly, the American social experiment could have taken a different social form. America might have just as well renounced Biblical moralism and adopted instead a neo-Darwinian, evolutionary, and racialist approach in its domestic and foreign policy. There were some serious academics in the first half of the twentieth century who used the field of eugenics in studying social changes, and who left some impact on decision making circles in America.

One may also argue, from a sociobiological and racialist perspective, that early Americans, at least until the mid 19th century, constituted a peculiar gene pool able to weather real or figurative storms which their European left-behinds, particularly in the 18th and 19th century, were neither physically nor emotionally capable of confronting. As transatlantic "supermen," early Americans must have had lots of stamina to answer the "cull of the wild" in their new homeland. It is unquestionable that the rigors of the weather and a harsh unpredictable life in the early South-West must have resulted in a sociobiological selection that in time gave birth to the famed American breed. The subsequent social cleavages between and among Americans, including their unparalleled social mobility, along with the profusion of different lifestyles, makes, therefore, impossible any preconceived stereotype of a "unique" American species, i.e., *Homo americanus.*"

The much decried American conformism, which Alexis de Tocqueville critically observed along with other European thinkers, must also be put in perspective. America is definitely more of a consensual society than Europe, and its bipartisan spirit is often wrongly interpreted in Europe as a sign of intellectual provincialism. Werner Sombart, a prominent German sociologist of the first half of the 20th century, writes that Americans "are inclined to striking uniformity"(...) and "they also show herd instincts."[31] Such quick judgments must be put in perspective. In early postmodernity, by the end of the twentieth century, American conformism proved to be the ideal social framework for the flawless functioning of a sophisticated high-tech industrialized society. European proponents of organic and traditional society, also known as traditionalists, nationalists, national revolutionary conservatives, etc., must, therefore, think twice before blaming America as a threat to historical memory. In a global postmodern system relying on satellite and fiber optic networks and rapidly evolving digital mindset, the former European conservative palaver needs to be reexamined. It is precisely the sense of social conformism that gave Americans a distinct ability for team work and functional solidarity that cannot be observed in Europe, yet which is indispensable for smooth functioning of a postmodern system.

In a similar manner, America became a military superpower often against its own will. Its military supremacy after the end of the bipolar world, by the late twentieth century, was more a chance result of a global power vacuum and less a product of America's will to hegemony.

While it is common for all peoples on earth to make stereotypes, or even crack racial jokes about their next door neighbors, different races, and different ethnic groups, no nation, or for that matter not a single individual likes to hear someone else making jokes about his country of origin, regardless of how much he may subconsciously hate his country, or the country of his ancestors' origin. After all, it is always the "Other" who is wrong or who incarnates Evil; it is "Myself" who is always right. And who likes to hear deprecatory remarks or jokes about himself or his native country? Europeans often talk about strange American eating and sexual habits, American superficiality in professional and intimate relationships, about the obesity of American women, and over obsessive lachrymal sentimentality of American politicians whose behavior is colored by fanatical moralism. Europeans also lambast Americans for their lack of historical memory, the American absence of a sense of the tragic and its infantile optimism. These remarks, which have been made by countless European observers of America, are more or less correct. But Europeans have to admit that they do not like it when Americans remind them of their own parochial customs, or when Americans make observations that the much vaunted European "historical memory" has led to countless nightmares for all European peoples.

Although the vast majority of both Europeans and Americans descend from the same racial stock, there are serious differences in their respective societies. However, with almost the complete Americanization of the European continent at the beginning of the 21st century, what is the point of studying *Homo americanus* in America only? Is not Europe an extended part of America—albeit in a reversed historical manner? The American species, *Homo americanus,* exists all over Europe now and has gained in visibility in each corner of Europe—both in the West and the post-communist East. Hence another paradox: the belated European version of *Homo americanus* appears often unnerving to American visitors in Europe in search of an elusive "true" Frenchman, German, or a Dutchman. In the process of world wide globalization and American cultural imperialism having become the main vector for new cultural hegemony, it is increasingly difficult to tell the difference in life styles between citizens of America and those in Europe.

The transnational uniqueness of the American system can be critically examined at the beginning of the 21st century by research work in different academic fields. However, the best approach to a critical examination of *Homo americanus* and Americanism, both in America and in its mimicked European version, can be achieved by means of interdisciplinary research and historical comparison. This interdisciplinary approach is important given the fact that the more one wishes to narrow down the field where *Homo americanus* thrives, the more this field becomes evasive. Alas, as long as there is a single American citizen who displays un-American or "anti-American" traits, it is not fair to place common labels on the entire postmodern American population. Just because most French love eating cheese does not mean that all Frenchmen are cheese lovers. Just because Russian Jews, in 1919, made up percentage wise the majority of early Bolshevik commissars, does not mean that all Jews were communists. Yet, one must be cautious when making such elegant disclaimers. Unlike political scientists or historians, many biologists and geneticists will not reject allegations that nations, races and ethnic groups share distinct behavioral and physical traits that facilitate our cognition and our perception of the "other" in our day to day life. And there should be nothing offensive about this. Pretending that racial or ethnic differences do not exist and that each man is a product of nurture and education only, does not sound convincing. This belated liberal dogma of equality, so powerful during the 20th century, is losing credibility in the postmodern world. Or rather, this dogma will sound credible but only from the angle of its advocates in academia and the political arena, including those opinion makers who shield their vested interests and who are interested only in their version of the truth.

Unquestionably, most fields in social science since the end of the Second World War have been heavily influenced by the left-leaning, Marxist, egalitarian, liberal and Lamarckian framework of analysis, to the extent that serious criticism of the egalitarian dogma is viewed as a threat to democracy and by extension a threat to modern Americanism and its twin brother liberalism. In the same vein, much of what has been written or published in the second half of the 20th century about America came from leftist and liberal sources—not from right-wing sources. Seen from the historical perspective, it must not be forgotten that the modern framework of political references, particularly since the end of the Cold War, has been based on the dogma of antifascism and multiculturalism, with both elements of this dogma well incorporated into Americanism, and with both reflecting the geopolitical configuration of Europe and America after World War II. Using other perspectives or quoting books by anti-egalitarian authors, let alone immersing oneself into the study of modern and postmodern belief systems from a historical revisionist or sociobiological point of view, is viewed with alarm and rejected as "unscientific." These fields of analysis, or authors who resort to these unconventional approaches, remain an isolated breed, often stigmatized as "fascists" and "racists."

The fundamental issue that needs to be addressed here, even when one deals with such an abstract notion as Americanism, is not what is true or false, but who is the master of modern Americanized discourse and who is in charge of defining what the concept of (anti)-Americanism means. And why not give a chance, for a change, to authors who have voiced different views on Americanism and its founding principles: consumerism, multiculturalism, egalitarianism and the myth of progress?

Following the Second World War, hundreds of European and American authors were removed from library shelves on the basis of their allegedly extremist, racist and unscientific character. The point one needs to make in this chapter is not whether these authors, politicians, and academics were "pro-American" or "anti-American," democrats or non-democrats, credible individuals, quacks, monsters, or angels, but rather to stress the fact that they deserve a fair hearing and should stop being subject to intellectual and academic ostracism. Otherwise, any critique of the American system, of modern liberalism, or for that matter any critical study of a social phenomenon related to postmodernity, will continue to be subject to preconceived notions that yield self-serving conclusions. This is all the more necessary, as after the end of the Cold War and the breakdown of communism in Eastern Europe, paradigms that were used during the preceding fifty year period of the Cold War in the social sciences are no longer valid.

Critical studies of Americanism are not new. *Homo americanus* and the American system have been the subject matter of critical study for a very long period of time, both from the left-wing and right-wing perspective. Indeed, one can also think of National Socialist and Fascist politicians and scores of their intellectual supporters who probed into the mechanism of modernity, who examined the American system, and whose analyses must not be rejected out of hand—just because they originated in a system which is abhorred by liberal democracy and by American elites. The fascist anti-American prose, when not forbidden, which is still the case in Europe by the early 21st century, is avoided or dismissed as "crazy" and "unscientific." It is a typical trait, particularly in higher American education and the American media to eulogize noble principles of intellectual detachment and impartiality. However, each time an intellectual inquiry turns towards the fascist epoch or to the cultural heritage of fascism, all hell breaks loose, all dirty epithets are allowed. An average reader, be he a European or an American, rarely has the chance to judge for himself the other side of the story surrounding the epoch in Europe that stretched from 1933 to 1945. This is relevant not just for that specific political period but also for the political ideas that were dominant during that time. Having been subject since 1945 to a deluge of liberal and communist interpretation of contemporary history, with the social science curricula impregnated by antifascist and egalitarian theorems and having been exposed to different schools of thought more in line with the spirit of Marxist and liberal times, the average reader or student of contemporary America or Americanized Europe may not be fully aware of the existence of other schools of thought or alternative historical perspectives.

Even the attempt to accept as a working hypothesis that due to a peculiar historical and political environment, the American system may have given birth to a more or less new type of citizen with distinct behavioral traits, is rejected as unscientific by mainstream opinion makers. If one accepts, however, as a working postulate, that "*Homo americanus*" is a distinct sociobiological specie and not only a derogatory label for an average American citizen, irrespective of the fact that he may be an Oklahoma hick, an Appalachian hill-billy, a red neck from Chicago's steel mills, a Joe Six pack from suburban Los Angeles, or a Jewish neocon journalist, then it may be easier to speculate about a set of evolutionary changes that have occurred in America over the last two hundred years.

Who defines Americanism, in which time frame, and in which location, and by whose vocabulary? When one speaks of the average *Homo americanus,* should one refer to an East

Coast banker or to an antebellum poet like Edgar Allan Poe? Is Americanism embodied in the American heretic Thomas Jefferson or an equally strong antebellum American heretic George Fitzhugh? One way or another, these individuals during their prime were also depicted as "un-American" by their political opponents. If we were to take some contemporary neo-conservative scholar as the ideal archetype of postmodern *Homo americanus*, then we might just as well use his judgments regarding the modern and postmodern American system with all its multiethnic facets. That way a Jewish neocon might consider himself to be as genuine and as equal an American as some Southern Agrarian American of yesteryear, although their respective racial, ethnic, and political views may be light-years apart. Therefore, the conclusion as to who *Homo americanus* is, will hinge on the social, intellectual, racial, and ethnic pedigree of the observer and the observed. It would be interesting to know what would happen with postmodern self-proclaimed Americans if their country started to rapidly fall apart. Who would be willing then to define America and the meaning of the American spirit?

Race and the 'Cull' of the Wild

In postmodern America and its cultural satellite the European Union, racial profiling is not a rewarding job. Making across the board and general statements about non-European peoples or ethnic groups can earn a politician, journalist, professor, or scholar a label of being prejudiced, or being a racist bigot. Even the word race, once frequently used in America and Europe, was replaced by the late seventies of the 20th century by a more neutral word "ethnicity." Simultaneously, multiracial societies were also euphemistically dubbed by the expression "multicultural societies," thereby adding more confusion into the original meaning of the word "culture" and "race." Asking officially somebody in postmodern America about his racial or his ethnic origins is viewed as an affront against his personality. Over the last half a century, due to immigration laws passed in

1965, America has fundamentally changed its ethnic and racial composition, a fact that has resulted in mandatory employment of different semantic locutions. It is seemingly a matter of time until different legal and political structures will also be added to those demographic changes that have been at work since the mid 20th century. How will one define the word "Americanism" in the year 2025, and who will qualify then as a "good American"?

The various scenarios about the possible Balkanization of America are legion and usually it is traditionalists and so-called right-wing authors and scholars who depict the future of America in catastrophic terms. Many of them are aware that once upon a time, "immigrants were met with the unflinching demand to 'Americanize.' Now they are told that they should retain and reinforce their diversity."[32] In the early 21st century racial diversity is causing in America serious legal problems as newcomers from Third Word countries display two different political and cultural loyalties.

Modern multiculturalism in America implies by definition social integration and stands in sharp contrast to the assimilation process which was once a mandatory scheme for newcomers in their acceptance of new identity. However, the notion of assimilation in America is rightly viewed by postmodern liberal theorists as an eraser of America's "ethnic diversity." Hence a paradox: on the one hand newcomers in America are encouraged to erase their non-American roots as soon as possible. On the other, they are encouraged, in the name of some romantic belief in multiculturalism and racial diversity, to retain their non-American roots, and this by means of integration. It seems, therefore, that the American legal system, when dealing with non-European immigration, has become a victim of its own suicidal vocabulary. Terms like "diversity" and "ethnic sensitivity" are just empty locutions in the liberal and multicultural arsenal. According to the English-American scholar Peter Brimelow, a strategy of forcible multiculturalism results in "positive discrimination" against European Americans. Therefore, the definition of what Americanism means at the beginning of the 21st century will remain an impossible task to solve.

The modern Western system incorporated in postmodern neo-liberalism and spearheaded by America and its carrier *Homo americanus*, has imposed its own vernacular, its own version of truth, and its own framework of analysis. The word race is avoided because, apparently, there is only one human race -except when one talks about racial profiling, racial discrimination, or racial harassment, which seems to be a daily topic in postmodern America. Multiracial diversity, as has been already seen in countless cases, both in America and Europe, is not a recipe for multiracial conviviality. The prospects for America's Balkanization are real as different non-European ethnicities "with disparate mores, verbal communication problems and different abilities provide a recipe...for social breakdown..."[33]

When facing their political adversaries, America's masters of postmodern discourse keep throwing around signifiers, such as "anti-American," "fascism," "communism," "Stalinism," "racism," whose signified and interpretation depend on their own good will. And even the signified is differently interpreted by dissimilar parties as long as it serves their political agendas or their vested interests. Nominally, both liberal America and its replica in Europe, claim to be highly tolerant systems allowing diverse critics to voice criticism of Americanism, however vicious or bizarre this criticism may sometimes be. Hundreds of different organizations, agencies, or sects throughout America and Europe, defend the rights of marginal social groups, ranging from political dissidents from different antipodes to local homosexuals, lesbians, or other gender bender minorities, including non-European religions of old and new. In theory, multiracial liberalism, with its main motor in America, tolerates any political view and life style—the point which it likes to stress on all wave lengths throughout the world. However, the more American society becomes heterogeneous the more this society needs to struggle for racial consensus. What may for instance be seen as a highly desirably topic in the study of European literature for an American student of European origin, may be viewed as a demeaning and degrading act for a student of non-European descent. In addition, there are social minefields engendered by political and academic elites in postmodern America that are meant to be "off limits" to intellectual scrutiny. In this sense, postmodern Americanism, which one may just as well replace by the word neo-liberalism, despite a torrent of eulogies about its tolerant nature, contains serious threats against its critics.

Admittedly, every epoch has its dominant ideas, and each ruling class in every country on earth is never too eager to discard its founding myths and replace them with other myths that may be seen as factors destabilizing for its political survival. Likewise, the dominant ideas at work in modern Americanism are often hailed by the ruling class and its court historians as "self-evident." Questioning the veracity of that self-evidence can cause serious troubles for an intellectual heretic and can even lead to the signing of a death warrant to their intellectual career. For instance, challenging the principles of American democracy or probing critically into the legacy of antifascist victimology must be strictly avoided. These prohibitions are not officially on display in America; they just constitute a public no-entry zone. An author or a politician who ventures into one of these forbidden fields is at best shrugged off as a crank by the masters of modern American discourse or labeled as a "prejudiced" person. At worst, he can end up in prison. In most cases, however, he will find himself cut off from academic discourse and political debate, which in effect means that he is intellectually sentenced to death.

Another American "self-evidence," which seems to be part of the American political theology, transpires in constant commemoration of the Jewish Holocaust—an event which has become a civic ritual all over the Americanized world, and which prohibits any critical inquiry. The topic of the Holocaust, along with the issue of multiculturalism, is one of those subjects of early postmodernity that can only be discussed by a chosen few—and usually in flattering terms. Professor Kevin MacDonald, an American sociobiologist writes: "The Judaization of the West is nowhere more obvious than in the veneration of the Holocaust as the central moral icon of the entire civilization."[34] On the basis of the incessant commemoration of the Holocaust, it can be easier to understand what postmodern Americanism means and which role this new ideology has played in the process of the Americanization of Europe and the entire world. The process of Americanization seems to be enhanced by the rapid growth of multiracial society, which has always had strong supporters among Jewish intellectuals in America who have never hidden "that making of the US into a multicultural society has been a major Jewish goal from the beginning of the nineteenth century."[35]

No wonder, therefore, that Americanism and Americanization are rapidly becoming terms devoid of original meaning. America is comprised of different peoples "who differed from one another so vastly in religion, race, background and education and lineage and who agreed to forget all these things."[36] Questioning critically, in the epoch of postmodernity, the meaning of Americanism, can earn a person the label of a prejudiced person. However, even the word "prejudice" must be put into linguistic perspective, as this word has the common root with the word "prejudgment," which is part of the biological and psychological makeup in human speciation without which any civilization would collapse. When properly used, writes Alan McGregor, prejudice serves as a useful intellectual tool in comparing and contrasting and as a short cut in reaching important decisions.[37] Undoubtedly, all humans discriminate, be that in the choice of their mates, friends, or against their political enemies. Nation-state building is a process carried out by the principles of "in-group" vs. "out-group" discrimination, wherein a tribe or an ethnic group, in a manner of an extended family, prefers to interact with its own in-group members. People of same racial ethnicity, in this case white Americans, are more or less genetically similar and will, therefore, tend to display overt or covert prejudices against other racial groups.[38] For numerous authors, particularly in the fields of sociobiology, xenophobia and racial prejudice are inherent in all human beings since they are "the natural and biological consequences of parental selections."[39] Ethnic or racial discrimination, let alone charges of anti-Semitism, are viewed in postmodern Americanism as the ultimate intellectual sin.

But is not, after all, friendship also a form of the most subtle form of discrimination in view of the fact that an individual cannot be friends with all people on earth? One discriminates when mating and in sexual relationships, a point often made by prominent sociobiologists, but who are often targets of criticism by their liberal opponents. Long ago, an American author close to the school of thought dealing with sociobiology, Dr. William Shockley, wrote that those who persist in holding views of ethnic exclusion regarding heredity and race "are denied tenure and research funds, physically threatened, and shouted off platforms."[40] Similar views on human diversity, let alone public ostracism of academics who argue that race and heredity play a significant role in social and political behavior, have been legion in Europe and America. However, in the best of all worlds, in so-called free America, certain dogmatic views, particularly those regarding the sacred Jewish question and inherent goodness of non- European races, are imposed by force and must be accepted by all.

When a human being makes a specific choice in his life, he automatically discards other options and rejects other propositions, even if his act may hurt a fellow human being. Examples abound: In postmodern America and Europe, if a citizen shows in public positive prejudices. i.e., by making laudatory comments about some racial groups, he can fearlessly resort to grammatical constructs without using embellishing qualifiers or disclaimers. Thus, one can hear in America that "African-Americans are good singers and basketball players." There is nothing wrong with this general statement which implies that *some* blacks are not gifted for playing basketball. By contrast, a general statement that "African-Americans are prone to violence and that they are not family-oriented," can earn a person who uttered those words the label of being a "racist." One can also sometimes hear general remarks that "Jews are good musicians"- and hardly anybody will object to this more or less well documented fact. However, avoiding the qualifier "some," and saying that "Jews are very rich," may cause social objections and is prudently avoided by many in America's public discourse. In other words, if an author were to display a critical view about some non-European ethnic group or a race in America, or for that matter if that European author lambasted the proverbial *Homo americanus* as a Jewish paradigmatic man of commercial and banking activities, he had better be prepared to use the whole arsenal of diminutives and make sure he frames his critical arguments in conditional sentences. By equipping himself with loads of disclaimers an author critical of Americanism and its numerous social derivatives such as globalism, liberalism, egalitarianism, can secure himself a professional exit, in case he needs one in an emergency. It may come in handy if he needs to plead professional ignorance.

Politics means comparing. The way Europeans traditionally perceive Americans differs from the way Americans perceive themselves—let alone how they both perceive each other's perceptions. In order to be aware not just of his object's difference, but also of his own subjective difference, a scholar, or for that matter an intelligent person, needs to put himself in perspective and try to observe himself through the eyes of his interlocutor or his political adversary, regardless of how stupid or intelligent his adversary or his interlocutor, or for that matter he himself may be or appear. This is important as the end of the Cold War brought about the necessity for a different type of political discourse. Words such as "left vs. right," "communists vs. fascists," are no longer appropriate for labeling political or ideological opponents, although these words are still in use by politicians and scholars. Unfortunately, these words are also used as derogatory labels for defaming or dismissing the adversary, despite the fact that they had lost their original meanings.

The verbal constructs *"Homo americanus," "Homo occidentalis,"* or *"Homo sovieticus,"* although voguish today, can be described as pejorative platitudes for somebody's ideological stance and someone's social views. Most likely in the foreseeable future they will disappear and be replaced by other verbal constructs, and rightly so. Former cleavages in the political landscape which marked the entire 20th century make little sense in postmodernity, as the entire political vocabulary has been subject to change. Similarly, with a changing world a new word came into usage by the end of the 20th century, namely the word "postmodernity." This vague, but also snobbish word is increasingly used in the description of America and Americanism. After the end of communism, America is rightly viewed by many as an ideal laboratory for the study, not just of political change in the Western hemisphere, but also as the place for the destined "end of history." If one were to follow this Americano-centric logic, no other historical meaning, other than Americanism, is allowed to thrive. By the late 20th century, America had already become the concave mirror reflecting, as well as initiating, postmodern changes all over the world.

Although viewed as a nemesis by its critics, America, nonetheless, exerts enormous social, political, and cultural attraction, even on those non- or anti-American scholars and politicians who resent America and Americanism. Baudrillard, in his perceptive work on postmodernity and Americanism, sees America as a compounded dreamland of all—including its critics:

> *America is neither dream nor reality. It is a hyperreality because it is utopia which has behaved from the very beginning as though it were already achieved. Everything here is real and pragmatic, and yet it is all the stuff of dreams too. It may be that that the truth of America can only be seen by a European, since he alone will discover here the perfect simulacrum—that of the immanence and material transcription of all values.*[41]

It is for this reason why every European, desiring to better understand himself and his European homeland, needs to observe himself through the eyes of postmodern America first. But are Americans, who reside in America, also capable or willing to observe themselves through the eyes of Europeans? This point, of course, depends on the ideological baggage of the observer or the lack thereof. Traditionally, both the European and American radical left and radical right have been critical of the American system, the only exception being that the European or American left, when criticizing America claim that America is "not American enough," i.e. that it has departed from its egalitarian founding myths. In other words, the Left claims that modern America has not achieved enough equality, enough democracy, and enough progress. Consequently, America should return to its originally charted goals. The same deductive logic could be seen, after the break-down of communism at the end of the 20th century among scores of disenchanted Marxist intellectuals, both in America and Europe, who argue that the Gulag and communist repression were unintended results of Marxism, and that true Marxian socialism was betrayed by Soviet reality. True communism (whatever "true" may mean), deserves, therefore, a second chance. When a Jewish-American left-leaning writer, Noam Chomsky, attacks in his books the American system for its alleged or real corruption, he never touches on the sanctity of the American founding fathers and the importance Jeffersonianism exerted on scores of American social scientists. Indeed, Chomsky sounds full of praise for the Jeffersonian legacy and acknowledges that "Jefferson and John Dewey today sound like crazed Marxist lunatics."[42] To similar conclusions regarding the American Declaration of Independence, comes Lawrence R. Brown in his magnum opus *The Might of the West*. But unlike the leftist Chomsky, Brown, despite his erudite and thoughtful analyses, is unknown in America. Brown acknowledges that the Declaration was a form of political theology, compatible with the spirit of the time of Enlightenment, and therefore replete with platitudes and "self-evident" truths. The Preamble of the Declaration could very well fit into the Middle Ages, albeit by changing the wording into a more divine language. "Custom does not permit us to call these Eighteen Century liberals what in historical perspective they really were: leftists."[43] In hindsight, the meta-language used by the framers of the American Constitution does appear as something quite normal to an observer in the 21st century.

Yet, during the period of the late Enlightenment the words uttered by the architects of the American Republic set the whole Western world on fire.

Many European authors, usually associated with the stigma of the "radical right," with notable American exceptions, reject any aspect of Americanism. When some French right-wing thinker or German philosopher Martin Heidegger voices criticism of the American system, he curtly challenges the very being of modernity. And this is something that needs to be pondered when dealing with the notion of postmodern Americanism vs. anti-Americanism:

From a metaphysical point of view, Russia and America are the same; the same dreary technological frenzy, the same unrestricted organization of the average man. At a time when the farthermost corner of the globe has been conquered by technology and opened to economic exploitation; when any incident whatever, regardless of where or when it occurs, can be communicated to the rest of the world at any desired speed...when time has ceased to be anything other than velocity, instantaneousness, and simultaneity, and time as history has vanished from the lives of all peoples; when a boxer is regarded as a nation's great man; when mass meetings attended by millions are looked on as a triumph—then, yes then, through all this turmoil, a question still haunts us like a specter: What for?- Whither.- And what then?[44]

The above passage summarizes what many European traditionalists and conservative thinkers in reality think of Americanism, although one must admit, one could find similar "anti-American" views among anti-egalitarian and antidemocratic American authors who would wholeheartedly agree with Heidegger's every comment. Authors, such as Ezra Pound, Lothrop Stoddard, Revilo P. Oliver, or Francis Parker Yockey, also viewed themselves as exemplary American patriots, yet they were denounced as "un-American" by their liberal opponents, although they did not hesitate themselves to hurl the same epithets of anti-Americanism at their detractors. However, when words of anti-Americanism come from such an important European heavy-weight philosopher as Martin Heidegger, who was linked for a while to the National Socialist experiment, then these words carried special weight. After all, Heidegger cannot be depicted as a right-wing crank. The reason Heidegger and other authors of his stature in Europe and America are often dubbed "anti-American" lies not so much in their criticism of American society. Their anti-American image is primarily due to the fact that they squarely rejected parliamentary democracy and the American-inspired myth of postmodernity. In the modern and postmodern Western world, saturated by the ideology of anti-fascism and democratism, their un-American prose will never sound credible enough and will be subject to ostracism. More likely, in a non-liberal climate, Martin Heidegger along with his American compatriots would become mandatory reading and would be held as major role models in the study of postmodernity. Alas, sympathy for anti-egalitarian ideas having their inspiration in the heritage of revolutionary conservatism, anarcho-conservatism, in the hierarchical non-parliamentary system, or in historically tarnished National Socialism or Fascism, however carefully these ideas may be voiced, will be denounced as "fascist" by postmodern opinion makers. Books by so-called fascist authors, even when their subject matter comprises of literal fairy tales, will not reach a wider audience.

In contrast to Heidegger's endless speculation about the loss of Being in the Americanized time, one may quote similar views, less colored by metaphysical lingo, yet similar in their anti-American and anti-modern message. After reading critical judgments about America and Americanism by the National Socialist heavy-weight Joseph Goebbels, a chief cultural propagandist in the Third Reich, one is struck by similarities with Heidegger's views, and with the similar opinions of latter-day European right-wing critics of the American system. Moreover, over the last past decades Goebbels' views on Americanism have been unknowingly used by leftist critics of America, although their antifascist pedigree secured them literary notoriety. Goebbels sounds postmodern when he

writes in the distant 1942, i.e. right in the midst of the Second
World War that "the less Americans know about some matter
the more they talk about it in an expert-like fashion. They quite
earnestly think that European peoples only wait to be taken
care of and led by them."[45] Similar critical views of America were
to be encountered among leftist and rightist French scholars
and critics in the second half of the twentieth century. With
or without the famed Goebbels, many Europeans today would
echo similar views about America and would privately complain
about the American compulsive drive to compartmentalize
each field of human existence. Probably, the major point worth
singling out in Goebbels' prose regarding Americanism is his
critique of American cultural decadence, especially when he
writes that "Americanization is a form of *Verkitschung*"(...). "If
Americans had no money they would probably be the most
despised people on earth."[46] After the Cold War, similar critical
views began circulating in European cultural circles across wide
segments of the intelligentsia. As the sole superpower on the
planet Earth, America, for each minor failure in its foreign or
domestic policy, turned into a subject mater of undeserved
criticism.

America's alleged materialistic civilization was bound to
give birth to new enemies around the globe. The American
religion of money, as a form of spiritual salvation, became the
main target of its critics — Goebbels notwithstanding. It was
America's excessive idea of progress and its overemphasis
on material well being that most European right-wing critics
found appalling. Goebbels acknowledges America only as high-
tech civilization, when he writes: "As much as we safeguard the
achievements of modern civilization and wish to make it ours
in the embellishment of our life, equally much are we convinced
that it cannot be seen as the meaning of Being."[47] Probably, if
one were to drop the name of Goebbels and leave out other pro-
fascist authors with similar anti-American views, similar views
about America and Americanism would have a safe passage in
contemporary academia and would likely capture the attention
of a postmodern reader. However, if an author is *a priori* designed

as a "fascist monster" or as a "supreme Nazi devil," as Goebbels has been, then such observations about America are likely to fall on deaf ears. Therefore, one is allowed to resort to critical observations about America only when quoting authors who abide by the canons of liberal and socialist dogma.

This brings up again the subject matter of ideology from which America has claimed itself to be spared, especially when describing its political arena. Hardly any American politician would admit that there is any ideology in America. American social scientists and politicians have traditionally associated ideologies with European power politics. For them, each ideology has something "un-American," something incompatible with the principle of freedom and parliamentary democracy, something usually linked to the discredited European ideologies of Communism and National Socialism. American elites, instead, prefer the word "policy," in which the omnipotent market does away with muscled politics. However, if one were to set out from the premises that America posits the market as the ultimate human goal, can one not argue that the veneration of the market becomes in turn another ideology?

American political elites have always stressed the notion of liberty in describing the American unique historical experiment, while carefully avoiding to state the obvious, namely that it was the dream of economic progress and not the abstract notion of liberty which had brought together the American founding fathers. Charles Beard, a prominent American historian, writes that America was founded on economic and capitalist premises, as "democracy of how to get rich" and that the framers of the Constitution literally "usurped the principles of Jeffersonian democracy."[48] If one accepts his thesis one may then conclude that American citizens, as a result of the two hundred years of racial and biological selection, constitute today a special infra-European breed that, although looking European by their phenotype, has a proclivity to act as economic agents. This negative biological selection affected the behavior of future generations of Americans. Americans whose values and interests were different had to be removed from mainstream

politics or could not play an important role in the making of
the American dream. One can, therefore, use the synonym of
Homo economicus for *Homo americanus* given that postmodern
Americans are focused exclusively on commodities amassment,
to the point of becoming perishable commodities themselves.

Some early European eugenicists did bring this point, i.e.
the American breed of *Homo economicus,* to larger academic
attention by noticing that "America was a result of economic
selection."(...) "On the whole, the dominant influence in the
making of America has been overwhelmingly bourgeois, and
the population has been selected by the requirements of the
capitalist regime."[49] If one accepts a hypothesis of a distinct
American genotype that has surfaced as a result of capitalist
social selection, then one may give some credence to Heidegger,
notably that both the Americans and Soviets had managed to
groom a special infra-racial breed—blacks, Mexicans, and other
non-European immigrants notwithstanding.

In view of this, European racialists and eugenicists
differ considerably from American racialists as the former
tend to emphasize more the role of historical community by
underlining the importance of the cultural-political arena in
human interaction. By contrast, liberalism and its embodiment
in Americanism, has brought about negative sociobiological
selection by fostering "the mercantile gene." America's dogma
of the survival of the fittest basically applies not the fittest in the
fields of arts, politics or workers solidarity, but to the fittest in
capitalist commerce. Ludwig Woltmann, an early German left-
leaning national-racialist scholar, who had a significant impact
on racial theorizing in Europe in the first half of the 20th century,
writes that "economic selection under given circumstances
can have specific and degenerative consequences, especially
when commerce and money hoarding play a prominent role in
human life..."[50] One must not, however, forget that racialism
and eugenics had numerous supporters in America and both
fields were well combined with early American liberalism. Even
modern liberalism, under cover of locutions such as "human
rights" and "democracy," promotes unabashedly fierce economic

selection in the free market, by rewarding only those who are most successful in it.

American eugenicists and white racialists also claim that the white race should have the upper hand in America. Their concern and anxiety over the dramatic racial demographic change in American seems to be justified. However, there seems to be a contradiction in their analyses regarding the waning of the Euro-American world. While they bewail the passing of the white race, they fail to critically examine the economic foundations of Americanism, i.e. an ideology that is fully propitious for low wage non-European immigrant workers. What role models will the withering white race of Euro-Americans endorse if American values have gravitated for centuries around the myth of economic progress regardless of whether white racialists or dark multiculturalists are in power? Why should one worry about the passing of the great white race if that race has only been involved in endless economic transactions?

It is a typical trait for a political system to project its goodness and to minimize its flaws, or at least to cover up its short-comings with trendy verbiage. Thus, many white Americans, when critical of their present rulers, often try to embellish the legacy of the American dream by extrapolating the alleged goodness of their previous rulers. This seems to be a feature of many white American racialists who stubbornly refuse to criticize capitalism—which has traditionally been the main motor for attracting European immigrants, including postmodern masses of non-European economic migrants. It would be interesting to find out the percentage of early American settlers who had come to their new American homeland for reasons other than "making a quick buck."

Prime Americanism and anti-Semitism

Modern American racialists and traditionalists examine the ugly results of multiracialism and multiculturalism, such as riots arising from racial tensions and ill-defined affirmative action programs favoring non European-Americans. However, they seldom look at economic motives that brought these different peoples and diverse races to the shores of America. Similar inconsistencies can be seen among white Europeans in Europe who, when angry at the present ruling class, project their wishful thinking into a romantically untainted all-white European past. A few American authors, such as Francis P. Yockey and Revilo P. Oliver did point to those contradictions among American racialists, especially when they criticized Americanism from an anti-egalitarian and anti-mercantile point of view. Their prose, hostile to liberal canons, has been subject to ostracism and denounced as "un-American." It is because American elites make stringent disclaimers on all ideologies, that it is worth while raising the question whether America's obsession with the market and its fanatical belief in progress also makes America an ideological system.

Yockey and Oliver could have easily passed for European revolutionary conservatives in the 1930s, or for that matter, as the godfathers of modern conservative anti-Americanism in Europe. Harshly critical of American ideology, of Yankeeism, of the American constitution, of Jewish "culture distortion" elements, Yockey echoes in anti-American European authors. Immediately after the Second World War, he wrote that the words "America" and "American" were stripped of all spiritual-national significance, and were given a purely ideological significance."[51] This was in particular true for his nemesis, American Jewry who, in his words, had succeeded in kidnapping political concepts and dubbed his writings "un-American." "(T)hey (the Jews) were able to identify their Jewish idea with America, and to label the nationalism of America with the term un-American."[52] Does this mean, therefore, that a correct definition of what Americanism and anti-Americanism is cannot be given by a European-American racialist or traditionalist, or some proverbial American right-winger? Jewish American scholar, Alvin H. Rosenfeld, half a century later, writes that "anti-Americanism is always similar to anti-Semitism; they relate to each other and empirically are almost always in close proximity, even if not totally identical. The overlap in bias between them has become more pronounced since the end of World War II."[53] Rosenfeld wrote those words during the American military campaign in Iraq in 2003, an event which was not welcomed by American right-wingers and traditionalists. At that time, criticism of American foreign engagements in the Middle East, particularly when coming from Europe, was interpreted by the American establishment as a new form of anti-Americanism.

In early postmodernity, many American Jews assume to have discovered in European anti-Americanism a veiled form of anti-Semitism. The early 21st century, for the first time after the Second World War, highlighted a tension between political elites in Europe and America, and brought to the fore unpleasant historical memories that are likely to grow in severity in the years to come. It is the past that does not want to pass away and it is Israel and the Jewish question that have become time again unavoidable topics in studying postmodern America, the ideology of Americanism, and its carrier *Homo americanus*. Seldom do European and American politicians wish to publicly mention those fateful words "the Jewish question" and the Jewish role in the process of Americanization, although they all know in private that the closest ally of America, Israel and American Jews, are indispensable factors in studying the different aspects of Americanism and anti-Americanism. "The dreaded word anti-Semitic functions like the word anti-Soviet. Being undefined it is unfalsifiable," writes the American journalist Joe Sobran, who once fell into disrepute with the American mainstream due to his probing into the semantics of the word anti-Semitism.[54] There has been a growing tendency in America ever since the fall of communism, to draw a parallel between anti-Americanism and anti-Semitism, which some Jewish-American neoconservative scholars have been very eager to emphasize.[55] It is a strange socio-political phenomenon, that despite much bragging about universal rights to freedom of speech, the subject of Jews, Judaism, and the role of Jews in Americanism is carefully avoided.

Does this mean that at the beginning of the 21st century, a genuine American is a Jewish American, or at least a European American sympathetic to Israel and Jews? This is the impression one gets after scanning the American media and the role of Jews in postmodernity. In the years to come, the Jewish question, which modern political and intellectual elites feel so uncomfortable talking about, will be a decisive factor in the future for America, Europe and the entire world. One needs only to look at the flurry of anti-European newspaper articles in America, following the invasion of Iraq in 2003 to realize the scope of lies and mendacities that could at any moment degenerate into open hostility between America and Europe on the one hand, and between Euro-Americans and non-Euro-Americans on the other.[56] It suffices to witness a major world crisis, following the terrorist attack on New York on September 11, 2001, or the subsequent American military involvement in Iraq in order to realize what Americans think of the outside heretic world and what this outside heretic world thinks of America. It should not come as a surprise that a number of prominent American Jews discovered their brand of American patriotism and began to support the flag-waving star and stripes Americanism in all its postmodern expressions. Respectable pro-American and pro-Israeli journalists, both in America and Europe, published after that fateful event of "9-11" a whole list of laudatory articles about America, always comparing anti-Americanism to anti-Semitism. "In the Jewish consciousness the attacks against America are simultaneously attacks against Jews."[57] One thing remains certain though; the more one looks for the true definition of who a true American is or what American ideology is all about, the more one gets bogged down in a semantic morass.

The term "un-American" seems to be a frequent word in depicting the foes of Americanism. It is an amorphous ideological term used by America's elites, however much they adamantly reject ideological denominations in depicting the enemies of America. In times of crisis, the term "un-American" has been hurled by American elites at heretics voicing criticism against different American administrations. By a curious semantic twist, in the late 20th century, criticizing the policy of American ally Israel, could easily earn an American or a European author the label of anti-Semitism. In reverse, it can garner him the label of anti-Americanism. Criticizing the American founding myths can earn an author, as apparently it did to Yockey, a double stigma: of being an anti-American and of being an anti-Semite. One must not rule out the possibility that criticizing the American system in the years to come will be seen as a hostile "un-American" act, like in the ex-Soviet Union where criticism of communism was considered a criminal offence. Both systems—one past, the other still present, under cover of democracy, progress, and boundless economic growth—were based on philosophical finitude, excluding other ideological alternatives. How dare one reject a system designed as the ultimate human achievement in goodness—as America portrays itself to be? By the beginning of the 21st century, after becoming the sole hegemon on the planet, one observes a greater dose of hubris in America's ruling class—a trait which usually appears when a system or an ideological system reaches the zenith of its might.

Chapter II

Twin Brothers: *Homo sovieticus* and *Homo americanus*

The closer one studies American ideology, the better one can understand its relationship with other political beliefs, be they of a secular or religious nature. At first sight it may seem preposterous to draw parallels between Communism and Americanism, between *Homo americanus* and *Homo sovieticus*. Americanism, after all, in the second part of the twentieth century, drew a solid part of its world legitimacy from strong anticommunist beliefs. Anticommunism was part and parcel of American foreign policy and hatred of communism constituted a solid arsenal among American conservative elites and the great majority of American citizens. One could ridicule Americanism and its moralistic escapades regarding the real or alleged "red scare," yet the fact remains that had it not been for America, had it not been for the massive American investment in the policy of containment, communism and its chief motor the Soviet Union would likely have become a reality of life for many people on earth. Surely, under such a scenario communism under Soviet hegemony would be less sympathetic to consumerism, permissiveness and less attractive to Third World immigration. Most likely the life style of Americans and Europeans would be less individualistic and their personal values would remain more conservative. Yet it is hard to deny that the drabness of communism and the machinery of its incarceration system would have left deadly traces on millions of its citizens.

Therefore, "warm death" in the fun-infested ideology of
Americanism seems to be more attractive for the masses world
wide, regardless of its deadly consequences for the cultural and
racial memory of every people on earth. Americanism, as a big
promoter of the "fun ideology" has had no problems in disarming
its opponents. Moreover, Americanism has had no difficulty in
creating consensus if not outright complacency of postmodern
world citizens, something unheard of in communism. Its
avoidance of physical terror, its recurrence to therapeutic social
programs, helped it secure lasting longevity. It is undeniable
that the vast majority of people, had they had a choice between
communism and Americanism, would have opted for the latter.
European conservative critics of Americanism often forget that
fact—because many never lived under communism. Worse,
communist genocidal legacy has not been graphically depicted
by the world media in the similar proportions as has been the
legacy of fascism. There are, of course, citizens in every system
who are born rebels and who do not easily fall into the dualistic
trap of "the good America vs. the bad Soviet Union," but who
search, instead, for a third social and political option. Yet these
individuals and heretics can be literally counted on the fingers
of one hand. Certainly, communism kills the body, in contrast
to Americanism which kills the soul, but even the worst type of
intellectual "soft-killing" in the postmodern American system
seems to be dearer to the masses than physical maltreatment or
a violent communist death.

This chapter does not dispute this fact. It only argues that
both the American and the Soviet experiments were founded
on the same principles of egalitarianism, however much their
methods varied in name, time and place. It is also questionable
how tempting the world would be today had the Soviet-style
communism won the political and intellectual contest during
the Cold War. Probably the communized masses in a Soviet
America would be today subject to the torrents of guilt feelings
regarding their real or alleged racist past, the displacement of
American Indians, the segregation of American blacks, and
in addition, they would likely be forced to critically examine

all facets of American foreign policy. Probably many former American vocal conservative patriots would be among the first to offer their service to the new communist ruling class, and would be among the most avid supporters of global communism. The trait of intellectual fickleness has been common to Western history and this point does not need more elaboration. For instance, at the end of the Cold War, Eastern European communist officials did not hesitate for a second to embrace the new creed of Americanism and to pay lip service to American anticommunist slogans. The same people, only a few months earlier, lambasted American capitalism and sang odes to the glorious communist future.

It is undeniable that during the Cold War, American ideology had at least the advantage of partly revealing to the wider public the communist killing fields in Eastern Europe and Russia, however much American elites had once helped the local Communists in setting up these same killing fields. In view of the sudden demise of Soviet style communism at the beginning of the 21st century, many American traditional conservatives must be out of a job. Their nemesis, the Soviet Union, is gone now for good with little chance of resurrection. Furthermore, American anticommunism has always had a superficial and self-defeating ideological substance, more in line with the Christian crusade against communist atheism, and with little or no focus on the egalitarian dynamics which underlines both communism and Americanism. After the demise of the Soviet Union, crypto-communist features which had lain hidden in Americanism, or were carefully hidden during the Cold War, suddenly began to emerge. This was to be expected in view of the fact that America, just like the ex-Soviet Union, has been legally anchored in the same egalitarian foundations. If the Soviet Union had only managed to achieve some type of an affluent society, as America has, very likely nobody in the postmodern world would have given a passing thought to the millions of citizens who perished in communist genocides. By the same token, if America had failed to achieve such surprising economic growth, it is questionable how many of its proponents and spokesmen would be preaching American ideology. Conversely, if one accepts the hypothesis that America has already achieved many communist goals, notably with the erection of its large multiracial universe, it is likely that less and less interest will be shown in the future to probe into the nature of the withering freedom of speech among Euro-Americans. Why examine freedom of speech if the legal foundations in America already posit freedom of speech as something "self-evident"?

Aside from natural geopolitical frictions which arose during the Cold War between the Soviet Union and the USA, both systems pursued the same goal of creating "a new man," stripped of his cumbersome past and ready to enter the lala-land of a radiant egalitarian future. The once much acclaimed Japanese-American author Francis Fukuyama, who had written about the "end of history" and whose books once stirred much feigned interest in America and Europe, had nothing new to transmit to those who had lived under communism and Americanism. Fukuyama's palaver about the end of history was just the replica of a discourse once aired on all wave lengths in the old communist universe; namely, with Communism history must have a stop. Similar discourse about the end of history has been a standard theme in America over the last two hundred years. Real historical time supposedly began in the Soviet Union in 1917 and in the USA in 1776. All other past events were and are still considered irrelevant at best, reactionary and barbaric at worst. Here lies part of the drama with most American elites who are unable to put themselves in historical perspective.

The former Communist nomenclature in the Soviet Union knew that it was living a historical lie; American elites seriously think that they live the historical truth. Yet history, as the events in post-Cold War Europe demonstrated, is always open, and the "problem is not that Americans do not have history; they do not wish to have one," writes de Benoist.[58]

Similar pessimistic remarks about the end of history in America were once made by the revolutionary conservative European philosopher, Julius Evola, who writes that "the structure of history is cyclical, not evolutionary. It is far from being the case that most recent civilizations are necessarily superior. They may be in fact senile and decadent"(...). For Evola, this linear and senile mindset is typical of Americanism and its carrier *Homo americanus,* who "has neither spiritual dilemmas nor complications; he is a natural joiner and a conformist."[59] The parallel with *Homo sovieticus* in the ex-communist Eastern Europe and Russia appears obvious.

Regardless of its verbal anticommunist crusade, America, although having rejected the outward signs of its former communist nemesis, has always resorted to the use of the same egalitarian principles; it has only given them a different name and veneer. It must be emphasized that political slogans and words have changed their meaning over the past decades, although certain principles inherent in communism had taken hold more properly in America than in the ex-Soviet Union. The American transmutations of those paleo-communistic virtues require from the viewpoint of a postmodern observer a different form of conceptualization for which, unfortunately, words are still lacking. It is therefore wrong to assume that just because the communist Soviet Union disappeared, the major discourse about equality, accompanied by the chiliastic principle of hope, will also disappear. Quite the contrary. At the beginning of the third millennium, the immense egalitarian meta-narrative, encapsulated in Americanism, is very much alive and kicking, which is particularly visible in America's academia and mass media. The utopian belief in equality represents the last big hope for millions of non-European newcomers living in America.

To a detached observer, communism had one distinct advantage over Americanism. Its repressive character made it look appalling even in the eyes of its erstwhile supporters. There is ample historical evidence, both in Europe and America, showing how the most ardent communist believers eventually became the most ardent critics of communism. Many of them, nonetheless, continue to think that communism can be better implemented by "non-communist" means, preferably in a country such as postmodern America.

As seen in the ex-Soviet Union, very early on communism started to breed enemies within its own body politic—both among its communized citizens and amidst communist party members. Consequently, and contrary to the pampered masses in America, the grayness of communism helped the citizens of Eastern Europe and Russia come to grips with an elementary political notion: the distinction between friend vs. foe. Thus, unlike Americans or Americanized West Europeans, citizens in communism had the immense political privilege of knowing how to decipher the communist enemy and how to fool the communist enemy. As communism began to wither away by the end of the 20th century, a myriad of communistic principles that had hitherto hovered only in the realm of theory took hold, more aggressively, in Western Europe and America. A large number of American left leaning intellectuals seriously began to think that "true" communism could have a second chance with a humane face in America, and this by means of employing different forms of social engineering. Some European authors observed that communism died in the East because it had already been implemented in the West.[60]

After the end of the Cold War, and particularly after the shock caused by the terrorist attack on America on September 11, 2001, *Homo americanus* turned into a finite postmodern global specie who, although originating in the USA, is thriving now in all parts of the world. He is no longer restricted to the territory of the United States or to a specific region of the world. He is an achieved global kind similar to his ex-twin brother, but also his ex-counterpart *Homo sovieticus*, who had pitifully finished his historical journey. In contrast to the Soviet system, the American system proceeds with philo-communist social engineering more efficiently than the ex-Soviet Union and in a fashion more digestible to the Americanized masses. The breakdown of communism in Eastern Europe played into the hands of American elites and helped them legally strengthen American ideology, both at home and abroad. The demise of communism in the East gave further legitimacy to American-style communism in the West. Alexander Zinoviev noted that "by idealizing the situation in the West, by exaggerating out of proportion in their imagination Western abundance, ex-Soviet citizens transferred to the West the communist promise of a terrestrial paradise."[61] Admittedly, with its strong egalitarian substance, Americanism has so far been much more receptive to a reenactment of a new proto-communist utopia.

During the Cold War, Americans liked contrasting themselves to Russians and often self-righteously declared their system to be superior to the Soviet system. In most cases, this comparison was made in the realm of economic growth and standard of living. At that time, it was considered natural by many Americans to refer in a derogatory manner to a slothful Soviet citizen, while proudly pointing out how American affluence and high tech remained unsurpassed in the world. Curiously, few American experts on communism looked into the hidden advantages of Soviet-style communism, such as guaranteed economic security and psychological predictability that the Soviet version of communism was able to secure better for its masses than the American system. During the Cold War, abstract principles of liberty, which American citizens liked gloating about, were primarily associated with the country's economic performance. At the same time, however, hardly anybody in the so-called free West thought it necessary to tackle the American psychology of proto-communist conformism and to critically examine the surprising communist-like sameness of *Homo sovieticus* and *Homo americanus*.

It was the author Zinoviev who coined the term *Homo sovieticus* for species living in a Soviet style communist system and also having the communized mindset. This is a curious specie of low integrity yet of phenomenal adaptability to all egalitarian experiments.[62] Zinoviev's understanding of communist psychology remains unsurpassed, all the more so as his description of communist psychology facilitates now a study of *Homo americanus* in postmodernity. Contrary to many other anticommunist dissidents, Zinoviev, after the breakdown of communism, did not hesitate to critically examine Americanism and its human carriers, which explains why his analyses are still ignored by many.

In the contest with the Soviet Union, America poured millions of dollars into projects known under the names of Sovietology and Kremlinology; America's different governmental think tanks developed during the Cold War a host of abstract theories regarding the future behavior of Soviet citizens and the communist nomenklatura. The Soviet Union was portrayed by professional American anticommunists as a totalitarian hell in comparison to which democratic America shined as a bright city on the hill. During the Cold War, the official American endeavor to inquire into the Soviet mind was further facilitated by the oppressive political situation in Eastern Europe as well as the dream of many East European citizens to immigrate to America. Ironically, the average East European and Russian anti-communists viewed America only through the prism of economic success, hardly paying attention to the flaws in the American system, including a well hidden American brand of thought control. Subconsciously, most Russians and East Europeans continued to remain "true communists" in their mind and merely conceived of the communist paradise as more easily attainable in America. During the Cold War period, there were thus more true "Americans" in Eastern Europe than in America itself!

After the breakdown of Soviet communism, the American method of negative legitimization, that is, the preceding invocation of the real or surreal communist threat, no longer sounds convincing. Needles to say that none of the American or Western experts could fathom the sudden demise of the Soviet Union, nor understand the root causes of the communist breakdown. Had they understood the origins of the collapse of communism, American elites would have had to focus critically on the same paleo-communist impulses within their own system and within their own populace. But how could they ever carry out this process of introspection in view of the fact that Americanism preaches the same principles of equality and progress — so dear to both *Homo americanus* and *Homo sovieticus?* The paradox is that citizens during Soviet communism never believed in the official communist version of their radiant future; they saw their radiant future only palpable in America — albeit under an anticommunist name.

It is fundamentally wrong to blame the communist party in the ex-Soviet Union or Eastern Europe as the only culprit for communist mismanagement or state-sponsored terror. The communist party in the Soviet Union was the repository of an egalitarian ideology whose goal was not to further the interests of party members only, but to serve as the operating philosophical principle governing social conduct of millions of its citizens.[63] A parallel could be drawn with the Catholic Church in earlier centuries, an institution which was not only represented by the Pope and the clergy, but which served as an organizational principle that provided a pattern of social behavior for countless individuals, irrespective of their personal feelings toward Christian dogma. Likewise, Americanism has never been an administrative foundation of the American political system, nor has it been embedded solely among the members of political elites in Washington. Americanism, as a common denominator for perfect egalitarianism, transcends different lifestyles, different political affiliations, and different religious denominations.

Contrary to the assumption of liberal theorists, in communist societies the cleavage between people and party was almost nonexistent since rank-and-file party members were recruited from all walks of life and not just from one specific social stratum.[64] The same parallel could apply to the circulation of political elites in postmodern America. Inevitably, the logic of the Declaration of Independence and its egalitarian discourse had to give birth to a multiracial society and to the ever increasing demands of non-European new comers for their share of the American dream. Many American conservatives and racialists wrongly assume that one could keep the legacy of the early founding fathers while establishing a strict hierarchical society based on the racial merits of dominant white European

Americans. Yet, the historical dynamics of Americanism has shown that this is not possible. Once the flood gates of egalitarianism open—however modest this may appear at the beginning—the logic of equality will gather momentum and will end up eventually in some protean form of proto-communist temptation.

It is a serious failure to disregard communism as something historically redundant or as a temporary zig-zag of history. Communism is the most logical form of perfect egalitarianism. It is the system which is dearest and nearest to the masses no matter how dreadful its consequences can be for the masses. Communism is a system which flatters the animalistic impulses of each human being and brings out the worst behavioral elements in all individuals. However, communism is also an ideal social model for future mass societies facing shrinking natural resources and rapid modernization. After its official disintegration in the Soviet Union, the main features of communism, such as the belief in progress and economic growth, have been brought to their perfection in America. In the decades to come the role of Americanism, even if America splits up into smaller geographical entities, will continue to be dominant, regardless of the alleged withering of the state in the global world. In the case of an emergency, such as a war, famine, terrorism, or some other unforeseen cataclysm, a future communized American mass society will be obliged to recur to *manu militari* in order to preserve its stability. At that point American elites will cease to resort to verbal abstractions such as the free market or individual human rights for all. In a perfect egalitarian system citizens are designed to be expandable since according to the canons of egalitarianism, everybody equals everyone. Thus, in order for the proper functioning of future Americanized society, the removal of millions of surplus citizens must become a social and possibly also an ecological necessity. The results of such new social engineering will be visible in America and Europe in the near future.

Admittedly, in Soviet-style communism the per capita income was three to four times lower than in capitalist America, and as the daily drudgery and bleakness of communist life indicated, life under communism was by no means pleasant. Yet, did the lower purchasing power in the ex-communist East necessarily indicate that the overall quality of life was inferior to life in the West during the same epoch? This judgment will depend on the criteria that a critic of both Americanism and communism uses. If one takes into account that an average worker in the communist system put in three to four hours every day in his work (for which he usually never got reprimanded, let alone ran a risk of losing his job), then his pay made the equivalent of the pay of a worker in a capitalist America.[65] Stated in Marxist terminology, a worker in the communist system was not economically exploited, but instead "took the liberty" of allocating to himself the full surplus value of his labor which the communist state never provided to him. Hence the popular joke, so firmly entrenched in post-communist Europe which still vividly explains the longevity of the communist nostalgia: "Nobody can pay me less than the little I can work." Speculations about the economic superiority of American capitalism over communism or fascism, or for that matter allegations that American capitalist economies are more efficient than communist economies, are groundless. Views by American plutocratic elites about the purportedly better life in America seldom take into account long-term social benefits and the quality of life provided by Soviet elites to their citizens. China is a case study of a gigantic mass society which in a pragmatic fashion managed to combine a command economy with a market economy. America will likely engage in a similar socio-economic experiment in the years to come.

And why also not measure the correlation of economic growth with social and mental stress and various other social abnormalities that characterize the American free market, yet which were virtually absent in the Soviet-style communist system? In the years to come, communist social advantages, however Spartan they once appeared to foreign observers, will be in demand by more and more citizens in America and Americanized Europe.

America in the Eyes of post-communist Europe

Post-communist Eastern Europe and Russia are ideal laboratories that help us understand the interaction between the two twin brothers, *Homo americanus* and *Homo sovieticus*. While a massive amount of both critical and laudatory literature about America has been circulating in Western Europe, only a few critical books about America and the American way of life have been published thus far in post-communist Eastern Europe.[66] At the beginning of the third millennium, America is observed by many people in post-communist and Third World countries as the only remaining dreamland on earth.

People living in Eastern Europe do not like being called Eastern Europeans; neither do they like being labeled with the term *Homo sovieticus*. Also the term "Eastern Europe" has the ring of an insult in their ears. They consider themselves, despite their region's communist past, to be full-blooded Europeans— as much, if not more so than West Europeans and Americans. There may be a grain of truth in this semi-complacent attitude. From a racial point of view, all post-communist countries in Eastern Europe are highly homogeneous, with relatively few non-Europeans living on their soil. Western Europe and America, by contrast, have been subject to increasing racial and demographic changes which, by the end of the 20th century, began to leave traces on the legal and political structure of their systems. Ironically, due to the closed nature of communism, Eastern Europe had never experienced a large influx of non-Europeans. By contrast, at the beginning of the third millennium, America and Western Europe are awash with non-European emigrants. It is often forgotten that quite in accordance with the stateless and multicultural ideology of Marxism, the communist system in Russia and Eastern Europe was originally designed as a multicultural system of mass foreign immigration. However, its Spartan nature in Eastern Europe could not attract many non-European immigrants or would be immigrants, who opted, instead, for a more financially promising West European and American itinerary. The irony of history is that the political rigidity and economic frugality of communist systems helped East Europeans and Russians remain racially homogenous. Another historical irony is that due to the repressive nature of communism, Eastern Europe is now more ready to face the challenges of multicultural postmodernity. Looming inter-racial riots in America, which will likely break up America, are hardly conceivable in post-communist Eastern Europe and Russia. However, problems of a different geopolitical nature and the creeping sense of a loss of national sovereignty are already looming large on the East European horizon. In addition, in the span of ten years after the end of the Cold War, the process of Americanization has made many regions in Eastern Europe look like a replica of distant America.

Although claiming to be one hundred percent European, East European nations, and particularly the newborn nation-states in the region, are well aware of their racial and European roots—more so than are West Europeans and Americans. For decades, during the darkest hours of communism, East Europeans showed strange love for white America, while displaying strange resentments toward their next-door white European neighbors. Despite their communized mindset and *Homo sovieticus*—inspired culture of sloth, most Eastern Europeans and Russians, at least in private, showed anticommunist, racialist, and even pro-American feelings. During the Cold War, in the eyes and ears of East Europeans, the West was not the nearby rich and opulent Western Europe, but rather the distant, Hollywood-hazed America. Former American presidents Richard Nixon and Ronald Reagan had more true, albeit hidden constituents in communized Poland, Hungary, and Albania than on the West or East Coast of America. It was difficult for many East Europeans, particularly those who had physically suffered under communism, to grasp the motives of left leaning Western critics of America. Their self-styled Americanism knew no limits. Of course, pro-American and anticommunist sentiments among wide layers of official Eastern European society had to be skillfully hidden. A great majority of people in Eastern Europe, despite their communist life style, privately cherished U.S. foreign ventures and America's harsh anticommunist rhetoric, and most were seriously persuaded that sooner or later American GIs would liberate their homelands from the red plague. After the end of communism and with the rapid Americanization of Eastern Europe, citizens in this part of Europe are beginning to realize that America had other fish to fry than liberating their region from communism.

To some extent, Eastern European attitudes toward America resemble those of West Europeans following World War II, when America, as a shining myth, surpassed its own gloomy reality. In early postmodernity, Eastern European politicians and their constituents still view with mistrust the European arbitration of their regional or ethnic disputes. They first turn their eyes toward distant America. Even among America-haters in Eastern Europe, the prevailing assumption is that America, due to its historical detachment and its proverbial geographical naiveté, can be the only honest broker in international affairs. Despite grotesque cravings to become part of the West, so vividly exhibited by East Europeans during the Cold War, the East European political class continues to view itself as a loyal progeny of Americanism. Former communist officials in Eastern Europe have good reasons to be vocal spokesmen of Americanism. The virulent economic competition in America, offering little safety net to American workers, can serve for them as a role model for their quasi lawless and clannish oriented post-communists societies. "The savage side of economic competition in the American manner (bankruptcy and corruption), can closely be related to the dynamics of post-communism."[67] Even the most cultivated Eastern European opponents of the American way of life or the harshest critic of U.S. foreign policy, cannot dispute the fact that America elicits awe and respect among Eastern European leaders and that, therefore, America is expected to be the only mediator vis-à-vis a pesky European neighbor. Such a view only gives additional credibility to the American expansionist experiment in Eastern and Central Europe.

Everybody in Eastern Europe finds something inexplicably

attractive about America. The servility of post-communist elites towards American elites is a natural and logical outcome of their colonial mentality. Once it were the Soviets who needed to be paid all due respect by Eastern European rulers; today they know that "it is the American ambassador, in the capacity of the proconsul, who commands behind the scene."[68]

But is America still the same role model country for East Europeans as it was prior to the dissolution of communism? America's racial profile has changed dramatically since the end of the Cold War, which is largely due to a massive influx of non-European immigrants as well as to the persistence of the pseudo-Marxist and neo-liberal role models of ethnic diversity who still frame the discourse in American universities. During the heyday of the Soviet Union, Eastern Europe's embellished image of America, accompanied by an often ludicrous love of an imaginary America, was a predictable gut reaction against the endless official anti-American rhetoric by the communist ruling class. Even when communist apparatchiks in Eastern Europe or the Soviet Union aired slogans that carried some truth about America's racial discrimination, poverty and high crime rates, East European masses across the board refused to believe in it. This was understandable. How could they ever believe communist propaganda given that the communist system in the East was founded on a big lie and could only function by lying on all wavelengths twenty-four hours a day. Instead, East Europeans opted for their own self-styled version of imaginary America, which real Americans would have found laughable and hard to believe in. The more realistic the picture of America was presented by the communist propaganda machine, the more East Europeans believed in its surreal and hyperreal side.

This has now slowly started to change. More and more East Europeans are beginning to realize the advantages of their "all white" post-communist Eastern Europe; more and more will tend, in the years to come, to close themselves off from multicultural Western Europe and America, a system whose social profile looks less and less European.

It might now take some time before East Europeans realize

that *Homo americanus*, similar to his twin brother in communism, also has its local taboos which must never be tackled. After the first euphoria, following the demise of the Soviet Union, Eastern Europeans are gradually toning down their illusions about quick Americanization and Westernization—which in their popular parlance was once a code word for becoming rich. By the end of the 20ᵗʰ century, communist mendacity, police repression, and economic scarcity prompted East Europeans and Russians to kick out communism from power. But would they have done the same thing had there not been the prospect of a better and a more affluent American "communist" counterpart? Had America failed in its headlong drive towards economic progress, most East Europeans would be still happy with their home grown communist systems. With the Soviet negative referent of comparison gone, and having now heard that the American-style egalitarian utopia requires private initiative and back breaking hard work, often in a climate of a dog eat dog mentality, East Europeans instinctively revert to demands for more communist-style security and for more social promiscuity which was once associated with their beloved breed of *Homo sovieticus*. "This anti-democratic disenchantment, shows again, how in the countries of the ex-Soviet block, parliamentary democracy is only a surface phenomenon," writes Claude Karnoouh.[69] Oh how beautiful it would be to live a life combining the glamour and glitz of the vicarious *Homo americanus*, as seen on the American TV screen, and enjoy the psychological security of *Homo sovieticus*!

And who says that America cannot engage in this project too? Who says, after all, that thought control cannot be carried out in a democratic fashion, and that individuals or masses always know what is in their best interest? Sometimes a leader, a strongman, a *fuehrer*, a *caudillo*, or a *vodj*, best knows the answer.

The psychological legacy of communism in Eastern Europe is hard to grasp even for those American thinkers of substantial cultural and intellectual probity. Communism had created distinct patterns of behavior that will take much longer to discard than its ideological or legal legacy. A shrewd American traveler to post-communist Eastern Europe, whether a businessman, a politician, or a student, will notice how citizens in post-communist Prague, Bucharest, Budapest, or Zagreb, despite their obnoxious flag-waving Americanism, continue to display the communist phenotype. Essentially, as Claude Karnoouh notes, political elites in post-communist Eastern Europe are the same communist apparatchiks who converted after the Cold War to the ideology of liberalism and Americanism, and "whose democracy is often reduced to lexical incantation."[70] The communist culture of social leveling had resulted in a considerable depletion of the gene pool and brought to the fore the most vulgar and the most mediocre communistic individuals, who in early postmodernity are dressed up in the garb of pro-American neo-liberalism. Earlier communist mass genocides, especially in the first phase of the communist consolidation process, had created a mind-set of base survivalism and fickleness, and gave birth, subsequently, to a peculiar Eastern European subspecie that still lives on today. Although this subspecie looks very European by its phenotype, its communist behavioral traits have not changed all that much.

For a variety of reasons, Western European and American elites have never been willing to reveal these gigantic sociobiological changes in Eastern Europe and Russia for fear of revealing their tacit approval of communist genocides. It is more convenient for American elites to narrate about real or alleged fascist crimes than to talk about the far bigger and more numerous crimes committed by their erstwhile communist allies. Thus, the entire postmodernity in Americanized post-communist Eastern Europe may be characterized as an epoch of an almost nauseating and continuous discourse of antifascist victimology mixed with pro-American sentimental incantations, with little to no mention of crimes committed by the local ex-post-communist elites. As a result, Americans should not be surprised if they witness how the new post-communist political elites in Eastern Europe conceptualize the capitalist American reality differently from what the American reality actually is. Beneath the style and the rhetoric of these new post-communist and pro-American elites, the substance of *Homo sovieticus* still lives on. Indeed, from the Balkans to Baltic countries, the majority of Eastern European politicians are basically the sons and daughters of recycled communists, who for obvious geopolitical and techno-scientific reasons converted to Americanism. Karnoouh adds that "within one day former professors of "scientific socialism," who were once in charge of inculcating the casuistic *doxa* to their students and to their colleagues, discovered in themselves, by some miraculous intervention of the Holy Liberal Ghost, fervent disciples of Hayek."[71] In hindsight, it is questionable to what extent these ex-Communists were true believers in their former communist deities, and for how long they will believe in their newly discovered theology of the free market.

The culture of *Homo sovieticus* cannot be wished away by State Department officials or would-be American moralists. Over the last half a century the American attitude toward Eastern Europe has been based on pragmatic (albeit too idealistic) models and schemes that foresaw a solution, or at least a contingency plan, or a formula for every crisis and for every nook and cranny of East European life. But America's endless formulas, which a good observer of America, Thomas Molnar derides, do not contain a ready made answer for post-communist Eastern Europe. Americans, unlike other peoples, like to have extended recipes for everything; how to teach democracy in Africa and Europe, how to have safe sex, how to become rich, and how to find a formula for political and economic success stories in post-communist Eastern Europe, and so on. "The Americans are at unease and have bad conscience as soon as they have to leave the magic circles of formulas," notes Molnar.[72] The quest for formulas is basically a logical product of American rationalism, which in practice explains why American elites lack the feeling and understanding of someone's else "suddenness," i.e. why they cannot grasp the concept of national state of emergency in Europe. It must, therefore, not come as a surprise that the average Eastern European or Russian will continue to display behavioral traits of *Homo sovieticus*, however much he may be subject to the American process of democratic re-education. An average post-communist Eastern European is prone to irrational emotional outbursts and he continues to harbor paranoid conspiracy theories about foreigners, including the Americans. Due to negative biological selection caused by earlier communist genocides, he learned, long ago, the basic formulas of survivalism. An Eastern European, although far less individualistic in his decision making, is more of a con man and less of a social conformist than his American counterpart. Since he often thinks that all American and Western foreigners are potential crooks, he will do his best to double-cross them. Civic loyalty, initiative, professional commitment, and economic self-reliance, which are still visible in America and Western Europe, are almost completely nonexistent in Eastern Europe. The prevalent opinion in the post-communist postmodern East is that in order to show self-initiative one must be a crook—in a positive fashion. The imbedded communist practices of double dealing present, thus, a formidable barrier for any long term Americanized alternative in Eastern Europe. Numerous American scholars and politicians think that these barriers will disappear with the brutal implementation of the free market. They are wrong. For Eastern Europeans, the American dream boils down to transplanting themselves vicariously into surreal American TV soaps—as long as these soaps last.

Conversely, white elites in America tacitly envy Eastern Europeans for something that America lost long ago and something Eastern Europeans are still not quite aware of: racial homogeneity and all out European roots. What contemporary Americans, along with Western Europeans, seem to envy among Eastern Europeans most is their sense of belonging to something more important than the mere individual self. Despite the depletion of their best genes, Eastern Europeans have retained a sense of historical and racial identity with a distinct feeling of nationhood. Thus far, they have been less bruised by consumerism and multiculturalism. One may argue, as does Jean Baudrillard, a theorist of postmodernity, that America, although being a utopia achieved at the beginning of the 21st century, remains a crippled utopia designed only for Third World immigrants.

Despite visible long term advantages, Eastern Europe, however, has skipped the most important part of modern history; it never carried out wholesale political decommunization, and it never began educating the masses in civility. But how could it, in view of the depletion of its best genes and the absence of real role models? Where exactly should Eastern Europe look for new inspiration? Should Eastern Europe look for guidance in multicultural and multiracial Western Europe? The tragedy of Eastern Europe consists in the fact that despite its racial homogeneity, it has functioned over centuries as a social laboratory for Russian or Soviet and Western elites, including America's present elites. The sense of civic identity is gravely missing there.

But equally true is that Western Europe and America never bothered to carry out the demarxification of their own public discourse; nor did America ever attempt after the Cold War, to seriously debunk Lamarckian methods which are still influential in Western higher education. It must not be ignored that Communism, as was once practiced in Russia and Eastern Europe, had intellectually been conceived in Western European and American universities. Trends may have changed by now but the communist substance of incivility has remained the same. America's postmodern exports to Eastern Europe, in the form of cheap video thrills, are replete with decadence and their aftershocks will be more damaging for Eastern Europeans than the legacy of communism. Once upon a time when serial communist killings were taking place in Eastern Europe, American universities were teeming with professors teaching Freudo-Marxian scholasticism and raving about alternative Cuban, Yugoslav, and Chinese communist models. Later, when communism in the East and the Soviet Union tempered its violent phase of political repression, the same American ex-Marxist professors and scribes deemed it necessary to replace

Marxism with liberalism and the capitalist creed. But their former goals of globalization and economic progress have never been abandoned.

During the initial post-communist phase, following the Cold War, Eastern Europeans thought that by shouting pro-American anticommunist slogans they would open up the road to rich Americanism. This was visible in 2003, when Eastern European leaders were among the first Europeans to endorse the American military intervention in Iraq. Their servility to Americanism knew no bounds as they seriously thought that by mimicking Americanism they would soon find the stepping stone for the much desired entry into an earthly paradise. A good observer of the East European mindset, Bruno Drweski, writes, how Eastern European elites have become "the Trojan asses of the United States of America."[73] It is no accident that the first governments in post communist Eastern Europe, shortly after the fall of the Soviet Union, were made up of radical anticommunist and nationalist politicians—acceptable but not much beloved by American elites. Later, during the second phase, which is still in progress, the Eastern European political class engaged in a grotesque emulation of America's multiculturalism, while rejecting its erstwhile tribal nationalism. Everybody started regurgitating words such as "economic growth," "privatization," "globalization," and "Euro-Atlantic integration," without knowing what those words actually stood for.

This phase of Americanization is now coming slowly to an end, leaving a dangerous vacuum behind and a minefield of mass anxiety ahead. One may not rule out that after the post-Cold War brief experiment "made in the U.S.A.," Eastern Europeans will suddenly, out of defiance, revert to their aged domestic hard-liners. Security comes first; liberty may be a distant second. The rapid process of Americanization in Eastern Europe, with its self-induced, self-gratifying dreams, has already had its nasty drawbacks, let alone that previous projected illusions have not been matched by the American reality. The Hollywood custom designed America for Eastern European has not materialized. If an American academic or politician recovers courage and starts raising similar questions about the rapid "de-Europeanization" and "communization" of America, then both Eastern Europe and America will be ready to abandon the American dream, and will get ready to face up to a new chapter of tectonic history. Eastern Europeans, for their part, will gladly flock to their treasure trove of myths and legends which lie in abundance beneath America's passing glitz.

The Meta-Language of Americanism

The political language in America is a potent weapon for legitimizing the system. Probably this book should have dealt first with the semiotics of Americanism given that the language in America has acquired a different meaning from the meaning used elsewhere in the world. The American meta-language, as used in the political arena, is reminiscent of the communist language in the ex-Soviet Union, although American politicians tend to use words and phrases that appear less abrasive and less value loaded than words used by European politicians. In the American academe, media, and public places, a level of communication has been attained which avoids confrontational discourse and which resorts to discursive vocables devoid of substantive meaning. Americans, in general, avoid political hyperbolas and qualifiers that the state-run media and Party nomenklatura in the ex-Soviet Union once used in fostering the veracity of communist ideology. Also, unlike West Europeans, and very much in line with the ideology of historical optimism and progress, Americans are enamored with the overkill of morally uplifting adjectives and adverbs. Their choice of grammatical embellishers is consistent with the all-prevailing market which, as a rule, must employ for the commerce of its goods and services adjectives in their superlative forms. By contrast, behind the communist semiotics in Eastern Europe, there always loomed a general doubt. Communism was a make-belief system in which, ironically, citizens never believed and which everybody, including communist party dignitaries made fun of in private. Eventually, verbal mendacity spelled the death of Soviet communism.

In America, by contrast, politicians and scholars, let alone the masses, passionately believe in every written word of democratic discourse. American official communication perfectly matches the rule of law and can, therefore, rarely trigger a violent or a negative reaction among the citizens. Surely, Americans like staging protests and marches; they are masters of organizing rallies against some unpopular governmental decision; they can easily drum up public support on behalf or against some issue—be it against American military involvement in a foreign country, or against fraudulent behavior of some local political representative. But, as an unwritten rule, seldom can one see rallies in America that challenge the democratic substance of Americanism or the ceremonial language of the American ruling class.

In his classic, *Metascience and Politics*, the American scholar James Gregor provides a solid theoretical account of the postmodern language and politics. However, his analysis of political meta-language appears to be too hermetic and it rarely provides a much needed example regarding political use and abuse of the language by American elites. Being also known as the foremost expert on intellectual fascism in Europe, Gregor certainly knows what he is writing about. One must give him credit for dissecting political semiotics—as long as the totalitarian systems of communism and fascism are involved— yet, he hesitates in lodging the same critique against political utterances by American elites and their court historians. Are not "normative locutions," as he calls political propaganda in fascism and communism, also part and parcel of the American ceremonial language that banks on the lowest impulses of the American masses in order to sell them the "best of all worlds?" Gregor, unfortunately, does not use the explicit word for American "double talk," preferring instead an arcane label of "the non-cognitive language which is used for manipulative or predictive analyses."[74] Despite valuable insights, Gregor fails to provide examples for propagandistic American rhetoric, although he notes that "social sciences have produced ample evidence that most people do not have clearly articulated values, much less any one specific subtending values."[75]

To put it crudely, postmodern Americans and the Americanized masses in Europe are better fooled and deceived by official propaganda than were the Sovietized and communized masses in Eastern Europe. Due to the torrent of meaningless vocables and idioms, such as "human rights" and "democracy," the thought control and intellectual repression in postmodern America functions far better. Therefore, in the American "soft" system, a motive for a would-be heretic to overthrow the system is virtually absent. The American system is posited as a historical finitude, simply because there are no competitors for another "freedom narrative" in the present world. Thus, America gives an impression of being the freest country and the best of political systems—when compared to any past or present system.

It is worth observing that millions of former communist sympathizers and opinion makers in the USA and in the European Union, after the Cold War, deemed it necessary to refurbish their former Marxist phraseology by substituting it with "soft" liberal locutions. Owing to its awesome technical know how, America became the first country on earth that managed to substitute its conception of political reality to a projected hyperreality. It managed to force upon the public eye the imagery which precedes a real political event. This is best observed on the American TV screen and in motion pictures, which endlessly rehash countless contingency plans about one single theme or one single topic. This surreal imagery has significantly helped the postmodern American intelligentsia in search of new "paradigms"- an endeavor which fully squares away with their definition of polymorphous postmodernity. It would be, therefore, wrong to interpret the sudden conversion to liberalism by the left leaning American intelligentsia as a sign of intellectual treason. After all, fickleness has always been a standard feature of Western intellectuals and at all times in history. Given that communism and Americanism share the same techno-morphic roots going back to the Enlightenment and its idea of progress, as well as the common parable of a new post-historical and a-historical man, both systems are compelled to inflate or deflate their respective languages. Hence the reason why former Marxists and communist intellectuals, turned liberal and pro-American after the Cold War, can easily shrug off with impunity their former "hard core" rhetoric revolving around Marx. In postmodernity they have no troubles embracing the more advanced form of "soft" rhetoric made in the USA.

Americanism and its accompanying dogma of liberalism came to be viewed, after the breakdown of communism, as a safe exit which enabled many leftist thinkers and authors to save face yet help them continue with the same sloganeering about egalitarianism and global humanity, albeit in a more respectable and non-violent Americanized fashion. An external ritual had to be changed too. At some recent point in history European and American left leaning intellectuals made pilgrimages to Havana and to Moscow. After the Cold War, with the beginning of postmodernity, it became mandatory, short of ruining one's career, to travel to the newly found super-egos: Tel Aviv and New York.

However much communism may be dead as a programmatic religion, its verbal substratum in Americanism is much alive, not just among left-leaning intellectuals but even among those Americans professing conservative beliefs. One must dismiss the communist signifiers, and look instead into the signified. In the USA there are surprisingly many academics who seriously believe in the veracity of egalitarian and pan-racial ideas, although they package these ideas in humanitarian or Christian ecumenical words. Red star and hammer and sickle are dated referents in America; what is crucial is the usage of new symbols conveying the same meaning, but in a disarming and more sentimental way. In order to enforce its paleo-communist goals, Americanism requires a different social setting than the one the Bolsheviks used in Russia at the beginning of the 20th century. Therefore, words and sentence structures conveying communistic messages in America must be framed by different signifiers.

Modern public discourse in the USA is also teeming with Soviet-style messages such as "ethnic sensitivity training," "political correctness," "affirmative action," and "holocaust studies." This is best observed in American higher education which, over the last thirty years, has transformed itself into places of higher commissariats of political correctness which consist of "committees on preventing racial perjuries," "ethnic diversity training programs," and in which racial awareness courses have become mandatory for the faculty staff and students. No longer are professors required to demonstrate skills in their subject matters; instead, they must parade with sentimental and self-deprecatory statements which, as a rule, denigrate European cultural heritage.[76] What strikes the eyes is that these new verbal constructs and neologisms resemble retarded and well masked carbon copies of the old Communist meta-language going back to the 50s and 60s, and which was once obligatorily parroted in different dialects by communized subjects all over Eastern Europe and Russia. These refurbished ritual utterances are now being mouthed by *Homo americanus.*

In trying to be original with their diversity, American government-sponsored multicultural groups and agencies tend to end up being the same. As much as these different groups, ranging from lesbian clubs and gay societies to fellowships of cat lovers to sun worshippers, often stress their diversity, the imagery and rhetoric they use is always the same — and therefore redundant. A theorist of postmodernity, Jean Baudrillard, writes that "it is in its resemblance, not only analogical but technological that the image becomes most immoral and most perverse."[77] By constantly stressing the same referent of "diversity," diverse American groups and infra-political tribes prove their sameness, making dispassionate observers easily bored and tired.

Nowhere is this sign of American hyperreality more visible than in the constant verbal and visual featuring of Jewish

Holocaust symbolism, which ironically, is creating the same saturation process among the audience as was once the case with former communist symbolism. Soviet communist truth, which also consisted of endless antifascist body-counting, eventually triggered the opposite result from what the Soviet politicians had initially expected. *Homo sovieticus* did not believe in communist victimology, even when that victimology contained elements of credibility. The best proof of communist mendacity was, ironically, laid barren not by the proverbial counterrevolutionaries or the world bourgeoisie, but by former communist apparatchiks themselves. This explains why after the breakup of the Soviet Union the same apparatchiks did not have qualms in rapidly converting to Americanism and anticommunism. One may conclude that if they so skillfully betrayed their self-evident beliefs once, very likely they will equally quickly discard their newly adopted American ideology—when time becomes ripe for new "self-evidences."

In a similar fashion, the American visual description of the hyperreality of Auschwitz will not enhance a better understanding of the Jewish question; it will cause more anti-Semitism. "It is the perpetuation of it in a different guise, under the auspices not of a site of annihilation but a medium of dissuasion," writes Baudrillard.[78] The larger postmodern narrative about the Holocaust runs thus the risk of no longer representing a historical event, but of turning into a massive media non-event.

❧

Both *Homo sovieticus* and *Homo americanus* were and still are the products of rationalism, Enlightenment, egalitarianism, and the belief in progress. They both believe that a glorious future is unfolding on the horizon. Both herald the slogan that all men are created equal. The early Bolsheviks were as much inspired by the French revolutionaries as were the founding fathers of America. Now, in hindsight, the famed Declaration of Independence, signed by Jefferson and stating that all men are "created equal," may sound to conservatives or racialists in the United States, let alone in Europe, as semantic nonsense devoid of any empirical basis. Yet, attempts to rectify the damage are coming too late. All academic discussions about genetic or racial differences are quickly neutralized by the all-encompassing words such as "racism" or "hate speech."[79] In multiracial postmodern society, as is America, this has been foreseeable and inevitable. It appears that a multiracial society, such as America, will soon become the least tolerant society, precisely because every constituent racial or ethnic group wishes to underline its own version of historical truth. For fear of being called confrontational or racist, an honest politician or an academic must practice self-censorship.

Left-leaning critics, who argue that the methods for measuring I.Q. are Western-biased and that they only reflect Western standards of measurement, are, from the methodological point of view, correct. But at the same token, it is also correct to state that social and anti-racist discourse in postmodernity, including egalitarian analyses in vogue and the methods of critical inquiry into the origins of European slavery and racism, are also Western and American made. In fact, even those non-white academics and politicians in America who resent each vestige of traditional Western discourse, are forced to admit that their own conceptualization and their own hatred against the white world, has been handed down to them by the sons and daughters of their former white masters. America created slavery and racial theories of inequality; it also created self-hatred and numerous theories of racial equality.

If something is "self-evident" it does not need to be repeated ad infinitum, it need only be stated once. Communist systems were replete with "self-evident truths" and questioning that truth could land a dissident in jail. One may surmise that if a political belief or an idea, such as is the case with Americanism today, is founded on strong empirical evidence, it does not need to be repeated *ad nauseam*. Conversely, if an ideology or a political belief is founded on frail evidence, its enforcers and disciples are obliged to resort to its constant repetition. The censorial intellectual climate in the American media, so similar to old Soviet propaganda, bears witness that American elites, at the beginning of the third millennium, are worried about the future identity of the country they rule. Surely, the American system doesn't yet need truncheons or police force in order to enforce its truth. It can remove, by using the syndrome of "guilt by association," all rebellious individuals from important places of decision—be it in academia, the political arena, or the media. Once the spirit of the time will have changed, the high priests of this new postmodern inquisition will likely be the first to dump their current truths and replace them with other voguish "self-evident" truths.

It would be a waste of time to speculate what was crossing Jefferson's mind at the time of the signing of the Declaration. Jefferson and his compatriots were people of the Enlightenment and Rationalism. Jefferson was a man of his epoch and his intellectual legacy can only be understood within the spirit of his time. American conservatives use him as a logo; liberals and leftists admire him; and even the pro-fascist poet Ezra Pound raved about Jefferson's "proto-fascist" legacy. Jefferson is considered a hero in America, although at some point in the future, he may be dismissed as a crook or a con man. The timeless quest for historical meaning will always depend on those who define that meaning as well as the truth seeker himself.

George Fitzhugh, a Southern racialist, and an antebellum author, was a person who intensely hated Jefferson. Yet, he viewed himself as a good American—but not in a Jeffersonian fashion. Being a keen observer of political semiotics, he knew well how words could historically be deployed—sometimes with positive and sometimes with negative results:

The true greatness of Mr. Jefferson was his fitness for revolution. He was the genius of innovation, the architect of ruin, the inaugurator of anarchy. His mission was to pull down, not to build up. He thought everything false as well in the physical as in the moral world. He fed his horses on potatoes, and defended harbors with gunboats, because it was contrary to human experience and human opinion. He proposed to

*govern boys without the authority of masters or the control of religion,
supplying their places with Laissez Faire philosophy...*[80]

Similar critical views of early American ideology were later
echoed by many American and European authors whom we
have already quoted in this book. Their un-American words may
sound offensive to the ears of a 21ˢᵗ century liberal spokesmen of
the American dream. One must admit, however, that Jefferson
certainly did not consider native Indians or Africans to be his
equals. But equally true is that the spirit of Enlightenment
gradually seeped over into the egalitarian dynamic of early
Americanism and gave birth, two hundred years later, to *Homo
sovieticus* and *Homo americanus.* The philosophical tenets of the
Declaration made everybody wish to be his own boss and not
to be bossed around by a king or a prince. The result of this
passionate drive for equality must lead, eventually, to mutual
suspicion and latent civil strife, as was observed in the ex-Soviet
Union. Needless to say, irrespective of their official *"braggadioccio,"*
regarding their lauded multicultural and democratic credentials
or the egalitarian dream which they like to sport, in private,
the vast majority of white European American politicians and
academics hardly believe in the equality of peoples and races.
But it is their haunting fear of falling into disrepute which
functions as a self-projected scarecrow and that prevents them
from saying these "self-evident" words aloud in public.

Is it not "self-evident" that men are different? But does
it matter at all? What Jefferson and his likes had in mind is
of little importance; what is important is what his successors
and non-European American interpreters had in mind two
centuries later. Jefferson's words could at any time be easily
taken out of context and used as a justification for copying
paleo-communistic practices.

In all fairness, one must give credit to those rare American
rebels mentioned earlier who fell out with the syndrome of
Homo americanus, yet who refused to embrace its communist
replica. Who says that the enemy of my enemy must be my
friend? Often my enemy's enemy can be even my worst foe. If
one was to calculate the ratio between true American rebels

and true European rebels, then one would need to question the often stated European cliché about the alleged American conformism vs. the alleged European non-conformism. The role of intellectual elites in Europe during the Cold War period, and especially after the end of communism, has been deplorable. Aside from a few intellectuals, as will be shown in the next chapters, European intellectuals and politicians have been masters of self-censorship self-delusion, as well as great impresarios of ideological mimicry. As a rule, they discard their ideas as soon as these ideas are no longer trendy.

From the European perspective one can welcome the fact that Europe has by and large been an area of cultural endeavors and of great history. Yet Europeans have also deftly proven to be experts in tribal warfare and mutual mayhem—which consequently renders their attempt at objectively describing *Homo americanus* as not credible. Europeans have lamented for centuries about the alleged Turkish, Arab or Judaic danger, often forgetting that they like carving each other to pieces when alien races and nations are no longer on their turf. There is, therefore, little reason to search for points of differences between America and Americanized Europe on the one hand, and between *Homo americanus* and *Homo sovieticus* on the other. At the beginning of the third millennium, americanolatry and democratic mimicry became a part of the common landscape in America, Europe and the ex-communist Eastern Europe. Each side is trying to outwit the other with a surplus of Americanized verbiage such as "tolerance," "democracy," and "human rights." "In the Americanized world of the present and the immediate future those forces are set against culture," noted Aldous Huxley, quite some time ago..."The born culture haters are much more numerous than the born culture lovers."[81] One can detect in the above Huxley quote a good understanding of Americanism, the results of which are reminiscent of communism whose mechanism Huxley also well understood.

Huxley knew what he was writing about when he observed the mimicry of Americans he met. He had detected similar mimicry amidst citizens in communism. His understanding of the egalitarian communist pathogenesis remains unsurpassed by his contemporaries, including the much quoted George Orwell.[82] *Homo americanus, Homo occidentalis,* or *Homo sovieticus,* are still thriving in postmodern Europe and America and their days are not numbered yet. These species harbor herd like instincts which are malleable for all egalitarian experiments. Huxley noted that all actions of extraordinary men in the Americanized future—given that their acts do not fall into the egalitarian social scheme—"will be regarded as a crime." He wrote, "In this reversal of the old values, I see a real danger, a menace to all desirable progress."[83]

Granted the ex-Soviet Union was a criminal enterprise, how about suggesting that Americanism may also have some criminal traits? Would it not be desirable in postmodernity, as Molnar suggests, to set up the studies of "Americanology," and to critically examine the "American man" and alongside him the entire American ideology? "We must look forward to a time where there will be 'Americanologists' in the same capacity as there were 'Sovietologists.'"[84] For those thinkers and advocates of the study of Americanolatry—or at least for those individuals who think critically—using the same analyses in studying the egalitarian obsessions in the United States, which were once applied in the Soviet Union, is a matter of civic honesty and intellectual integrity. By probing critically into Americanism and *Homo americanus,* one could probably set the stage for a better understanding of postmodernity and also better grasp the Americanized system in any corner of the world.

It must be recalled that the passionate American desire to make the world safe for democracy also led, after World War II, to the creation of the Nuremberg Tribunal whose legal structures make up the judicial framework of the postmodern European Union, including the European Criminal Code. Some eloquent European and American authors and historical revisionists, who examined the American system during and after the Second World War, certainly do not fall into the category of *Homo americanus.* They opened up, long ago, a Pandora's Box that may lead to new paths in the search for new social models and a new historical meaning.

Chapter III

The Origins of Political Correctness and America's Role in its Perfection

"Political correctness" is a euphemism for intellectual censorship whose legal and cultural origins can be traced to America and Europe, immediately after the Second World War. For the first time in European history, a large scale attempt was made by the victorious United States of America, the Soviet Union and their allies, to condemn a large number of thinkers and writers from defeated Germany and its allies to intellectual oblivion. Social engineering, channeled thorough various forms of intellectual self-policing and self-censorship, became mandatory after 1945. Although Fascism, as an organized political system, no longer poses a threat to Western democracies, any criticism—however mild it may be—of egalitarianism and multiculturalism can earn the author or politician the stigma of "fascism," or even worse, of "anti-Semitism." Any revision of the intellectual heritage linked to nationalism and racialism is severely reprimanded. Principles of vilification of an intellectual opponent or a political adversary have become the rule in postmodernity.

The modern thought police in both the USA and Europe are hard to spot. They make themselves invisible as they seek cover under soothing words such as "democracy" and "human rights." While today each member state of the European Union likes to show off the beauties of their constitutional paragraphs, seldom do these constituent states attempt to tackle the ambiguities of their criminal codes. At issue is the enactment of ever new legislation whose objective is to counter the growing suspicion about the viability of a multiracial America and European Union. In addition, following the terrorist attacks on America on September 11, 2001, and in the wake of occasionally veiled anti-Israeli comments by American and European mainstream journals, the wish of the European Commission is to exercise maximum damage control via maximum thought control. This became visible when the European Commission sponsored legislation regarding legal provisions against "hate crimes"—which was meant to be the best tool for muzzling free speech.

One of the salient features of Americanism and its pendant of European neo-liberalism is to reverse the meaning of words, which in turn can be aptly used by the judiciary of each European state for silencing its heretics. The judiciary of any individual EU member state in which an alleged "verbal offence" has been committed, no longer carries legal weight. Legal proceedings and "appropriate" punishment have become the prerequisite of supra-national courts. Pursuant to this law's ambiguous wording of the concept "hate crime" or "racial incitement," anyone convicted of such an ill-defined verbal offense in country "A" of the European Union, can be fined or imprisoned in country "B" of the European Union. In reality, this is already the case with some European and American authors, right-wing militants or journalists, who to be sure, do not necessarily end up in prison, but whose lives are ruined by defamation and smear campaigns orchestrated by the ruling class and the media. In hindsight, the enactment of EU "hate crime" laws appears like a reenactment of the communist criminal code of the late Soviet Union. For instance, the communist judiciary of the now defunct communist Yugoslavia had for decades resorted to a similar legal meta-language, such as the paragraph 133 of the Yugoslav Criminal code, mentioning "hostile propaganda." Such semantic abstraction, i.e. "hostile propaganda," could apply to any political heretic—regardless of whether he had committed acts of physical violence against the communist Yugoslav state, or simply cracked a joke critical of communist ideology.[85]

At the beginning of the 21st century, the United Kingdom enjoys the highest degree of civil liberties in Europe; Germany the lowest. Since 1994, Germany, Canada, and Australia have strengthened laws against dissenting political views, particularly against historical revisionists who question the official truth regarding modern historiography and in particular the number of Jews killed during the Second World War. Several hundred German citizens, including a number of high-profile scholars, have been accused of incitement to racial hatred, "defamation of the memory of the dead," or of denying the Holocaust, on the basis of the strange German legal neologism of Section 130, notably "incitement to popular hatred," (*"Volksverhetzung"*), as stipulated by the German Criminal Code. From this clumsily worded yet overarching German-Orwellian grammatical construct, which is hard to translate into English, it is easy to place a German journalist or a professor in legal difficulty in Europe if he questions official historiography or if he happens to be critical about the rising number of non-European immigrants in Europe.

How did this happen and who introduced this climate of intellectual censorship and self-censorship in America and Europe at the beginning of the third millennium?

Brainwashing the Germans

In the aftermath of World War II, the role of the American-based Frankfurt School scholars and European Marxist intellectuals was decisive in shaping the new European cultural scene. Scores of American left-leaning psychoanalysts—under the auspices of the Truman government—swarmed over Germany in an attempt to rectify not just the German mind but also to change the brains of all Europeans. Frankfurt School activists were mostly of German-Jewish extraction who had been expelled by the German authorities during National Socialist rule and who, after the Second World War, came back to Europe and began laying the foundations for a new approach in the study of the humanities. But there were also a considerable number of WASP Puritan-minded scholars and military men active in post-war Germany, such as Major General McClure, the poet Archibald MacLeish, the political scientist Harold Laswell, the jurist Robert Jackson and the philosopher John Dewey, who had envisaged copying the American way of democracy into the European public scene. They thought of themselves as divinely chosen people called to preach American democracy—a procedure which would be used by American elites in the decades to come on each occasion and in every spot of the world.[86]

Most of the new American educators, however, were former disciples of Freud and Marx, who considered that the best approach in curing defeated Germany was by treating Germans as a nation of "clinical patients" in need of a hefty dose of liberal and socialist therapy.[87] The Frankfurt School, during its days of American exile, had already drafted various social theories as to how to cure Germany of its "authoritarian character." Accordingly, its major spokesmen argued that "the German petite bourgeoisie has always demonstrated a sado-masochistic character, branded by veneration for the strong man, hatred against the weak, narrow-mindedness, pettiness, hostility, thriftiness, often bordering on miserliness (both in terms of their feelings and money)."[88] In the decades to come it sufficed to be labeled a "Neo-Nazi" or a "radical right winger" in order to lose the right of free speech and become an intellectual pariah. Although the American provisional military government in Germany pursued the hunt for National Socialist dignitaries and brought many to justice, it used the same tactics in the realm of German education and the media. It never crossed the mind of American post-war educators that their actions would facilitate the rise of Marxist cultural hegemony in Europe and lead to the prolongation of the Cold War.

As a result of Frankfurt School reeducational endeavors in Germany, thousands of book titles in the fields of genetics and anthropology were removed from library shelves and thousands of museum artifacts were, if not destroyed in the preceding Allied fire bombing, shipped to the USA and the Soviet Union.

The liberal and communist tenets of free speech and freedom of expression did not apply at all to the defeated side which had earlier been branded as "the enemy of humanity."

Particularly harsh was the Allied treatment of German teachers and academics. Since National Socialist Germany had significant support among German teachers and university professors, it was to be expected that the US reeducational authorities would start screening German intellectuals, writers, journalists and film makers. Having destroyed dozens of major libraries in Germany, with millions of volumes gone up in flames, the American occupying powers resorted to improvising measures in order to give some semblance of normalcy in what later became "the democratic Germany." The occupying powers realized that universities and other places of higher learning could always turn into centers of civil unrest, and therefore, their attempts at denazifaction were first focused on German teachers and academics.[89]

From the Allied viewpoint, and particularly from the viewpoint of the American military government, the universities, despite their undoubtedly great academic achievements in the past, were the breeding ground of reactionary nationalism conducted by the conservative oligarchy of professors. The focus of the universities was overspecialization by means of sharp delimitation between students as a unique elite versus the rest of the society. Moreover, education at the universities transmitted technical competence while neglecting social responsibility.[90]

During the post-war screening of well-known figures from the German world of literature, thousands of German intellectuals were obliged to fill in questionnaires known in post-war Germany as *Fragebogen*. These questionnaires consisted of sheets of paper containing well over one hundred questions probing into all spheres of private, sexual, and political affinities of German suspects. The questions had many misspellings and their ultra-moralistic wording was often difficult for Germans to grasp. Had those "Fragebogen" not acquired a doomsday meaning for many Germans, they would have made good material for a Hollywood vaudeville. A German novelist and a former conservative revolutionary militant, Ernst von Salomon, describes in his satirical novel, *Der Fragebogen*, how the American "new pedagogues" extorted confessions from German captives, who were then either intellectually silenced or dispatched to the gallows.[91]

There is still a perception in the liberal American establishment and its academia that women in National Socialists Germany were deprived of their rights and that their role consisted of shuttling from the church to the kitchen and then back to the children. Such comments, often to be heard and read by respectable liberal scholars in America, do not further the study of Fascism and National Socialism. They do, however, throw additional light on the genesis of political correctness in post-war and postmodern Europe. In many ways German women in the Third Reich had higher cultural and political visibility than anywhere else in Europe or America during the same epoch. Actresses like Leni Riefenstahl, Zarah Leander, and Joseph Goebbels' friend (a Czech woman) Lida Baarova, or test aviation pioneer Hannah Reitsch and many other German women, played significant cultural roles in the Third Reich.[92] Among the new American educators, the opinion prevailed that the allegedly repressive European family was the breeding ground of political neurosis, xenophobia, and racism among young children:

> *Whoever wishes to combat fascism must start from the premises that the central breeding ground for the reactionary person is represented by his family. Given that the authoritarian society reproduces itself in the structure of the individual through his authoritarian family, it follows that political reaction will defend the authoritarian family as the basis for its state, its culture and its civilization.*[93]

Patrick J. Buchanan, an American conservative Catholic author and a former American presidential candidate, observes that Frankfurt School intellectuals in postwar Germany, bankrolled by the American military authorities, succeeded in qualifying National Socialist sympathizers as "mentally sick," a term which would later have a lasting impact on political vocabulary and the future development of political rectitude in Europe and America. Political prejudice, notably, a sense of authority and the resentment of Jews, were categorized as mental illnesses rooted in traditional European child-rearing. Therefore, in the eyes of the American reeducational authorities, the old fashioned European family needed to be removed and with it some of its Christian trappings.[94] Similar antifascist approaches to cultural purges were in full swing in Soviet-occupied Eastern Europe, but as subsequent events showed, the Western version of political correctness proved to be far more effective. In the early postwar years the Americans and their war allies carried out large scale intellectual purges in the media, notably with issuing special licenses to newly launched newspaper outlets in Germany. The words "Nazism" and "Fascism" gradually lost their original meaning and turned, instead, into synonyms of evil. The new educational principle of *"reductio ad hitlerum"* became a new paradigm for studying social sciences. A scholar who would slightly diverge from these newly installed antifascist pedagogical methods would have meager chances for career advancement if not outright fired. In some cases, even sixty years after the end of World War II, he would have to face stiff penalties, including a jail term.[95]

During the same postwar period in communist Eastern Europe, Soviet-led cultural repression was far more severe, but, ironically, its vulgar transparency, as seen in previous chapters, gave its victims an aura of martyrdom. In addition, as the Cold War, by the end of the 40s, began to pit the communist East against the capitalist West, the ruling Western elites deemed it appropriate to come to the moral rescue of Eastern European anticommunist dissenters—less on the grounds of their anticommunist views, but more as a sign that the American liberal system was more tolerant than communism. However, at the end of the twentieth century, with the breakdown of communism and with Americanism and liberalism having become the dominant ideologies of the West, this ceased to be the case. The ideology of antifascism became by the late 20th century a form of negative legitimacy for the entire West. It implied that if there was no "fascist threat," the West would cease to exist in its present from. Therefore, the simulacra of ever-resurgent fascism and anti-Semitism needed to be kept alive.

Shortly after 1945, and largely due to the process of reeducation of German society, Marxist theoreticians and militants in Western Europe implanted themselves as a "counter-power" in places of opinion making, although legally speaking, the West had never embraced communist ideology. Western European and American universities, particularly in the fields of social sciences, were thus in a position to field more true Marxist believers than their communist fellow travelers in Eastern Europe. In the following decades Western European political elites went a step further: in order to show to their American sponsors democratic credentials and their philo-Semitic attitudes, they introduced strict legislation forbidding historical revisionism of the Second World War and any critical study of mass immigration into Western Europe, including the study of negative socio-economic consequences of multiculturalism and multiracialism.

After the Cold War, despite the increasing thought control in higher education, America remains, legally speaking, just about the only country in the West upholding some elements of free speech. By contrast, the much vaunted constitutional provisions stipulating freedom of speech and expression in other European countries, stand in blatant contradiction to their individual penal codes which stipulate a prison sentence for a written comment or an uttered word that minimizes the Jewish Holocaust or trivializes the dogma of multiculturalism.[96] Revisionist authors, or for that matter authors and academics critical of modern liberalism, are obliged to resort, more and more, to marginal publishing companies or strictly to the internet in order to have their words heard. The impression prevails that an author sympathetic to the legacy of right-wing conservatism must be mentally disturbed. At the beginning of the 21st century, the whole intellectual climate in America and especially in Europe came to resemble the medieval period by forbidding critical inquiry into "self-evident truths" of liberal democracy and its chief mentor, America.

The case in point is postmodern Germany. Following the end of communism in the East, the German Criminal Code appears in its substance more repressive than the former Soviet Criminal Code. When silencing their critics, the German authorities do not need to resort to violent means. They usually create a cultural smearing campaign whereby a cultural heretic is portrayed as a funny, pseudo-scientific crank that does not merit a place in mainstream publishing houses. Moreover, the heretic is often induced into self-muzzling behavior, thereby disabling himself from being portrayed as a victim of state repression.

This postmodern mimicry of political rectitude has attained the same mendacious proportions regarding the relationship between America and Europe. In Germany, for instance, the country's perception of the USA must coincide with its own self-perception as a self-flagellating pupil labeled once by the Frankfurt School as a chronically sick patient state. Day after day Germany has to prove that it can perform self-educational tasks better than its American tutor. It must show signs of being the most servile disciple of the American hegemon, given that the "transformation of the German mind (was) the main home work of the military regime."[97] If one wishes to grasp the concept of modern political correctness, one must study in detail the political psychology of the traumatized German people.

In Germany, contrary to England and America, there is a long legal tradition that everything is forbidden that is not explicitly allowed. In America and England, legal practice presupposes that everything is allowed that is not specifically forbidden. This may be the reason why Germany adopted after the Cold War stringent laws against independent minded intellectuals, often dubbed as "right-wingers," or "Neo-Nazis."

In addition to frequent media vilification of local intellectual trouble makers, Germany also requires from its civil servants, pursuant to the Article 33, Paragraph 5, of its Basic Law, the obedience to constitutional commands, and not necessarily their loyalty to the people or to the state of Germany.[98] Germany's looming constitutional agencies, designed for the supervision of the constitution, have the task to control the purity of American imported democracy and the appropriate usage of the democratic meta-narrative. The famed "Office for the Protection of the Constitution" ("*Verfassungschutz*"), as the German legal scholar Josef Schüsselburner writes, "is basically an internal secret service with seventeen branch agencies (one on the level of the federation and sixteen others for each constituent federal state). In the last analysis, this boils down to saying that only the internal secret service is competent to declare a person an internal enemy of the state."[99]

Given that all signs of nationalism, let alone racialism, are reprimanded in Germany, on the ground of their real or purported unconstitutional and undemocratic character, the only patriotism allowed is "constitutional patriotism." "The German people had to adapt itself to the constitution, instead of adapting the constitution to the German people," writes the German legal scholar, Günther Maschke.[100] This new form of German secular religion, i.e. "constitutional patriotism," which has now become mandatory for all citizens in the European Union, encompasses a belief in the rule of law and so-called open society. Under cover of tolerance and civil society, it is considered legally desirable to hunt down European heretics who voice doubts in the legal premises of parliamentary democracy or who criticize some aspects of modern historiography.

Furthermore, in view of the fact that Western societies have also changed their social and ethnic profile, the interpretation of existing laws must also be subject to the political circumstances on the ground. German constitutionalism, continues Schüsselburner, has become "a civil religion," whereby "multiculturalism has replaced Germans with citizens who do not regard Germany as their homeland, but as an imaginary "Basic Law

Land"(...). As a result of this new civil religion, Germany, along with other European countries, has now evolved into a "secular theocracy."[101]

Since the end of the Cold War, all over Europe, the social arena has been designed as a replica of a huge market. In America and Europe, the free market itself has become a form of an additional secular religion whose principles must be encompassed in the judiciary of each country. In a similar fashion, raising critical questions about the viability of the market can also cause an author professional troubles. It is considered conventional wisdom that any flaw of the market can and must be cured by the infusion of more free market principles and more "invisible hand" friendly policies. Economic efficiency is seen as the sole criterion for any social interaction. Hence, individuals, who may have some second thoughts about the founding myths of liberal economy, are seen as enemies of the system.

Also, books dealing with themes that critically examine parliamentary democracy, or the role of America in World War II, or authors questioning antifascist victimology, are less and less accessible in mainstream publishing companies. Books or journals challenging the official number of fascist crimes during the Second World war or disputing the body-count in the Jewish Holocaust, are banned and their authors often end up in prison.[102] Similar to Communism, historical truth in Western Europe is not established by an open academic debate but by state legislation. In addition, scientists whose expertise is in genetically induced social behavior, or who lay emphasis on the role of I.Q. in human achievement, while downplaying the importance of education and social environment, are branded as racists. The entire West, including America itself, has become a victim of collective guilt which, strangely enough, is induced more by intellectual self-denial and by Christian inspired atonement, and less by state repression.

In politically correct America, the academic language is also subject to hygienic rules. New qualifiers emerge among would-be heretics serving as disclaimers for their controversial thoughts. In the eyes of new inquisitors an intellectual right-wing heretic must be monitored—not on the basis of what he has said or wrote, but on the basis of whom he saw and met. "Guilt by association" hampers someone's career and ruins the life of a diplomat, a politician, or an academic who ventures as a speaker into some right-wing or racialists literary circle, or who attends a venue where the contents of a revisionist book are discussed. Any idea critically examining the foundations of egalitarianism, democracy, and multiculturalism becomes suspicious. Declaring oneself a "conservative" is also dangerous. Even the mildest forms of cultural conservatism are gradually pushed into the category of "right-wing extremism," or "white supremacism." And these qualifiers are disarming enough to silence even the most vocal heretic. "There is a typical European form of political correctness, which consist, in seeing fascism everywhere," writes the French Jewish philosopher Alain Finkielkraut, although with his former endorsement of the previous antirevisionist laws in France, from 1990, it is questionable whether Finkielkraut always means what he writes. In November 2005, Finkielkraut was himself called to account by the French antiracist agency MRAP for his alleged deprecatory statements against rioting French blacks and Arabs in France, an event which the author described in an interview to the Israeli newspaper *Haaretz*.[103] Thy irony is that Finkielkraut, along with many French and American court historians and philosophers of postmodernity, and very similar to American neoconservatives, was once upon a time a supporter of Marxist-inspired multiculturalism. Now, wearing his neo-con skin, he seems to be the victim of his own theories. The "Finkielkraut" syndrome is quite common among former communist sympathizers, who became ardent anticommunists and liberals when Marxism ran out of fashion. The only problem is that a lot of people have died in the process—as a result of their erstwhile intellectual Marxist and antifascist fantasies.

As much as American imported liberalism rejects and punishes racial stereotypes, it does not hesitate to use stereotyping when depicting its own cultural or political enemies. When Muslims and Islamists residing in America or Europe become the perpetrators of street riots or terrorism, the modern system tolerates name calling and the sporadic usage of anti-Arab slurs. Conversely, a Muslim American resident or a Muslim living in Europe can often get away with anti-Semitic or anti-Israeli remarks, which a Gentile citizen, or a scholar, cannot even dream about—for fear of being called by the dreaded word "anti-Semite." Thus, the ruling class in America and Europe successfully resorts to the scarecrow of debate stopping words, such as "anti-Semitism" and "Neo-Nazism," as an alibi for legitimizing its perpetual status quo. The specter of a projected catastrophic scenario must silence all free spirits. Naturally, if fascism is legally decreed as absolute evil, any aberration in the liberal system will automatically appear as a lesser evil. The modern liberal system, which originated in America, functions as a self-perpetuating machine of total mind control.[104]

Publish and Perish

It would be false to blame only America and Americanism for the climate of political correctness which has engulfed the European intellectual scene. The ongoing inquisitorial atmosphere in postmodern Europe is due to Europe's own ideological divisions going back to the Second World War, and even earlier to the French Revolution. The climate of intellectual censorship became salient after the breakdown of communism and the emergence of Americanism as the only remaining cultural and political referent. It needs to be added that the communist version of the Cold War had only given the finishing touches to a future tide of European thought police.

In late 1944, prior to the establishment of the provisional military government in Germany, France was subject to severe communist inspired intellectual purges which overshadowed the subsequent American-led denazifaction process in Germany. In order to grasp the repressive laws which are in effect in France, at the beginning of the third millennium, one must first delve into the period of the French civil war among

its intellectuals—which raged during the Second World War. In
1942, under the prodding of U.S. authorities, the London based
exiled deputies and politicians (Pierre Bloch, Pierre Mendès
France, etc.), issued a statement that "the French opinion would
not understand why the accomplices and helpers of the
enemy could continue exerting any authority whatsoever in
the liberated territories."[105] Their elaborated programs for
intellectual purges were later endorsed by the provisional
Assembly of the new French Republic in Algiers, on July 10,
1944, a month which coincided with the American invasion of
France. Thus, the exiled French politicians in Northern Africa
and London, who were backed up by the American authorities,
looked also for American moral and legal guidance in settling
their scores with French fascist and pro-fascist sympathizers
and collaborators.

The aftermath of the American invasion of France in June
1944 opened up the flood gates of domestic reprisals and barbaric
retributions in France and in the rest of Europe—often with the
tacit approval of the American provisional military authorities
in Germany. The problem was further aggravated by the fact
that the vast majority of pro-Fascist French, Flemish, Walloon,
Danish and Norwegian politicians and intellectuals, charged for
collaborating with National Socialist Germany, were once former
left-leaning and Marxist intellectuals and politicians. Former
French communists and socialists, who in the mid-thirties
participated in the setting up of diverse antifascist "committees
of vigilance" in Europe, welcomed the German occupation of
France in 1940. In many cases they fully endorsed Germany's
racial policies. Some of them did it on purely opportunistic
grounds, although many had become in the meantime aware of
communist heritage and its incarnation in the species of *"Homo
sovieticus."*[106] As history amply shows, "true believers" have no
qualms in switching from one religion or ideology to another.
Likewise, by gauging the psychological profile of liberal thinkers
and politicians in Europe and America today, one cannot rule
out that with different winds blowing tomorrow on the horizon,
these postmodern self-proclaimed democratic vigilantes, vying

for the constant favor of Israel or American Jews, would become ardent anti-Semites. If one studies the psychological legacy of anti-Semitism in Europe, one can never discount that this may happen again.

In the wake of the antifascist purges in France in late 1944 and early 1945, the majority of prominent French writers and artists, i.e. former fascist "opinion makers," disappeared from the public eye, only to be replaced by French and German Marxist-oriented authors, who were to become the new trend-setters in the realm of mores, the arts and esthetics for the next half a century all over Europe and America.

Of all professional categories journalists and writers were hit the most. This underlines the ideological character of the conflict and the ensuing purges. The proportion of writers and journalists who were shot, imprisoned, and barred from their profession surpasses all other professional categories. Do we need to be reminded of the assassination of Albert Clément, Philippe Henriot, Robert Denoël, of the suicide of Drieu La Rochelle, of the death of Paul Allard in prison prior to court hearings and of the executions of Georges Suarez, Robert Brasillach, Jean Luchaire (..)...The death sentence pronounced in absentia or a commuted prison sentence for Lucien Rebatet, Pierre-Antoine Cousteau, etc.) The targets were the providers of the ideas more than the entrepreneurs who had contributed to the German war industry. By 1944 the professional interdiction decreed by the CNE (Comité nationale des écrivains) targeted approximately 160 journalists and writers.[107]

After the Second World War, an *ex post facto* law was adopted in France, making some political opinions a crime, and which was primarily designed to monitor French revisionist historians. Often, these newly adopted laws were pushed by the same individuals who only a few months earlier had themselves collaborated with the Germans in pro-fascist Vichy France. From then on, in French intellectual life, "journalist, just as new politicians, of whom most did not have any professional competence, came into possession of journals, of the offices and

the material, and this contrary to the customary laws," writes
a French novelist, Marcel Aymé, himself a victim of postwar
antifascist purges.[108] Many French authors were hit by the legal
verbal construct of "national indignity" (*indignité nationale*) which
meant in practice that they were deprived of literary exposure.
Mutual denunciation became part of European intellectual life
as former colleagues vying for literary and artistic fame began
blaming each other for their real or purported "Nazi sympathies
or collaboration with Fascism." The French Academy, once full
of praise for Marshal Pétain, quickly expelled from its ranks
several major academics on the suspicion of their war time
collaboration with the Germans.[109]

The subsequent social and cultural unrests in Europe,
particularly the student revolts in May 1968 that were sponsored
by crypto-Marxist intellectuals and carried out under the
banner on "anti-Americanism," were not intended to challenge
prevailing American cultural dominance in Europe. In fact, for
many leftist French intellectuals, America was not antifascist and
procommunist enough. Very much in contrast to them, during
the same period, European conservative intellectuals imagined
that America was the only barrier against the communist threat.
As mentioned earlier, however, America, other than using its
policy of military containment of the Soviet Union, had never
seriously envisioned the intellectual roll-back of Marxism.
Had it ever contemplated waging a serious culture war against
Marxism, it would have been obliged to retroactively repudiate
its cultural policy in postwar occupied Germany.

On July 14, 1990 a law, known by the name of French
Communist and Socialist deputies Laurent Fabius and Jean-
Claude Gayssot, respectively, came into effect in France. The
law forbade critical inquiry into the troubled French past and
the minimizing of Jewish plight during World War II. The
legal precedent of this new French law, whose goal was also
to institutionalize political correctness in the realm of French
scholarship and the media, was basically the tardy legacy of the
Nuremberg Tribunal of 1946. "The law has its origins in this
process (Nuremberg), or rather in its judicial masquerade. This

law is its retarded offspring; its debility is congenital"[110], writes French attorney Eric Delcroix, himself once a victim of the French thought police.

Moreover, any critical inquiry into the dominant ideas surrounding France's multiculturalism, or any critical examination of anti-Fascism during the period of the Second World War, are legally considered to be a criminal offence in France. Also, the opinions of dissident scholars, attempting to resurrect French authors who were once sympathetic to fascism or who collaborated with the short-lived Vichy France, are considered a threat to public order in France. "Here we are again, we must have landed into an epoch of permanent political processes," writes Delcroix. "Worse, we are in the permanent ideological process. The defendants are not blamed for their acts—provided there were any—but for their ideas."[111] At the beginning of the 21st century, as a result of this repressive intellectual climate in Europe, hundreds of French and German authors showing sympathies for anti-liberal authors or who voice criticism of multicultural experiments in postmodern Europe or America are subject to legal sanctions and public ostracism.

One would have expected that after the Cold War, and especially after the end of communism in Russia and Eastern Europe, a more tolerant intellectual climate would have developed in Europe and in America. But this has not been the case. Leftist cultural hegemony continues unabated; this time under the guise of liberal rhetoric. Freedom of speech must only be defined within the framework of the liberal parameters and possibly contain some laudatory remarks about Jews and other non-European residents. Paul Gottfried, an American-Jewish scholar, argues how the American Left, particularly after the end of the Cold War, became the fundamental pillar of intellectual reference for the European ruling class. His thesis supports the much debated idea in postmodernity; namely, that Communism fell apart in the East because it had fully been implemented in the West.[112]

At the beginning of the new millennium, the feigned pro-American conduct by European elites becomes even more obvious. Any form of power politics has been handed over to the Americans on the grounds that America is the only country which knows how to decide who is the enemy of democracy and who is the friend of democracy. As a result, European states have become handicapped in their own foreign policy dealings and devoid of any independent decision makers. This, in turn, has made them incapable of containing even local interethnic wars in their own backyard, such as the one that occurred in ex-Yugoslavia in the 1990s. Moreover, as one can observe, wars, contrary to America's messianic wishes, have not become restrained in their violence. Since they are *a priori* viewed as illegal and criminal enterprises by American elites, wars tend to become more savage, losing their limited nature altogether.

It is true that Western Europe, unlike Eastern Europe, could escape the naked terror of communism, although Western Europe's own subspecies, the *antifascist homunculi*, as German scholar Günther Maschke derogatorily calls modern Americanized opinion makers in Europe, tirelessly watch for any sign of a nationalist revival. The apprenticeship of American democracy must be, therefore, constantly waved in Europe as a sign of political rescue. "In order to venture out onto the field of democracy, a reeducated person is obliged to lie successfully. And so the lie became the essence of the hitherto unknown freedom in Germany!," writes Maschke.[113] The image of Hitler and National Socialism has become so negatively popular in both America and Europe, it has guaranteed that Hitler himself is destined to live forever. Despite the fact that under the American-sponsored Basic Law of 1949, Germany acquired all the prerogatives of a sovereign country, its sovereignty has in reality been nil.

After the end of the Cold War, which began with the fall of the Berlin Wall, many scholars and politicians in Europe assumed that antifascist rituals would be superseded at least briefly by some mild forms of anticommunist rhetoric, or at least some sporadic acknowledgments that communism had left rivers of blood that needed to be drained too. Nothing of this sort has ever happened. One wonders, why does not the Communist criminal legacy trigger a similar negative outcry in the wider public as the fascist legacy? Why must the public stay tuned to endless recitals of National Socialist crimes, whereas rarely ever does it have an opportunity to hear something about Communist horrors? Arguably, one can conclude that if the public was more sensitized to the communist syndrome, one could not rule out that National Socialism and Fascism, if not pardoned, could at least be better understood. But this is where a serious ideological problem could occur since such an intellectual endeavor could easily cripple the legitimacy of the ruling class in America and Europe. In hindsight, after reading National Socialist politicians and their accounts of the psychology of communism, one gets a better sense of what communism was all about.[114] Invariably, if one were to examine in detail the legacy of communist anthropology, one does not have to read modern and postmodern mainstream democratic conservative authors who have made valiant strides in describing the communist system. All that they have said and written since 1945 about communist terror had already been graphically described in detail by preceding fascist politicians and their opinion makers. The only problem is that these forgotten or demonized fascist anticommunist authors do not have any credibility in the eyes and ears of the liberalized and Americanized postmodern masses. This confronts us again with the fundamental question: In order to understand the barbaric aspects of communism, must one embrace the theoretical foundations of Fascism and National Socialism?

Political correctness, as a peculiar type of thought control, will not disappear overnight from the political and intellectual life in postmodern America and Europe. In fact, at the beginning of this new millennium, it has strengthened its hold in all spheres of social, political and cultural activity. Its chief standard bearers, as regards the antifascist struggle, are alive and well and in charge of the grand democratic narrative. Post-communist and post-Marxist intellectuals, as seen earlier in our descriptions, continue to thrive and control modern discourse in the higher echelons of the media and opinion making. They may have discarded their Freudo-Marxian scholasticism of yesteryear, but they continue to relentlessly advocate the ideology of multiculturalism, egalitarianism, and globalism—that is, all those doctrines which were once destined to make up the perfect communist system. The only difference is that the Americanized version of political correctness has become more effective through the adoption of managerial capitalism and Judeo-Centric modern historiography. Whereas the average American and European citizen is a daily witness to a constant barrage of antifascist Holocaust victimology that has obtained religious status in Europe, hardly any mention is made against former left-leaning intellectuals who once marched in the footsteps of Maoism, Trotskyism, Titoism, and who are still entrenched in the media and educational system. Thus, in postmodern interregnum, both America and Europe appear hardly distinguishable. They function symbiotically in a mimicking manner, as if each is trying to prove that it does not lag behind its overseas fellow traveler and its own antifascist therapeutic rhetoric. Ironically, as Europe and America move further and further away in time from the epoch of Fascism and National Socialism, the more their public discourse revolves around an endless antifascist theme. Never has the West preached so much tolerance and so much multiracial conviviality, at a time when the whole system is ripe with all forms of subterranean violence and mutual hatred.

The West, with American elites at the helm, like to admonish countries not to their liking, about the need to uphold human rights. Yet, daily occurrences where individuals in America and Europe are fired, penalized, or sent to prison on charges of racism, xenophobia or a "hate crime," go mysteriously unnoticed. The larger public in America and Europe have little knowledge that in Germany alone, in the last decade of the twentieth century, thousands of individuals, ranging from German youngsters cracking jokes about non-European immigrants, to scholars dealing critically with the Jewish Holocaust, have been sentenced to either financial fines or to considerable prison terms. In the political and academic environment, writes the modern German heretic Germar Rudolf, it must, therefore, not come as a surprise that "political scientists, sociologists and historians do not wish to call things by their names."[115] They are afraid of being called "Nazis" or anti-Semites and lose their perks, a fact which Rudolf, as a former chemical scientist experienced first hand when doing research on forensic details related to the Auschwitz concentration camp museum. By the mid-nineties of the previous century, for his politically incorrect views he was obliged to flee to America. However, his revisionist writings and books in America, which continued to probe into the official veracity of the Holocaust narrative, could not find a safe haven there either. His appeal for political asylum in 2005 was rejected by the American authorities as "frivolous."[116] Subsequently, he was deported to Germany in order to stand trial for the previous charges filed against him by the German authorities regarding his "incitement to public hatred."

The spiral of intellectual cowardice only reinforces the Americanized system's thought control. The silence of American academics and prominent human rights advocates, following the arrest of Rudolf in America, proves time and again that American intellectuals realize that there must be limits to their freedom of speech, however much they all like eulogizing the alleged academic freedom in Western democracies. Consequently, it is not far fetched to say that Western intellectuals, as has been observed on many occasions, are also among the first to embrace new utopias and new academic paradigms when the old ones become outdated. Rudolf notes in his earlier writings age old wisdom, i.e. that "dictatorships generate fear, because only the fearful subject is a good subject."[117] The American brain child, the post-war Federal Republic of Germany, might enter some day into history books as the most bizarre system ever seen in Europe. It uses American post-World War II ukases and institutionalizes on a grand scale mutual snitching and intellectual self-surveillance. Such a paranoid climate has already resulted in the loss of elementary civic courage among most German intellectuals.

Despite its vaunted First Amendment, America has also shown on countless occasions how it rids itself of its own heretics—often under cover of free speech and in the name of proverbial human rights. American politicians and academics are aware of the fact that even a minor critical comment about Jews and Judaism can ruin their career—and life. The Russian author, Alexander Solzhenitsyn, noted long ago, how the decline in courage had become the hallmark of America. America seems to have lost its civic courage, both as a whole and as a state of individual citizens. Such a decline in courage is particularly noticeable among the American ruling class and intellectual elites, and has created the impression of a complete loss of courage by the whole of American society. "Of course," writes Solzhenitsyn, "there are many courageous individuals but they have no determining influence on public life. Political and intellectual bureaucrats show depression, passivity and perplexity in their actions and in their statements and even more so in theoretical reflections to explain how realistic, reasonable as well as intellectually and even morally warranted it is to base state policies on weakness and cowardice."[118] This cowardice has today become the main political and academic pillar in America and Americanized Europe.

Contrary to a widespread belief, political correctness, as a bloodless version of intellectual repression, is not a result of a violent ideology espoused by a handful of thugs, as was once observed in the ex-Soviet Union. Civic fear, feigned self-abnegation, and intellectual abdication create an ideal ground for the loss of freedom. Under the influence of American neo-liberalism and European Marxist-sponsored multiculturalism, political rectitude has been fueled since 1945 by a popular belief that somehow things will straighten themselves out. But growing social apathy and rising self-censorship only boost the climate of intellectual and political mendacity. Essentially, the spirit of political correctness is the absence of all spirit.

Chapter IV

The Biblical Origins of American Fundamentalism

A merica is a land of the Bible. In America, it is virtually unheard of to openly declare oneself an agnostic or an atheist and to aspire at the same time to some high political office. No country on earth has ever known such a high degree of biblical influence as the United States of America. Over the last two hundred years, biblical vocabulary has played a much stronger role in American public affairs than the much lauded American constitutionalism or the praised rule of law.

While trying to decipher the intricacies of the American system, one must unavoidably look at the religious phenomenon of Biblical Puritanism and the role of early American pilgrims in New England. Calvinism, although originating in Europe, reached its moralistic climax in America and its message marked forever subsequent American politicians. Later, despite the fact that America's founding fathers were men of the Enlightenment, opposed to religious fanaticism of any sort, the Calvinist heritage continued to have the upper hand in formulating the American political character and American society at large. America is indeed a unique country, where all church denominations—unlike in Europe—are strictly separated from the political arena, yet where Biblically derived ethics plays a decisive influence in American political behavior.

As was to be expected under the influence of the Enlightenment and the progressive secularization of America, the legacy of Biblical Puritanism lost its original theological God-fearing message and adopted, at the turn of the 20th century, a secular neo-liberal form of the human rights gospel. Subsequently, by a bizarre twist of fate, the Calvinist legacy of Puritanism that had been chased from Europe by the end of the 17th century started its journey back home to Europe— particularly after America came out victorious after the Second World War. Although Europe remains a much less Bible- oriented society than America, the moralistic message, as an old Bible derivative, is making strong headways in the postmodern European social arena. However much the surface of America shows everywhere signs of secularism, rejecting the Christian dogma and diverse religious paraphernalia, in the background of American political thought always looms the mark of the Bible.

In hindsight, in the British context of the 17th century, the strongest political standard bearer of Puritanism, Oliver Cromwell, appears as a passing figure who did not leave a lasting political impact on the future of the United Kingdom or on the rest of continental Europe. Yet Cromwell's unwitting political legacy had more influence on the American mindset than Lenin's rhetoric did on the future of communized Russia, or for that matter on millions of leftist intellectuals in Europe. Just as Cromwell used the Bible in justifying the murder of King Charles and later in his expeditions against the Scots and Irish, so did his American Puritan progeny provided a framework for the rise of American moralistic zeal in conducting the policy of world improvement. Regardless of the fact that millions of Americans adhere to various Christian and non-Christian sects and denominations, or even belong to anti-Christian tribes or cults, the mindset of the majority of Americans is shaped by the Bible. Christopher Hill, the English foremost scholar on the English civil war and early Calvinism in England, writes in his books about the often forgotten period of religious fanaticism in England in the mid 17th century and the ensuing civil war. Having in mind a revolutionary fervor which had swept England, as well as the subsequent birth of proto-communist millenarian

Christian sects, such as Levellers, Ranters, and Quakers, with each having little tolerance for the other, one wonders whether the 17th century was the most intolerant century in Western history? The same Biblical fanaticism that had accompanied the Civil War in England was to be detected in the English colonies overseas—in what was to become America.[119]

Puritanism was an ideal religion for American pilgrims as it fostered social discipline and hard work, urging avoidance of violent rhetoric, while promoting a remarkable degree of civic decency. The American way of life and the so-called "have a nice day" mentality, which Europeans wrongly deride as a form of hypocrisy or a capitalist facade, are direct behavioral products of early Puritanism. In Geneva in the 16th century, Calvin himself did not see anything wrong in mercantile activities—a credo gladly accepted by his American successors in the late 17th century. Calvin's teachings perfectly matched the early development of capitalism in America and later, during the period of Enlightenment, they gave birth to the liberal belief in the ideology of progress.

Although America prides itself on a high degree of social tolerance and rejects in practice political interference of any organized church, its obsession with moralistic preaching borders on mass delirium. Most Americans are hardly aware of it and usually take their moralistic stance as something desirable for all human beings. Foreigners, by contrast, and particularly Europeans, immediately notice in American behavior strong pedagogical outbursts which they wrongly interpret as camouflage for capitalist hypocrisy. In the eyes of Europeans, even among those who are highly religious and Bible-oriented, the American type of moralism is viewed as something odd. This can be observed in constant references by many Americans to Jesus and the Bible, which happens to make up the main rhetorical ingredient of all American politicians. The former president Ronald Reagan used to say that "the prosperity and might of America are the proof that America is blessed by God."[120] "The country which is closest to God must also be Gods' representative on Earth with the three godly characteristics; omniscience, omnipotence, and generosity.[121] Similar biblical nebulosity can be heard over and over again in all walks of life in postmodern America. Therefore, it is questionable to what extent America can be a free country for all if the Biblical moralistic framework, however secular it appears, is a precondition for professional success.

Freemasonry followed later in the footsteps of Puritanism and found its adherents among the framers of the American Constitution. U.S. society is that "which forbids any religious discord in its offing; yet allows the belief in divine providence. This is, therefore, a typical American phenomenon."[122] Again, this is additional proof that America is a land of extreme biblical fundamentalism, albeit perfectly compatible with the most violent capitalist endeavors. Although no church in America is allowed to exert political power, the Biblical message is viewed as a fundamental moral decorum in social and political affairs. Whichever side one turns to in America, left or right, Catholics or Methodists, the center or periphery, to hippies, junkies, blacks, or whites, the inevitable moralistic formula aiming at the world improvement, always points to the ever present Bible.[123]

In contrast to European Catholicism or Lutheranism, Calvinist Puritanism managed to strip Christianity of pagan elements regarding the transcendental and the sacred, and reduced the Christian message solely to the basic ethical precepts of good behavior. American Puritanism deprived Christianity of its aesthetic connotations and symbolism, thereby alienating American Christians as well as American cultural life in general, further from its European origins. In this way, Americans became ripe for modernism in architecture and new approaches in social science, while at the same time readily embracing pseudo-historicism which was coherent with sentimental relationship to religions and the concept of the sacred.

In the Land of Hypermoralism

Puritanism played the starring role in so far that it introduced into American political behavior a high level of hypermoralism and self-serving messianism. The German anthropologist, Arnold Gehlen, an author who was close to the legacy of European revolutionary conservative thought, notes that the American system and its later liberal expression are deeply embedded in hypermoralism, which in postmodern America often spills into political fundamentalism. This Biblical fundamentalism has different turns and shapes, and it usually functions without a reference to classical political ideas or symbols. It is often formulated in petty sentimentalism, passing pep talks, gigantic fake smiles, verbiage teeming with bombastic adjectives, and a vicarious "love thy neighbor attitude," always accompanied by a strong desire for social conviviality.

It is a common sight in America to witness an endless stream of new sects, interest groups, and life-styles. Many of these sects are of a bizarre and passing nature, passionately advocating the rights of birds, insects, animals, but always enveloping their agenda in a hypermoralistic discourse that resembles "some sort of a new humanitarian religion."[124] This hypertrophy of moralism had its birth place in New England during the early reign of the Pilgrim Fathers, which only proves our thesis that New England and not Washington D.C. was the birth place of Americanism. Therefore, understanding postmodern American man means tracking down his roots in New England of the early 17th century.

The moralistic message of the American founding fathers spread later to nations around the world. This effort by American elites was facilitated in so far as the new secular human rights oriented moralists could well combine their rhetoric with the advocacy of total sexual permissiveness and hyper-consumerism. Also, the obsession with hypermoralism could be perfectly linked to war mongering and American bellicosity; it could be a tool for preaching peace too. American hypermoralism is a timeless *pret à porter* for any occasion and for any life style. Early Puritan asceticism, the cult of work, the spirit of saving money, gave birth after World War II to a new hero who was both the opposite of the old American ideal yet at the same time his logical postmodern extension. One can speculate whether under the impact of Puritanism a new sociobiological selection has also occurred in America just as it once did in the ex-communist Soviet Union, following large scale communist genocides. The Puritan mindset must have provided an ideal social framework for a distinct biological selection that predetermined future generations for activities in limited fields of human endeavor, notably in the all-encompassing free market. Early American individuals, who were genetically not endowed for such Bible inspired moralistic outbursts, could hardly fit into American society. The Bible and business became two pillars of Americanism. This point was underlined by Louis Rougier, a European philosopher who depicts *Homo americanus* and his mercantile embodiment as a new species "who spends his time evaluating everything in dollars and who sets up the monetary equivalent for all objects he encounters, and for all people he meets..."[125]

It was to be expected with the Puritans' idea of self-choseness that Americans took a special delight in the Old Testament. "From it, almost exclusively, they drew their texts, and it never failed to provide them with justification for their most inhuman and bloodthirsty acts" (...) Their God was the God of the Old Testament, their laws were the laws of the Old Testament, their guides to conduct were the characters of the Old Testament. Their Sabbath was Jewish, not Christian. In New England, in their religious persecutions and Indian wars, the sayings of Christ never prevailed to stay their hands or to save the blood of their victims."[126] Early Puritans viewed themselves as self- righteous dissenters fighting for the ultimate goal of spiritual salvation, whereas their new American homeland was welcomed as God's special gift. The Old Testament was their book of reference, whereas the "positive sides of the New Testament seem to have left them singularly cold."[127] Early English Puritans had much in common with the intolerance and fanaticism of early Muslims, and as the German philosopher, Oswald Spengler notes, "the people surrounding Mohammed, such as Abu Bekr and Omar, were closely related to the Puritan leaders of the English revolution, such as John Pym and Hampdon."[128] With its departure to America in the 17th century, Puritanism turned into the "American religion," adds Spengler."[129]

All three major monotheistic religions, Islam, Christianity and Judaism share the same source, although often despising each other. The likeness and difference between Islamism and Americanism can be observed at the beginning of the third millennium, as the American political establishment and Islamic radicals around the world clash with each other in open warfare. A French philosopher critical of American Puritanism, Alain de Benoist, goes a step further and writes, "not only did the Americans desire to break away from Europe. They also wanted to found a society which would be capable of regenerating the whole of mankind. They wanted to create a Promised Land which would become a universal republic. This Biblical theme which is at the heart of the Puritan mind comes back over and over again as the real leitmotiv in the entire American history."[130]

It is a widespread view that America is a tolerant country. In light of the endless wars and carnage that have accompanied Europe over the last two thousand years, America appears, at first sight, as a land that has remained virtually immune to nationalist infighting and civil wars. But then one must also define the meaning of tolerance and look at its definer. What is the point of talking about tolerance in a system where Biblical conformism is considered a norm by all? De Tocqueville writes that the American form of materialism does not corrupt the soul but softens it up and extends all its substance.[131] Likewise, if an intellectual in America strays away from the common moralistic consensus and moves beyond the Biblical dichotomy of "good vs. bad," he will not be persecuted or go to prison. He will, however, get into trouble with his immediate pontificating environment and will likely become a moral outcast. This was well noted, not just by European right-wing authors, but also by rare American left wingers, however much they themselves ignored the later reincarnation of the Puritan substratum in their neo-Marxian and liberal thought. An early American Jewish activist and feminist, Emma Goldman, noted how Puritan chastity removes all esthetics and leads to a gloomy and uniform life in America. Puritanism, for her, is an enemy of the American people since it is itself a creator of "most unspeakable vices." She realizes that Puritanism inevitably leads to the "stifling of free speech and creates a culture of mediocrity."[132] Half a century after her writings we will be witnessing the same type of American-based political Puritanism—albeit this time around under the name of leftist "hate speech" and various forms of moralistic witch-hunts against critics of liberal democracy. It is questionable whether Goldman and her likes would still be critical of the modern version of neo-Puritan political correctness, whose genealogy we traced to Biblical Puritanism, and whose modern versions have adopted a different political message. Modern American heretics are summarily dismissed as the "enemies of democracy" or "racists," or "right-wingers." How on earth dare one question American democracy and the free market if these elements make up the foundation of liberty? How can somebody resent American democracy if that democracy is destined to bring peace and prosperity to the entire globe?

With the rising affluence of American society, followed by the rapid secularization of the West, and accompanied by a silent Freudo-Marxian "counter-revolution" in the early 1960s in American universities, it become fashionable for the offspring of American Puritans to engage in the same moralistic escapades—this time, however, in a reversed manner and with a different signifier. The new neo-Puritan offspring advocate now "safe and clean sex," "safe and clean politics," "affirmative action," etc. The ideology of political correctness, which was described in the previous chapter, also originated in America in the 80s as a form of intellectual self-censorship. Yet it also represents the postmodern version of the old Puritan mindset. Today this political correctness ruins the careers of independent American and European free minds and makes intellectual inquiry into modern American taboos virtually impossible. In America, at the beginning of the 21st century, the castrated usage of verbal structures is just a graphic offshoot of the old proto-Puritan secular avatars, so typical of postmodernity.

"Judeo-American" Monotheism

American founding myths drew their inspiration from Hebrew thought. The notion of the "City on the Hill" and "God's own country" were borrowed from the Old Testament and the Jewish people. The Biblical idea of predestination served the early American founding fathers as a launching pad for their own concept of democratic self-righteousness. Of all Christian denominations, Calvinism was the closest to the Jewish religion and as some authors have noted, the United States owes its very existence to the Jews. "For what we call Americanism," writes Werner Sombart," is nothing else than the Jewish spirit distilled."[133] The author, a disciple of Max Weber, was sympathetic to Jews and, therefore, when he describes the overwhelming influence of the Judaic spirit in American life, he cannot be accused of having a bias against Jews. Similar remarks will be found later among legions of European authors, most of who fell into oblivion or disgrace given their ties to antidemocratic and racialist schools of thought. Sombart further writes that "the United States is filled to the brim with the Jewish spirit."[134] Many wide-spread customs in America, such as giving new-born children Judaic names, or administering circumcision to young new-born males, come from Jewish heritage.[135] Very early on America's founding fathers, pioneers, and politicians identified themselves as Jews who had come to the new American Canaan from pestilent Europe. In a postmodern Freudian twist, these pilgrims and these new American pioneers were obliged to kill their European fathers in order to facilitate the spreading of American democracy world-wide. "Heaven ha[s] has placed our country in this situation to try us; to see whether we would faithfully use the incalculable power in our hands for speeding forward the world's regeneration."[136] Even American Christian anti-Semites are subconsciously enamored with the Jewish idea of predestination, while at the same time harboring anti-Semitic sentiments. In fact, American anti-Semitism can be described as a distorted form of hidden philo-semitism which, while not able to materialize itself on its own American choseness, projects its would-be supremacy through its hatred against Jews. It is not far fetched to argue, as some authors do, that the American dream is a role model for universal Jewishness that must not be limited to a specific race or tribe in America, as is the case with ethnocentric Jews who are well aware of their in-group racial feelings. Americanism is designed for all peoples, races and nations on earth. America is, by definition, an extended form of globalized Israel and not reserved for one specific tribe only. Does that, therefore, mean that our proverbial *Homo americanus* is a universal carbon copy of *Homo judaicus*?

Of all topics in the twentieth century and particularly at the beginning of the third millennium, critical analyses of Jewish influence in America or overt description of the preponderant Jewish role in public life in America, is tantamount to intellectual suicide. The legacy of the Second World War, the narrative about endless Jewish suffering, and the referent of the Jewish Holocaust form the basic framework for political, social, and academic discourse of Americanism. In a country whose ideological principles are entrenched in an aggressive rhetoric about free speech, only few authors dare critically address the issue of Judaism in America. Most Americans, along with most Europeans, and particularly their respective political elites are very aware of the influence of Judaism in America, yet for reasons of self-induced fear or hypocrisy, this subject matter is never openly and objectively discussed in public. When the role of the Jews in America is critically discussed, the author runs the risk of being branded an anti-Semite, or simply end up on the social and intellectual margins.

American Neurosis: Love or Hate for the Jews?

At the beginning of the third millennium, Jews happen to enjoy a privileged place in the American limelight, with their entire past continuously portrayed as a story of endless suffering at the hands of their non-Jewish enemy. In his well documented book on the psychology of Judaism in postmodernity, the French scholar, Hervé Ryssen, examines the genesis of the concept of anti-Semitism and its multiple verbal distortions in daily political discourse. The word "anti-Semitism," unlike words "anticommunism," or "antifascism," does not reflect political beliefs or critical views of the Jews. This term is exclusively used as a lexical label to depict a person's grave mental illness. As a perceived medical or judicial illness, anti-Semitism must never be debated; an anti-Semitic patient must not be a partner in scholarly duels; his sick views must not be the subject of academic inquiry and counter-inquiry. As an element of medical pathology, anti-Semitism must only by treated by doctors, preferably by a Jewish psychoanalyst, or legally, by a liberal prosecutor in court.

The word "anti-Semite" will likely be studied one day as a telling example of postmodern political discourse, i.e. as a signifier for somebody who advocates the reign of demonology. "Many world-know Jewish authors, haunted by the either real or surreal menace of anti-Semitism, consider it a sickness, which enables them to avoid any form of introspection," writes Ryssen.[137] These remarks support our thesis that the present—however much it may be viewed as post-historical in America—is connected to the recent memory of the past, as both the present and the past affect civic identity, nation-state building, and the memory of Americans, and by extension that of postmodern Europeans. How does one dare critically talk about the predominance of the Judeo-American spirit in America without running the risk of social opprobrium or of landing into psychiatric asylum, as Ezra Pound once did? While it is a common place for the vast number of white American elites to crack jokes in private about Mexicans, Africans, or for that matter deride their fellow Gentile citizens, without looking over their shoulder, a critical comment about the staggering influence of Jews in America, even when that comment is founded on empirical facts, is viewed as a grave insult to Jews.[138] If a serious American scholar or a politician ventures into this forbidden field, his gesture is interpreted as a sign of being an *agent provocateur*, or worse, as a sign of somebody who decided to write his obituary. Such a schizophrenic climate of self-censorship in America will sooner or later lead to dramatic consequences for both American Jews and Gentiles. The lack of healthy dialogue can last for a century or so, but feigned conviviality between American Gentiles and American Jews cannot last forever and remain based on distorted perceptions of the Other and how this Other should behave. Mendacity carries the germ of a civil war. The entire Western history, particularly since the First World War, has abundantly proven that distorted self-perceptions, as well as the romanticized perception of the "Other," if based on negative wishful thinking, lead to war and chaos. Eventually, both American Jews and American Gentiles will be pitted into an ugly clash from which there will be no escape for any of them.

While a great many thinkers in America unabashedly challenge modern myths and sport staggering erudition and courage in their demolition, the most sensitive point of reference in the twentieth century, i.e., the Jewish question, is carefully avoided. If the subject of Jews is mentioned in America, then it is usually in a laudatory fashion, which clearly points to a morbid desire of postmodern American white elites to curry favor with the Jews. These same individuals will be the first to declare themselves certified anti-Semites when an opportunistic moment becomes official enough for pogroms and Jew baiting. It is the lack of open discussion about the topic of the Jews that confirms how Jews play a crucial role in American conscience building, and by extension, in the entire West. This is an additional sign of how past times interact with present times. Twentieth century experience with National

Socialism still serves as a powerful red flag in a political semantic field which must be carefully trodden upon.

But contrary to classical anti-Semitic arguments, strong Jewish influence in America is not only the product of Jews; it is the logical result of Gentiles' acceptance of the Jewish founding myths that have seeped over centuries into Europe and America in their diverse Christian modalities. Postmodern Americanism is just the latest secular version of the Judean mindset. Hypothetically speaking, if Jews, by some miracle, were to play a marginal role in America—as they claim they do—then, logically, they would be the subject of a normal critical discussion, just like other American ethnic groups, races, or next door neighbors are.

Blaming American Jews for extraterrestrial powers and their purported conspiracy to subvert Gentile culture borders on delusion and only reflects the absence of dialogue. American anti-Semitic delusions only provide legitimacy to American Jews in their constant search for a real or surreal anti-Semitic boogieman around the corner. Without the specter of anti-Semitism, Jews would likely assimilate quickly and hence disappear. Thus, anti-Semitism provides Jews with alibis to project themselves as victims of Gentile prejudice. Consequently, it assigns them a cherished role of posing as the sole educational super-ego for Americans and by proxy the entire world. In his book on the social role of Jews, a prominent Jewish-French politician and author, Jacques Attali, writes: "As Russian Jews invented socialism, and as Austrian Jews invented psychoanalysis, American Jews in the forefront, participated in the birth of American capitalism and in the Americanization of the entire world."[139] For some Jewish authors, like Attali, such a remark is easier to write down than for a Gentile thinker, who with the same comment, would be shouted down as an "anti-Semite."

Each time American Gentiles write critically about the Jewish role in twentieth century America, they are likely to find marginal readership, and will hardly garner credibility in the mainstream media environment. But when some prominent Jewish author talks about the same issue, notably the phenomenal Jewish role in social and political affairs in postmodern America and in the rest of the West, then his prose will elicit awe and respect. A critical Jewish author may be accepted with apprehension and irritation by his fellow Jews, but his words will nevertheless likely find their place in the ears and eyes of a larger audience.

It is an open secret that Jews played a disproportionate role in the Bolshevik revolution, and more precisely in the early Soviet secret police. It is also a fact that although being a tiny minority in America, Jews play an influential role in the opinion making industry, i.e. the film industry, the media, and higher education. "Jews are simply indispensable for other nations," notes Ryssen again.[140] There were literally tons of books published in the early and late thirties of the preceding century in America, Germany and France that provided detailed accounts of the role of the Jews and their number in different important professions in America and Europe, and that specifically discussed Jewish numerical overrepresentation in the early Soviet Union and America respectively. The government in National Socialist Germany had harnessed the best anti-Semitic brains in order to document every nook and cranny of Judaism in the Soviet Union and America.[141] But at the beginning of the 21st century, these books are either banned or derided as unscientific and anti-Semitic prose. In mainstream political discussions their authors are ignored. Their prose seems to be only savored by readers who are already hostile to Jews, and who usually explain away the entire human drama by reducing it to an alleged Jewish conspiracy.

Therefore, a comment or a book by a Jewish author, who preferably sports a politically correct liberal pedigree, and who tackles this greatest taboo topic of postmodernity, i.e. the role of Jews in America and Russia in the twentieth century, must be accepted with welcome. Such is the book of a liberal Jewish-Russian-American scholar, Yuri Slezkine, whose research does not reveal to someone already knowledgeable about the Jewish question any new insights regarding the Jewish role in America and the ex-Soviet Union. However, in view of the fact that these views are formulated by a Jewish scholar, they may be used as a standard reference by a reader. Slezkine notes how Jews played a prominent role in the early Soviet terror machine and in the Soviet secret police, the NKVD, but they did it "because they fought for the state in order to become free of Jewishness."[142] In other words, they happened to be Jews against their own will. They apparently wanted to leave the image of being first and foremost cosmopolitans wishing to improve humanity. Slezkine also confirms that America was an ideal promised land for the Jews in view of the fact that it "has no state bearing natives."[143] It was to be expected that with the collapse of the Marxist mystique, Americanism, at the turn of the 21st century, became a favorite ideology for disenchanted Jewish Marxists.

In the German language during the National Socialist epoch, the term "state bearing citizens," used by Slezkine was "*staatsgestaltende Volksgenossen*," the term which the National Socialist propaganda reserved for German citizens only, but the term and status which was legally denied to European Jews. Slezkine notes that America became a Jewish substitute utopia because, unlike Europe and Germany, with their strong tribal adherences, "America knew only vestigial establishment tribalism."[144] America, as a country of deracinated individuals, has never been in the position to put up ethnic or racial barriers against Jews and other non-European ethnic groups, as has been the case with racially homogenous European states and empires. From its inception, America was an ideal country for Jews; it was designed to be a prime laboratory for diverse multicultural and academic experiments, be they of intra-European or extra-European nature. This multiracial social engineering was facilitated by the ecumenical and globalistic framework of the early American Puritans—who had considered themselves as spiritual Jews. What Jewish intellectuals could not attain in Europe, or later in the Soviet Union, was at hand in America where "Jewish power, economic status and cultural influence have increased dramatically since 1960."[145]

On a different level of analysis, one can notice the American absence of what the Germans call *Kulturvolk,* i.e. a rooted cultural and national community (and not just the adherence to the white race), which is the main prerequisite for any sound state-anchored nationalism. The absence of a common cultural identity among white Americans seems to be the fundamental weakness of postmodern American nationalists, racialists and conservatives who, while not hiding their hostility to Jews, are unable to muster up common cultural and national energy for establishing their similar cultural and national uniqueness. Harping only on genetic determinism, as many eugenicists and modern American racialists do, in order to promote an abstract white man identity is self-defeating. Therefore, the question comes back again: What does it mean to be an American in postmodernity?

One can naturally concur that Americans are influenced by Jews, but then the question arises as to how did it happen? Was not Christianity the offspring of Jewish monotheism? Was Jesus himself not a Jew? Jews in America and their overrepresentation in powerful media positions and political appointments, which many Americans in private complain about, did not drop from the moon. Jewish social prominence, both in Europe and America, has been the direct result of the white Gentile's acceptance of Jewish apostles—an event which was brought to its perfection in America by early Puritan Pilgrim Founding Fathers. Be it in Europe or in the USA, Christian religious denominations are differentiated versions of Jewish monotheism. Therefore, the whole history of philo-Semitsm, or anti-Semitism in America and in Europe, verges on serious social neurosis.

American pro-Jewish or "Jewified" intellectuals often show signs of being more Jewish than Jews themselves. Their excessive love for Jews stems from their subconscious hatred of Jews, a fact that most Jews are perfectly aware of, and which only gives further legitimacy to Jewish social prominence in America. Indeed, at the beginning of the 21st century there can be no worse insult than qualifying a prominent white politician or an academic in America as an "anti-Semite." And often this derogatory noun or adjective does not originate with persons labeled as anti-Semites, but are hurled by Jews or Gentile intellectuals sympathetic to the Jewish cause. Americans, hostile to Jews, often forget that the hypothetical disappearance of Jews from America or their lesser role in public life would not open up a golden era of Americanism. The entire history of all European peoples, be that in Europe or in America, be it before Christ or after Christ, has abundantly proven that when Gentiles run out of Jews, then they start hacking each other to pieces—often for trivial reasons. As the latest version of Christianized and secularized monotheism, Judeo-Americanism represents the most radical departure from the ancient European pre-Christian *genius loci,* which Europeans have managed to preserve better than Americans. How then to counter strong Jewish influence in Americanism without lapsing into anti-Semitism?

It is the proximity of Christians with Judaism, writes de Benoist, which explains their phony mutual love and their frequent murderous wars. Christian anti-Semites in America often forget, in their endless lamentation about the changing racial structure of America, that Christianity is by definition a universal religion aiming to achieve a pan-racial system of governance. Therefore, Christians, regardless whether they are hypermoralistic Puritans or more authority prone Catholics, are in no position to found an ethnically and racially all white Gentile society while adhering at the same time to the Christian dogma of pan-racial universalism. "Anti-Semitism was born from the Christian desire to fulfill Judaism, to "finish it up," to attribute to it its "real" meaning."[146] The Pilgrim Fathers had exactly this globalistic and ecumenical approach in mind when they arrived in New England. Their secular successors are obligated in postmodernity to resort to democratic and human rights gospel as well to export ecumenical Americanism to the different antipodes of the earth. In the eyes of Christians "just as the Law, with Christ, had come to its *end* (in both senses of the word) and has become useless, in the same vein each distinction between Israel and other nations has become redundant: there are no more Jews or Greeks (Gal. 3, 28). It is universal Christianity which is *verus Israel*.[147] De Benoist writes further:

> "*This process, which emerged with the Pauline reforms had a double consequence. On the one hand it ended up with the persecution of the Jews, who were depicted as the worst enemies of Christianity, on the ground of their genealogical proximity and their refusal to convert, that is, to recognize Christianity as "true Israel." On the other hand, as Shmuel Trigano noted, while setting itself up as "new Israel," the West recognized to Jewishness a factual, if not a juridical jurisdiction over itself. And this boils down to saying that the West has become "Israelite" to the extent that it forbade to Jews to remain Israelites. It follows from this that the name "Judeo- Christianity" is a double incarceration; it imprisons the Christian West, which by its own act subordinates itself to a jurisdiction which is not its own, and in order to regain it, puts it in a position to deny this jurisdiction to its legitimate keepers.*"[148]

The West, at its zenith in America, has become anti-Semitic to the extent that it has always yearned to become Israelite. The West, and particularly America, will cease to be Israelite once it leaves this neurosis, once it returns to its own local myths, and "by stopping to be what it is not and by allowing the "Other" to continue what it is."[149] The Judeo-Christian embrace, resulting in a mutual love-hate relationship, has been going on for centuries, and at the end of the 20th century it attained its final neurotic peak in America. This corroborates our thesis about the strong link between Puritanism and Judaism, with both being the "proposition myths" of pre-modern and postmodern Americanism. These two beliefs do not exclude each other.

Many Jewish scholars rightly acknowledge deep theological links between Americanism and Judaism.[150] Also, American traditionalists and conservatives are correct in denouncing secular myths, such as Freudism, Marxism, and neo-liberalism which they see as ideologies concocted by Jewish and pro-Jewish thinkers. They fail to go a step further and examine the Judaic origins of Christianity and mutual proximity of these two monotheist religions that make up the foundations of the modern West. Only within the framework of Judeo-Christianity can one understand modern democratic aberrations and the proliferation of new civic religions in postmodernity. When, for instance, a number of American revisionist scholars critically point to factual inconsistencies regarding the historical narrative of World War II, or when they critically examine the Jewish Holocaust, they seem to forget the religious Judeo-Christian bonds which have shaped the historical memory of all European peoples. The words of historical revisionists will have, therefore, very little consistency. Denouncing the alleged myth of the Jewish Holocaust, while believing in the mythology of a Jesus Christ rebirth, is a proof of moral inconsistency. No wonder that the level of Jewish outcry against critical writings about the Holocaust will be very strong. The scarecrow of anti-Semitism or the charges of Holocaust denial are the best weapons to silence postmodern heretics. How can one dismiss the self-evident Holocaust story yet at the same time embrace a self-evident story of a Jew Jesus Christ? Both stories show inconsistencies. "Instead of submitting anti-Semitism to the free play of ideas, instead of making it a topic for debate in which all can join, Jews and their liberal supporters have managed to organize an inquisition in which all acts, writings and even thoughts critical of Jewry are treated as a threat to the moral order of mankind."[151] This brings us back to the point made earlier about the notion of "self-evidence." If something is proclaimed to be self-evident, as the postmodern narrative of the Holocaust is, it does not have to be stated over and over again. Conversely, when something is of dubious nature, its propagators turn it into a self-evident dogma that must be repeated *ad nauseum*, thus trivializing the very sacred idea which they attempt to uphold. The highly neurotic subject regarding the Jewish question will sooner or later result in another conflict between Gentiles and Jews.

The frightened attitude of American and European intellectuals, who often extol the concept of "intellectual freedom," is best seen in their servile attitude toward Jews in their proximity, to the extent that "(T)he pro-Semite has consequently made himself a mirror image of the anti-Semite."[152] The danger of this fatal embrace lies not with Jews, but with American Christians. After all, an American Christian-inspired anti-Semite must appear in the eyes of Jews like a bizarre specie. On the one hand he hates the alien Jew; yet on the other, he lugs behind himself a Levantine deity that is not of European cultural origin. Many American conservatives, and particularly American Christian Zionists, believe in the immaculate conception of the Virgin Mary, and equally much in the future conversion of American Jews to Christianity. This monotheistic linage, however contradictory it looks, makes sense. After all, just like Mary immaculately conceived her Jewish son Jesus, she remained an immaculate Jewess by birth.

The feigned fraternity between the postmodern American "shabbath" goyim and American Jews is veiled in servile mendacity and mutual make-belief mimicry which can be spotted in the postmodern American political establishment and its media. At the beginning of the third millennium, feigned love for the Jews is mimicked tirelessly by American vassals in Europe. Admittedly, this will give rise to a proverbial Jewish hubris which will continue to grow as long as it receives the appropriate Biblical fodder from Christian Americans and the self-censored European sheep which, after 1945, learned the lessons of tacit self-surveillance.

Also, the reason America has been so protective of the state of Israel has little to do with America's geopolitical security. Rather, Israel is an archetype and a pseudo-spiritual receptacle of American ideology and its Puritan founding fathers. Israel must functions as America's democratic Super-Ego.

American Neo-Paganism

Whatever one may think about the seemingly obsolete or even derogatory connotation of the phrase "paganism," it is certain that it best represents the antidote to Judaic spirit and anti-Semitism and can best protect America against Biblical fundamentalism. Etymologically, paganism is related to the beliefs and rituals that were in usage in European villages and the countryside. But paganism, in its modern version, can also mean a certain sensibility, and a "way of life"—a phenomenon that stands in sharp contrast to the Puritan heritage in America. To some extent, the European peoples in America still continue to be "pagans" because their national memory often contains allusions to ancient myths, fairy tales, and forms of folklore that bear the peculiar mark of pre-Christian themes. The omnipotence of Jewish-Christian beliefs has not completely silenced those ancient customs; it has only suppressed them into the shadow of the unconscious. In European culture, polytheistic beliefs began to dwindle with the rise of Christianity. In the centuries to come, it was to be expected that the polymorph system of explanation, whether in theology or later on in sociology, politics, history, or psychology, in short, the entire perception of the world, would gradually come under the influence of Judeo-Christian monotheistic beliefs. Unquestionably, the two thousand year impact of Judeo-Christian monotheism, with its latest distilment in Americanism, has considerably altered its approach to politics as well as the overall perception of the world. Following the consolidation of Judeo-Christian belief in its Puritan form in America, the world and world phenomena came to be observed by the American elites according to fixed concepts and categories governed by the logic of "either-or," "true or false," "good or evil"- with seldom any shading in between. But can the Judeo-Christian mindset continue to be a valid approach in twenty first century America, e.g., in a complex world replete with choices and intricate social differences that stubbornly refuse categorization?

In modern popular consciousness, the centuries long and pervasive influence of Christianity has significantly contributed to the modern view that holds any glorification of polytheism, or for that matter nostalgia for the Greco-Roman spiritual order, as irreconcilable with contemporary Americanized society. Modern individuals who reject Jewish influence in

America often forget that much of their neurosis would disappear if their Biblical fundamentalism was abandoned. One may contend that the rejection of monotheism does not imply a return to the worship of ancient Indo-European deities or the veneration of some exotic gods and goddesses. It means forging another civilization, or rather, a modernized version of scientific and cultural Hellenism, considered once as a common receptacle for all European peoples. Hardly can one argue for the conquest of the planet; rather, polytheism means envisaging a new community of European peoples in America whose goal should be the quest for their ancestral heritage and not the rejection of it—as has been hitherto the case with Europeans coming to America's shores. A return to European roots means not a sectarian approach to some out of this world religion, as is often the case in postmodern America. It means the recapturing the lost transcendental pre-Christian memory. At this stage, America is already replete with awkward non-Jewish and often anti-Jewish political groups, which are frequently embodied in weird sects and do not offer serious political alternatives. What makes these sects bizarre is less their refusal of Judeo-Christian monotheism but more their polytheism under primitive and puerile forms, related to what Oswald Spengler called "second religiosity" (*zweite Religiosität*). This second religiosity appears with rapid urbanization and corresponds usually to a phenomenon of evasion, alienation, or confused compensation and without any serious repercussion on reality. "It appears in all civilizations as they achieve completion and then move to an ahistorical status."[153] This is true today in America more than ever before, especially when one observes the myriad of quasi "pagan" sects or cults which in most cases render impossible any positive meaning of paganism.

The Jewish spirit and its distilled version in Puritanism has also introduced into the American mindset an alien "anthropology" that is today directly responsible for the spread of an egalitarian mass society and the rise of a "soft" liberal thought police. Americanism represents an ideological system of a unique truth; a system that upholds the idea of an absolute good versus an absolute evil; a system described in the Old Testament in which the idea of the enemy must be assimilated to evil—and an enemy who is, therefore, to be physically exterminated.[154] In short, Judeo-Christian universalism, practiced in America with its various multicultural and secular offshoots, set the stage for the rise of postmodern egalitarian aberrations and the complete promiscuity of all values.

That Americanism can also be a fanatical and intolerant system "without God," is quite obvious. This system, nonetheless, is the inheritor of a Christian thought in the sense in which Carl Schmitt demonstrated that the majority of modern political principles are secularized theological principles. They bring down to earth a structure of exclusion; the police of the soul yield place to the police of the state; ideological wars follow up religious wars. Such views are shared by many American non-Christian traditionalist and eugenicist authors whom we have quoted here, and whose philosophical research is directed toward the rehabilitation of European non-Christian thought, but who also reject any form of anti-Semitism. Louis Rougier argues how Christianity came under the influence of both the Iranian dualism and the eschatological visions of the Jewish apocalypses. Accordingly, Jews and later on Christians adopted the belief that the good, who presently suffer, would be rewarded in the future. When human beings lose the capacity to govern themselves, they resort to some sort of strange belief system; they create a salutary fiction which is necessary to them in order to transcend their earthy existence. The new postmodern fiction in America is called global democracy.

In the more rationalist and more developed countries, such as in America, one is witnessing the birth of a myriad of strange religious beliefs and cults. "Only in the USA, over 1300 different cults share some 155 million believers."[155] Over a period of time, the consequences of this largely dualistic vision of the world, inherent in Judeo-Christian monotheism, had to result in the portrayal of political enemies as always evil by American elites, as opposed to system of Americanism, which is always considered a good value system. The Greco-Roman intolerance of foreign belief systems had never assumed such total and absolute proportions of religious exclusion. The intolerance towards Christians, Jews, and other sects was sporadic and usually aimed at certain religious customs deemed contrary to Roman common law (such as circumcision, human sacrifices, sexual and religious orgies, and so on).

The most serious reproach that one can level against the Judeo-American mindset is that it has inaugurated secular versions of an egalitarian cycle, notably the idea of political progress, while introducing into the mind of its constituents a revolutionary anthropology with a universalistic and globalistic character. Judeo-Christian monotheism, along with its secular liberal exclusiveness, presupposes an underlying idea of universalism, as well as the establishment of one undisputed truth. The consequence of the Judeo-Christian belief in ontological oneness, i.e., that there is only one God and, therefore, only one democratic truth, resulted, over a period of time, in an effort to obliterate or downplay any other possible political truth or any other value system. Accordingly, American intolerance of other political systems can be interpreted as a violent response against those who have departed from Yahweh's path, or to put it in a secularized language, those who have strayed away from democratic finality. In America, this is best visible in the passionate desire among American elites to make the "world safe for democracy"- whatever the price may be. It should not come as a surprise that one often encounters among American elites the behavior of "false humility," particularly in regard to American Jews and other racial minorities. Although almost identical in their worship of one God, the mutual clash between American Jews and American Christians is waiting to occur. How can fanatical Christian-Zionists in America reconcile themselves with the fact that they must worship a deity of a *deicide* people? Jews by contrast, thanks to their religious exclusiveness, thrive in a system which is both theologically and ideologically predetermined to accommodate their deities, as well as their own secular aspirations. Whereas Christianity of Gentile Americans is meant to be a universalistic religion whose goal is to proselytize in all corners of the world, American Jews can dispense with these efforts. Judaism must be an ethnic religion of only the Jewish people. Judeo-Christian monotheism in America has substantially altered the modern approach towards understanding history and politics. Consequently, American elites consider themselves obliged to assign to the American dream a history with a specific goal, the end result of which would be a gradual but definitive devaluation of past historical events that do not display signs of God's theophany. And this theophany must end in a much cherished "end of history." Accordingly, the Judeo-American rationalization of historical process precludes the reassessment of America's own national or racial past, and in addition, it contributes to the "desertification" of American society. This disenchantment with Nature started with the biblical notion of Creation. The Judaic rationalization of religious life, which was adopted by the early Puritans, stems from the ultra-rational character of Mosaic and Talmudic laws, which were incorporated into American legalism and the so-called rule of law. More than in any other monotheistic religion, Americanism, similar to Judaism, has rationalized (and imposed the formulas) for all aspects of man's life, and this by means of a myriad of prescriptions, laws, and interdictions. The excessive American legalism has thus resulted in the desacralization of Nature and the devaluation of all cultural activity. One may conclude that if European Americans are to stave off spiritual anarchy, they would need to replace their monotheistic vision of the world with a polytheistic vision of the world—which alone can guarantee the "return of the Gods," that is, the plurality of *all* values. In contrast to Christian false humility and fear of God, polytheist and pagan beliefs stress courage, personal honor, and spiritual and physical self-surpassing. Early American settlers had a golden opportunity to create a new society as they had all the biological and racial prerequisites for it. In addition, they were not burdened by dated tribal memories from Europe. Early settlers in America, particularly those trekking southwest, consisted of a special breed of European people whose sense of courage and sacrifice could hardly be encountered in Europe at that time. The American archetype of this super hero could still be seen in a "lone cowboy" who essentially represents a modern version of Prometheus fighting against all odds. Even nowadays one can encounter in the so-called Bible belt of rural America individuals who seem to have retained better ancient European principles of communal solidarity and self-sacrifice than Europeans in Europe. Many characters from Jack London's novels display Promethean superhuman and pagan traits.

But the problem is that the overkill of Biblical hyper-moralism has created a mindset which has invariably caused false consciousness and which had made Americans willfully embrace the alien "Other." The future of America looks gloomy, as MacDonald remarks. Having become a "proposition nation," America and its ideology of multiculturalism will likely become a religious symbol with "sophisticated theories of psychopathology of majority group ethnocentrism, as well as with the erection of police state controls on nonconformists thought and behavior."[156] This behavior is already present in America, as Americans increasingly resort to a system of self-surveillance and exclusion for their intellectual undesirables.

At the beginning of the third millennium, America has no other choice than to export its universal Gospel of democracy and import endless masses of non-European individuals who do not comprehend ancient European values. America is bound to become more and more a racial *pluriverse*. Had the early American settlers accepted into their legal structures elements of biological Darwinism, as was briefly the case with some states in the early 20th century and had they rejected Judeo-Christian monotheism, probably America today would have become a different system—an empire similar to the Roman empire—yet limited only to the European genius. But guilt feelings inspired by the Bible, along with the belief in economic progress and the system of big business, pushed America onto a different historical path of no return.

Unlike an American Christian, a man with "polytheist values"- be he an "agnostic," or an "atheist," is encouraged to assume his entire responsibility before history because he is the only one who gives history a meaning. In pagan cosmogony, man alone is considered a forger of his own destiny *(faber suae fortunae)*, exempt from historical determinism, from any "divine grace," or economic and material constraints. Life, which is all the time faced-to-death and with-death, renders the future permanent in each instance; it becomes eternal by acquiring an inscrutable depth by assuming the value of eternity. In order to face off with the crisis of postmodernity, Americans could possibly abandon the dualistic logic of Judeo-Christian exclusion, that is, a logic of exclusion which has been responsible for extremism, not only among individuals, but also among parties and peoples and which, starting out with the American civil war in the 19th century, has disseminated into the world this dualistic split that has acquired deadly planetary proportions. In its present fashion, due to the legacy of the Bible, American monotheism excludes the possibility of historical return or "recommencement." History is destined in America to unfold in a predetermined way by making inroads towards a final goal of permanent economic bliss. The American concept of history suggests that the flow of historical time is mono-linear, and therefore, limited by its significance and meaning. Henceforth, for American Jews and American Christians, history can only be apprehended as a totality governed by a sense of an ultimate end and historical fulfillment. Small wonder that America is designated as the promise land for all peoples; no wonder that the creation of a distinct American nationalism appears to be a historical oxymoron.

History for *Homo americanus* appears at best *parenthetical,* at worst, an ugly episode or a "valley of tears," which must one day be erased from earth and transcended by economic paradise. Modern liberal ideas that are encountered today in America are aiming at replacing immemorial time by authorizing all uprootedness, all "emancipations," which, as a rule, always lead to new disappointments. The Utopian American future is meant to replace the mythical American past. Incidentally, it is always the generator of new deceptions, because the best that it announces must constantly be put off to a later date.

Temporality is no longer a founding element for the deployment of a Being trying to grasp the game of the world; temporality is pursued from one goal and reached from one end. The American concept of time resembles chiliastic expectations and no longer a national or racial communion. According to American liberal precepts, to submit historical becoming to an obligatory final outcome means in fact to enclose American history into the reign of objectivity, reduce its choices, its orientations and projects on behalf of economic commodities and instant gratification. Welcome to the club of Francis Fukuyama and American neo-cons!

Consequently, Americanism places all hope in the future since the future is thought to be able to "rectify" past errors and thereby assume the value of redemption. The concept of Time for Americans and their world acolytes is no longer reversible and, therefore, each historical occurrence must acquire the meaning of divine providence, of "God's" finger, or theophany. Moses received the Laws at a *certain* place and during a *certain* time and Jesus later preached, performed miracles, and was crucified at a *specifically* recorded time and place. In the same vein, the liberal *pax americana* wishes to bestow on all peoples world-wide a static and eternal bliss—notwithstanding the firebombings of Dresden, Tokyo, or Baghdad. The American monotheistic mindset interprets world events by giving them a new meaning and by stripping these events of their true historical meaning. When the American Messiah comes, the world will then be saved once and for all, and history will cease to exist. But how many more eons must one wait for it to happen? How many more cultures need to perish in this endeavor? If one accepts the idea of "the end of history"—as American globalists maintain, to what extent then can the entire history of suffering be explained? How is it possible, to "redeem" past oppressions, collective sufferings, deportations, and humiliations that have filled up the history of the West? This is a fundamental problem to which modern liberal American authors provide no answer. Suffice to say that this enigma only underscores the difficulty regarding the concept of distributive justice in egalitarian (both

American and Soviet) societies. If a truly egalitarian society ever becomes a reality in America, it will be inevitably a society of the elected—of those, who managed to escape the pressure of history by being born at the right time, at the right place, and in the right country. One will become "elected" by virtue of his affiliation to Americanized Yahweh. Yet, just like his future secular successors, Yahweh could not be other than a jealous god and in that capacity he was always opposed to the presence of other gods, i.e. to other political values. He is a "reductionist" and whatever exists beyond his fold must either be punished or destroyed. Not surprisingly, throughout American history, Biblical zealots and their secular liberal progeny in Washington D.C. have been encouraged, in the name of higher goals, to destroy those who have strayed away from Yahweh's assigned path.

Undoubtedly, many American atheists and agnostics also admit that in the realm of ethics all men and women of the world are the children of Abraham. Indeed, even the bolder ones who somewhat self-righteously claim to have rejected Christian or Jewish theologies, and who claim to have replaced them with "secular humanism," frequently ignore the fact that their self-styled secular beliefs are also grounded in Judeo-Christian ethics. Abraham, Jesus and Moses may be dethroned today, but their moral edicts and spiritual ordinances are much alive in American foreign policy. "The pathologies of the modern world are genuine, albeit illegitimate daughters of Christian theology," writes De Benoist.[157] One could add that the global and disenchanted American world, accompanied by the litany of human rights, ecumenical and multiracial society, and the "rule of law," carries the principles that can be directly traced to the Judeo-Christian messianism and which resurfaces today in secular versions under the elegant garb of American ideology.

By contrast, a system that recognizes an unlimited number of gods acknowledges also the plurality of political and cultural values. A polytheist system offers homage to all "gods" and, above all, it respects the plurality of all customs, political and social systems, and all conceptions of the world—of which these gods are sublime expressions. One must bear in mind that the Western world did not begin with the birth of Christ or in America. Neither did the religions of ancient Europeans see the first light of day with Moses—in the desert. Nor did the much vaunted concept of democracy begin with the proclamation of American independence. Democracy and independence—all of this existed among the early predecessors of Americans in ancient Europe, albeit in its own unique social and religious settings. America's Greco-Roman-Nordic ancestors also believed in honor, justice, and virtue, although they attached to those notions a radically different meaning. Attempting to judge these old European political and religious manifestations through the lens of postmodern America-centric and reductionist glasses means losing sight of how much America has departed from its old European heritage. Just because one professes historical optimism, or believes in the liberal "therapeutic state," does not necessarily mean that the postmodern world must be the "best of all worlds." Who knows, with the death of communism and the exhaustion of postmodern Americanism, one may be witnessing the dawn of a new American culture and a return to ancient European heritage. Who can dispute the fact that Athens was the homeland of European America before Jerusalem became its painful edifice?

Chapter V

In Yahweh We Trust: A Divine Foreign Policy

It was largely the Biblical message which stood as the origin of America's endeavor to "make the world safe for democracy." Contrary to many European observers critical of America, American military interventions have never had as a sole objective economic imperialism but rather the desire to spread American democracy around the world. This objective became obvious, when America, following the end of the Second World War, became a major global power. After the Cold War, America also became the arbiter of world affairs and the interpreter of international law. Whoever militarily challenged America ran the risk of being placed outside the category of humanity or labeled as a terrorist. Once declared outside humanity or declared a terrorist, a person, a nation, or a regime could be disposed of at will. When the Soviet Union and communism were gone, other negative archetypes had to be invented in order to better profile America's unique democratic zeal. By the beginning of the third millennium, the negative fixation on the *Other* found its substitute in Islam and the official mantra of "fighting radical Islamic terrorists" all over the world. It is striking how America, ever since its foundation, has resorted to negative profiling of other political actors, seldom looking at the specific root causes of the problem that stood behind their hostile un-American behavior.

Although postmodern America has assigned itself the role of being at the forefront in combating ethnic prejudices and racism, its own racial heterogeneity is having an impact on its foreign policy. As a multiracial society with over 25% of its citizens of non-European origin, America's role in world affairs can no longer be the same. The September 11, 2001 terrorist bombing of the Twin Towers in New York came as a small respite in forbidden ethnic stereotyping. From then on, a joke or a deprecatory remark against Arabs or the religion of Islam could get a safe passage in America's media. Many American conservatives and radical right-wingers, including white racialists, fell into the trap of such negative stereotyping of Muslims, and their hatred of Islamic fundamentalism turned into an excuse for xenophobic sentiments against all non-white immigrants. General resentments against Islam became a common denominator for many white Americans as they could finally and safely vent their frustrations against social experiments carried out in their home grown ideology of multiculturalism.

But why not point out that Bible-inspired American ideology can be as intolerant as Islamism, and why not recall that many Muslims living in Europe are of white European origin? Furthermore, the outbursts of anti-Islamic feelings in America became a handy instrument of different pressure groups including Jewish-American lobbies that had traditionally been on guard regarding the real or alleged rise of radical Islam in the Middle East. Therefore, in examining American foreign policy, particularly towards Muslim countries in the Middle East and Central Asia, one must ask the standard question: *cui bono?* Who benefits from it?

The American target of Islamism in the postmodern age should not come as a surprise. Similar negative stereotyping of the *Other* had its origin in the preceding vilification of Germany and Japan, the two countries which during the Second World War found themselves in a deadly military conflict with America and Americanism. The consequences of that military and ideological clash are visible to this day and they continue to shape the political agenda of the political elites both in America and Europe. It was to be expected that after the disappearance of Fascism and National Socialism in 1945, other negative stereotypes had to be used in order to legitimize the new American world order. One must raise the question whether Americanism can survive at all without constantly looking over its shoulder for some negative political counter-model? To a large extent, the real or alleged Islamic threat, which became part of an American orchestrated global concern in the early 21st century, is the logical continuation of America's compulsive quest to cleanse its own household of evil.

Europe and its heartland Germany experienced during World War II a full para-Biblical swing of American foreign policy, although the interests of American political elites in Europe were more complex than just removing "Nazi Evil." After all, Germany was on the way of becoming a major Euro-Asian steam-roller ready to challenge America's access to energy sources in the rimland countries of the Middle East and the Pacific Basin. Carl Schmitt, the well known German jurist and a theoretician of international law, who also experienced for some time the wrath of American world improvers, writes that America's hubris received another boost after the Second World War as America had become a first rate economic and military superpower. After 1945, America came to be viewed by reeducated European leaders as the economic embodiment of the spirit of the Enlightenment and as a pristine country of the state of nature that best reflected the dominant ideas of peace and progress. Later, even if many of America's foreign policy decisions were often looked down upon by European leaders, America's astounding economic growth, coupled with amazing technological discoveries, earned it the reputation as a miracle do-gooding country. Psychologically, not a single European leader or a would-be hegemon could dismiss the fact that America represented something all political actors in Europe and elsewhere in the world had always dreamed about. America was destined to push aside Europe and begin to function as its embellished substitute. It already had the ideological asset of having established its own city on the hill in a self-appointed desire to make the entire world safe for democracy. "The new West, America, will remove the old West, i.e. Europe from its own historical location, that is, from the old center of the world."[158]

Regardless of the negative portrayals of American foreign policy by European traditionalist and right-wing authors, America and Americanism cannot accommodate for a long period of time of other ideological alternatives. America can often be on friendly terms with smaller countries of different un-American and even anti-American ideological persuasions, provided these countries never compete with it for world supremacy. Hypothetically speaking, even if there were some replica of America, with the same geographical size, the same military capability, and sharing the same democratic values—it is very likely that present day America would sooner or later find itself on a collision course with this "other-sameness." Finally, the question should be raised not how harmful or beneficial American foreign policy is, but whether there is any other alternative to American hegemony at all. And if there were other non-American alternatives, who can deny that they cannot be worse? Over the last two thousand years, European politicians and thinkers have been sagely discussing about a common European homeland and a common European foreign policy. The results of such well thought-out wisdom became obvious by the beginning of the third millennium, notably when European elites failed again to rearrange their endless tribal disputes in a newly launched entity, the so-called European Union. How then can European elites project their Europeaness in other parts of the world if they are not capable of finding consensus on their own small peninsula which is one third the size of America? If America was to miraculously disappear, and with it all of its social and political ills, it is questionable whether some new European or some Asian superpower would be able to guarantee global security.

The Insular Mind vs. the Continental Mind

America has been a superpower often against its own will. It is a sole military powerhouse because at least for now there are no contestants for hegemony in the world arena. As an American author, a former diplomat and opinion maker, Zbigniew Brzezinski notes, "America was able to combine during the course of the twentieth century, four major factors in order to preserve its superpower status: it had a first-rate military capacity; it was a world locomotive of economic growth; it made path-breaking innovations in the computer industry. Finally, America's popular culture and its diverse leisure-oriented paraphernalia made the American life style acceptable by the whole panoply of word actors—even by those who profess 'anti-Americanism.'"[159] Indeed, this fourth point is the most important as it gives America cultural legitimacy which it can at any time translate into a military quest for power. Technically speaking, it is probable that the jurisdiction of America and its citizens can be projected into some other corner of the world, as this happened after World War II with the Americanization of Europe. It cannot be ruled out that even if America, with its present geopolitical location and its capital in Washington D.C., disappeared from the map, America and Americanism could relocate to some Euro-Asian or African region of a similar size. America may have its own sense of order, which may be accepted or rejected by other world actors. America does, however, have its own list of priorities that are often rejected by foreign powers, but which have sustained, over the last one hundred years, some sort of world order. Different theories, concocted by European anti-American theoreticians, notably about some Berlin-Paris-Moscow axis or a Euro-Asian empire in the offing, look silly and they reflect the typical fantasies of right-wing Europeans on their own self-imposed political margins. These theories are not based on solid empirical facts.

The Euro-Asian continent and especially the European powers have traditionally been torn apart by different political narratives, and nothing indicates that Europe, or for that mater China, is capable of forming a common entity to counter America's present or future ambitions. In fact, America does not even need to have outstanding geopolitical ambitions; they become available to her as a result of constant Euro-Asian infighting. For instance, the much vaunted European Union, ever since its foundation in 1957 and its refurbishment in 1992, has been mired in bureaucratic horse trading. Paradoxically, the much-acclaimed European cultural diversity hinders Europeans from having a common foreign policy. By contrast, the big advantage of America is its monolithic character, its linguistic unity, and nation-less ideology of a one world government. Therefore, the American system has thus far been in a better position than any other to foster world hegemony.

Undoubtedly, at the beginning of the third millennium, America began to show ambitions in Central Asia that will inevitably clash with the future interests of China, Russia, and Europe. This area represents a gigantic space, replete with energy sources which could possibly feed world energy demands for centuries to come, regardless of the Middle East imbroglio which has marred America's foreign policy energy and absorbed most of its foreign aid over the last several decades. But given the long standing ethnic, racial, and cultural bickering of a myriad of actors in this large area, it is highly unlikely that some Euro-Asian empire hostile to America or Israel will emerge any time soon. Viewed from another angle, is it not preferable to have some sort of stability and security—however criminal or hypermoral that stability may sound—to living in an ethnically independent and balkanized world governed by semi-anarchical regimes? Political disruptions in the Balkan Peninsula, following the end of the Cold War, the incapacity of Europe to halt the carnage in the ex-Yugoslavia, that is, in its own backyard, the call for America to intervene in order to stop the Yugoslav killing fields, confronts us with the same age old dilemma: Is it not, after all, preferable to have American-staged security to some vague notions of liberty replete with fear and violence?

These remarks cannot be an excuse for American political theology which most foreign leaders comprehend with great difficulty. Since its inception, America has been a victim of equivocal attitudes towards other political actors, a practice which has reflected itself in its foreign policy decision making to this day. On the one hand, American decision makers adhere to political autism, called isolationism; on the other, they often break into spasms of global military quests, frequently conducted by violent methods against the "Other," i.e. the "Non-believers," "the Axis of Evil," the "Empire of Evil," the Communists, the Fascists, the Muslim Fundamentalists—that is, against all those who oppose the American religious crusade against "Evil."

Similar to Bolshevik Russia, America introduced into the rules of military engagement a discriminatory factor against its military opponents who are no longer regarded as "just adversaries" *(justus hostis)*, but instead, as absolute foes that merit total annihilation. Naturally, absolute foe needs to be destroyed absolutely. This discriminatory factor first appeared during the American Civil War. Later, American engagements in Europe, particularly in the aftermath of World War I, followed a similar patter of Biblical exclusion and discrimination; American wars became total wars aiming at eradicating "evil" and regenerating humanity.[160] The firebombing of defenseless European cities during the Second World War, the destruction of Germany, as well as the bombing of other European countries[161] by the Anglo-American forces, must have served, if not as an example, then at least as a moral excuse for similar destructions carried out by America's communist allies in Eastern Europe.

Towards the end of the Cold War, some American and European scholars opened up a Pandora's Box by openly addressing the issue of American war crimes and "other losses" inflicted by American forces on war-ravaged Europe.[162] This topic deserves a special chapter, as with the opening of numerous German files and archives, American-made myths are subject to different academic scrutiny. Here again we seem to be confronted with the same legal dilemma encountered earlier; notably, who defines what is historical truth, and what is a historical lie? What is an act of humanity and what is a crime against humanity? The advantage of America, particularly in the latter half of the twentieth century, was its ability to justify the destruction of enemy forces by using the euphemism of "collateral damage," and by wrapping up its military engagements in the rhetoric of human rights and democracy.

Other than the omnipotent Bible that has traditionally served as a moral cover for providing good conscience to American political elites, the true advantage of America lies in its unique geopolitical position. No country on earth has been blessed by such a splendid insular location as America. Nor could America have prospered without constituting a common geopolitical whole, stretching from Alaska to Arkansas, from New York to New Mexico, without encountering political or cultural barriers or alien systems hostile to America's interests. America, unlike any empire so far, has a coastal line stretching for over 10,000 miles from the East to West coasts. As a result, America has been in a position to directly immerse itself in the affairs of Pacific Rim countries and in the affairs of Europe, yet always being able to retreat into isolationism. Spatial insularity permits America, even when it commits a cardinal error in foreign policy, to return to its home affairs. In addition, unlike other empires in history, America does not have to deal with militarily and industrially sophisticated neighbors in its immediate vicinity. America's ability to project its might to the different antipodes remains, therefore, unchallenged. Geography is America's destiny despite the fact that the academic field of geopolitics has never stirred much interest in America.[163] Geography is the advantage of each insular country, as was once the case with Great Britain, in contrast to land-locked countries on the Euro-Asian continent. Continental countries in central Europe are surrounded by unpredictable neighbors, as has been the case with Germany since the break-up of Charlemagne's empire. Had Germany not been constrained by its claustrophobic and land-locked space, very likely it would have become, a long time ago, a major Euro-Asian world power and would likely play today a major role in world affairs.

The Monroe doctrine became the major centerpiece in the formulation of American geostrategic calculations. Named after its architect, President Monroe in 1823, this doctrine had at the beginning a limited geographic scope which extended only to Central and Latin America. After Word War I, however, with Woodrow Wilson as President, the Monroe Doctrine was to encompass the entire globe. On January 22, 1917, Wilson officially declared the Monroe Doctrine the guiding principle of American foreign policy. Thus America could reserve for itself the right to project its military might to any corner of the globe, while using the same principle to prevent foreign encroachments in its own backyard.[164] During its inception, the Monroe Doctrine was purely a defensive mechanism of American foreign policy, primarily designed as a tool to hedge against European colonial powers. At the beginning of the nineteenth century, America, other than benefiting from its insular position, was far from becoming a major naval world power able to police the oceans. Following the Napoleonic Wars and the establishment of the European Holy Alliance, colonial and maritime Spain was still the major power in the Caribbean, that is, in the very vicinity of new-born America. Since then, with the gradual decline of European empires, America began to emerge as the only sea power, which in turn enabled it to conduct a single handed policy of unilateralism.

The new thalassocratic policy of America has always been more of a reactive and less of a proactive nature. American leaders are aware that any geopolitical void, wherever it may appear, will be eventually detrimental to America's long term interests. Any geopolitical vacuum leads to anarchy. Be it in the Caribbean, in the early twentieth century, or in the Balkans at the end of the twentieth century, or in Central Asia at the beginning of the 21st century, distant America cannot tolerate political vacuum for an extended period of time. For reasons of its own geopolitical security, America will, therefore, team up with anti-American regimes as long as these regimes provide stability and do not geopolitically pose a threat to America's interests. Despite its lachrymal Bible-inspired rhetoric, despite its obsession with political preaching, American political elites have demonstrated over the last two hundred years a remarkable sense of geographic realism. It is wrong, therefore, to accuse its elites of naiveté or ignorance in world affairs, as many Europeans wrongly do. America's good understanding of the complexity of the globe appears all the more puzzling as America is spatially and historically a "suspended" country whose perception of the enemy differs from the enemy's own self-perception, or the enemy's perception of America. Biblical fanaticism has only been one distinct trait of American ideology; sound analysis of geopolitical issues, a field in which America has been quite successful, is another phenomenon. By failing to distinguish between these two different issues of American foreign policy, many European observers make fateful conclusions about America's long term objectives.

The Monroe Doctrine, as Schmitt notes, was basically a unilateral decision. "It is not a treaty signed with other European countries."[165] It is very general in its wording and can be interpreted at will by its architects, while providing America with an astounding weapon to counter hostile interests. The Monroe Doctrine, over the last two hundred years, has served its purpose; it subjected the Western hemisphere to American influence and military control. America has achieved something which other powers have never been able to dream about. The Monroe doctrine is "extremely vague and its equivocal principles cannot be disputed by anybody. Other nations can never extract anything from America by means of this doctrine; America can always demand anything from any political actor, whatever it desires."[166] Despite the fact that America recognizes the sovereignty of the countries in its close and distant vicinity, it is actually American elites who define their concept of sovereignty and their concept of the political.

Later, after the First World War, the practice of

unilateralism continued unabated as America became the architect of the Geneva-based League of Nations—from which it quickly withdrew several years later when the legal provisions of the League were deemed contrary to America's own security interests. After the Second World War, America adopted the same detached attitude towards the United Nations and the Hague Tribunal, as well as to other international bodies—which it had once contributed in creating. So long as these international bodies further American interests they are propped up and used as a legal cover for America's decision makers; when America, by contrast, deems their actions hostile to its interests or unfriendly to the interests of its favorite ally, Israel, it ignores them. Whenever other countries are concerned, America insists on their full cooperation with the UN and Hague Tribunal and their strict adherence to the letter of international law. Seldom do these rules apply to America or Israel when the interests of their countries are at stake.

In the late twentieth century, having become a master of political semiotics, the dynamics of Americanism reached all corners of the world. The crucial moment, both from the semantic and political perspective, occurred in 1928, with the so-called Briand-Kellogg pact. By declaring that wars should be put "outside law," America became the sole interpreter of a political meta-language which later enabled it to define what was internationally "good" and what was "bad;" who was the aggressor and/or who was the victim of aggression. "This is the great superiority of the astonishing political mastership of America; its systematic recourse to general concepts that are open to any interpretation," writes Schmitt (...) "The one who has real power also defines words and concepts." As a result of the introduction of this new political meta-language, American future military engagements, particularly those in Europe and in the Pacific Basin during World War II, found ample legal justification. Often those engagements were not viewed by American elites as full scale military interventions; they were euphemistically labeled as "humanitarian police actions."[167]

Later, in the first half of the twentieth century, America's foreign policy took on even stronger messianic traits that were boosted by its tireless efforts to spread the gospel of democracy. Undoubtedly, the foreign policy of any country on earth must have a sound basis in some belief or some dogma, however angelic that dogma may appear to its architects and no matter how criminal it may appear to its victims. Therefore, a good analyst of a country's foreign policy must carefully study the founding myths of that state and project himself into the mind of his opponent from that state. But how many modern and postmodern American politicians have gone through the trouble of observing—let alone of judging themselves—through the hostile eyes of their opponents whom they often regard as ignorant recipients of America's divine deeds? Generally, only a few American authors acknowledge the self-serving influence of the Bible in American political and military affairs. One can find in Europe a large number of authors critical of American hyper-moralism and the role of the Bible in American political conduct. It is a common practice among American elites, regardless whether they consider themselves "liberals" or "conservatives," to sermonize other nations against real or alleged religious fanaticism; yet the response of America against the real or alleged Islamic fundamentalism, in the wake of the September 11, 2001 terrorist attack on Washington and New York, has largely been veiled in a very dogmatic Christian-crusading spirit.

If one studies American political behavior, one is struck with a large dose of simplistic rhetoric. Even the modern liberal ideology of "human rights," so dear to secular American opinion makers, may be seen as another expression of the primeval Biblical code of good ethnical conduct.[168] Words such as "humanity" and "democracy" have constantly been on the lips of American foreign policy architects and these words also left a strong aftertaste on the American public in the twentieth century. American statesmen have used words such as "providence or destiny." From John Adams to Andrew Jackson, from Franklin Roosevelt to George W. Bush, American politicians have resorted to a rhetoric that leaves other foreign actors puzzled and shocked, particularly when they become themselves targets of American biblical millennialist and their sponsors in the White House. "These are the same definitions that serve to justify (their) military aggression without justification under international law..."[169] As some critical, mostly European authors argue, American involvement in Europe during World War II and the later occupation of Germany were motivated by America's self-appointed do-gooding efforts and the belief that Evil in its fascist form had to be removed, whatever the costs might be. Clearly, Hitler declared war on "neutral" America, but Germany's act of belligerence against America needs to be put into perspective. An objective scholar must examine America's previous illegal supplying of war material to the Soviet Union and Great Britain. Equally illegal under international law was America's engaging German submarines in the Atlantic prior to the German declaration of war, which was accompanied by incessant anti-German media hectoring by American Jews—a strategy carried out in the name of a divine mission of "making the world safe for democracy." "The crisis of Americanism in our epoch," wrote a German scholar Giselher Wirsing, who had close ties with propaganda officials in the Third Reich, "falls short of degeneracy of the Puritan mindset. In degenerated Puritanism lies, side by side with Judaism, America's inborn danger.[170]

Nor have global issues surrounding America's messianism changed much today. Some modern authors call the postmodern American policy "neo-Jacobin," although this term may sound equivocal. "These new Jacobins (or neo-globalists), typically use democracy as an umbrella term for the kind of political regime that they would like to see installed all over the world."[171]

The concept of American democracy in postmodernity is also all-disarming. To oppose America's drive to democracy and peace must be seen as lunatic behavior. It then becomes clear why America has been such an avid lecturer in foreign affairs and why it has been able to foist its hegemony on all states in the world. Irving Kristol, a prominent Jewish-American opinion maker, and a true spokesman of Americanism, writes that America's world mission "is that of an exceptional nation founded on a universal principle, on what Lincoln called 'an abstract truth, applicable to all men and all times.'"[172] It is the simplicity of American political discourse, ignoring the shades of meaning, which has led, thus far, to untold misunderstandings and conflicts world-wide. Towards the end of the 20th century, however, American unilateralism provoked serious rifts with America's allies and may be seen as the first sign of America's decline.

A War Crime of the Bible

In the first half of the twentieth century American Biblical fundamentalism resulted in military behavior that American postmodern elites are not very fond of discussing in a public forum. It is common place in American academia and the film industry to criticize National Socialism for its real or alleged terror. But the American way of conducting World War II—under the guise of democracy and world peace—was just as violent if not even worse. Puritanism had given birth to a distinctive type of American fanaticism which does not have parallels anywhere else in the world. Just as in 17th century England, Cromwell was persuaded that he had been sent by God Almighty to purge England of its enemies; so did his American liberal successors by the end of the 20th century, think themselves elected in order to impose their own code of military and political conduct in both domestic and foreign affairs. M.E. Bradford notes that this type of Puritan self-righteousness could be easily observed from Monroe to Lincoln and Lincoln's lieutenants Sherman and Grant. "As an American long exposed to political Puritanism, I cannot help thinking of Cromwell by way of analogy to other men 'on an errand'; to our version of the species, and especially to the late gnostics who in God's name forged a Union of 'fire and iron' in our great Civil War (...) "The Southerners are puzzled at such schizophrenia. They should have studied the life of Cromwell and then emptied the house."[173]

Similar discriminatory acts against ideological opponents were reserved for Germany during and after World War II. Whereas everybody in American and European postmodern political establishment are obliged to know by heart the body count of Fascist and National Socialist victims, nobody still knows the exact number of Germans killed by American forces during and after World War II. Worse, as noted earlier, a different perspective in describing the US post-war foreign policy toward Europe and Germany is not considered politically correct. After the ill-fated American military excursion into Iraq in 2003 and the subsequent media coverage of American crimes committed there, the question in retrospect needs to be raised as to the behavior of the American military in Germany in 1945 and after. The American mistreatment of German POWs and civilians during World War II must have been far worse than that in Iraq after 2003.[174]

Just as communism, following the Second World War, used large scale terror in the implementation of its foreign policy goals in Eastern Europe, so did America use its own type of repression to silence heretics in the occupied parts of postwar-Europe. Purges carried out by the American military authorities in postwar Germany remain an uneasy topic for many official American historians who mostly study the Allied version of war events. Many European conservative scholars have also been unable to comprehend sudden shifts in American political behavior, because many have traditionally assumed that America is a cultural and spiritual extension of Europe. American political behavior in war ravaged Europe could only be understood and judged within America's own judgmental parameters. Using classical European value judgments regarding the notion of limited vs. unlimited warfare, yields different results that are often rejected by American elites.

The American crusade to extirpate evil was felt by Germans in full force in the aftermath of World War II. Freda Utley, an English-American writer depicts graphically in her books the barbaric methods applied by American military authorities against German civilians and prisoners in war ravaged Germany. Although Utley enjoyed popularity among American conservatives, her name and her works fell quickly into oblivion. Nonetheless, it is worth reminding that when an American author of her stature writes about American war crimes in Europe, she or he will naturally elicit more credibility than when a German or a French historian writes about the same topic. Utley's book throws additional light on the other side of America's much vaunted humaneness. In hindsight one wonders whether there was any substantive difference between warmongering Americanism and Communism? If one takes into account the behavior of American military authorities in Germany after World War II, it becomes clear why American elites, half a century later, were unwilling to initiate the process of decommunisation in Eastern Europe, as well as the process of demarxisation in American and European higher education. After all, were not Roosevelt and Stalin war time allies? Were not American and Soviet soldiers fighting the same "Nazi evil"?

It was the inhumane behavior of the American military interrogators that left deep scars on the German psyche and which explains why Germans, and by extension all Europeans, act today in foreign affairs like scared lackeys of American geopolitical interests.

A thoughtful American professor, whom I met in Heidelberg, expressed the opinion that the United States military authorities on entering Germany and seeing the ghastly destruction wrought by our obliteration bombing were fearful that knowledge of it would cause a revulsion of opinion in America and might prevent the carrying out of Washington's policy for Germany by awakening sympathy for the defeated and realization of our war crimes. This, he believes, is the reason why a whole fleet of aircraft was used by General Eisenhower to bring journalists, Congressmen, and churchmen to see the concentration camps; the idea being that the sight of Hitler's starved victims would obliterate consciousness of our own guilt. Certainly it worked out that way. No American newspaper of large circulation in those days wrote up the horror of our bombing or described the ghastly conditions in which the survivors were living in the corpse-filled ruins. American readers sipped their fill only of German atrocities.[175]

Utley's work is today unknown in American higher education although her prose constitutes a valuable document in studying the crusading and inquisitorial character of Americanism in Europe. There are legions of similar revisionist books on the topic describing the plight of Germans and Europeans after the Second World War, but due to academic silence and self-censorship of many scholars, these books do not reach mainstream professional and academic circles. Moreover, both American and European historians still seem to be light years away from historicizing contemporary history and its aftermath. This is understandable, in view of the fact that acting and writing otherwise would throw an ugly light on crimes committed by the Americans in Germany during and after the Second World War and would substantially ruin anti-fascist victimology, including the Holocaust narrative.

American crimes in Europe, committed in the immediate aftermath of the Second World War, included extra-legal killings of countless German civilians and disarmed soldiers, while tacitly approving serial Soviet genocides and mass expulsions of the German civilian population in Eastern Europe.[176] As Utley notes, the sheer sight of the horror and destruction which American warplanes had inflicted on German towns and cities, from the psychological point of view, must have prompted the American military authorities and subsequent American administrations, academics, journalists, historians, and opinion makers to cover up America's own misdeeds. Consequently, a whole new industry of story telling regarding real or alleged National Socialist crimes was established in the West. As years and decades went by, crimes committed by the Americans against Germans were either whitewashed or ascribed to the defeated Germans. Utley describes in detail how thousands of German captives, before being dispatched to the gallows, were molested by the American interrogators. Charges filed against them were based on flimsy evidence, with no chance for a suspect of standing a fair trial.[177]

The exact number of German casualties during and after the Second World War remains unknown. The number of German dead varies wildly, ranging from 6 to 16 million Germans, including civilians and soldiers.[178] The official American hesitancy to establish the precise number of German war losses is understandable, as this is a topic that American court historians do not find compatible with the spirit of Americanism. It is only the fascist criminology of World War II, along with the rhetorical projection of the evil side of the Holocaust that modern historiographers like to repeat, with Jewish American historians and commentators being at the helm of this narrative. Other victimhoods and other victimologies, notably those of people who suffered under communism, are rarely mentioned. Although Germany was the direct party involved in the war, the entire European continent was affected by the American military victory. The American supreme military headquarters, under the general Dwight Eisenhower, withdrew after May 8, 1945, the POW status to German soldiers who had earlier been taken prisoners. According to some German historians over a million and a half German soldiers died after the end of hostilities in American and Soviet-run prison camps.[179]

Political events in America and Europe since 1945 bear a strong mark of the Manichean approach in American foreign policy and hark back to the struggle which pitted the nations of European ancestry against other European nations, albeit with three radically different world views. There is a large and impressive "un-American" revisionist legacy in America depicting various aspects of American foreign policy during and after the Second World War. These revisionist scholars do not shy away from describing the plight of Germans and other Europeans at the hand of their American victors. However, their prose, although having legally a right of entry in America, has not had to date much of an impact on public consciousness and political decision making. The answer is not difficult to guess. The masters of discourse in postmodern America have powerful means to decide the meaning of the historical truth and provide the meaning with their own historical context.

Mentioning extensively Germany's war losses runs the risk of eclipsing the scope of Jewish war looses, which makes many Jewish intellectuals exceedingly nervous. Every nation likes to see its own sacred victimhood on the top of the list of global suffering. Moreover, if critical revisionist literature were ever to gain a mainstream foothold in America and Europe, it would render a serious blow to the ideology of Americanism and would dramatically change the course of history in the coming decades. Having this in mind, America's former foes, Japan and Germany, as well as other European countries, must continue to toe the line of American "cognitive warfare" in postmodernity.

Despite frequent reversals in its foreign policy, America's self-perception at the beginning of the new millennium continues to abide by the same concepts of self-choseness, mixed with puritanical moralism. Irrespective of many experts and scholars who craft American foreign policy and who are in charge of improving America's "cognitive warfare" abroad, the idea prevails among many that there cannot be an alternative to the American system. This type of hubris is quite natural in view of the fact that America is the richest country on earth and that it does not have to face other challengers yet. How can one reject the American system if America is seen and described by its ruling class as "the last best hope on earth," or according to the former American secretary of State, Madeleine Albright, as an "indispensable nation"?[180] Obviously, American elites use a different logic and make different judgments when trying to understand a non-American perception of their own Bible-inspired foreign policy. As the French philosopher Louis Rougier writes, a true believer will continue to believe in his self-styled dogmas, however aberrant these dogmas appear or sound in the eyes and ears of future generations. "What matters is not the true or false foundation of a religion, but how the believers live this religion. A historical truth, or a golden legend—but who cares!? It is in the hearts of the believers that gods live and resurrect."[181]

Likewise, the goddess of American democracy must be grounded in an evangelical millenarianism that America has used in its foreign policy ever since its inception. Since its birth, America has defined the foe in a way that has best suited its own moralistic and legalistic principles. With this goal in mind, the American language was also skillfully revamped for the description of America's future foreign policy gains or failures. As a result, many political concepts have acquired the role of a new political theology in American foreign policy. "The language became a deception: it was infected not only with those great bestialities. It was called to enforce innumerable falsehoods," writes George Steiner.[182] Therefore, it is indispensable for a student of Americanism, before studying any move or shake of American decision makers, to carefully look at the American political meta-language and the meaning this language has acquired. This is especially important when studying America's political behavior in postmodernity.

In the second half of the 20th century, it was again a Biblical narrative mixed with democratic babble that made the Americans embrace the new state of Israel, an act that triggered unforeseen consequences for the whole of the Middle East and for the rest of mankind. Most American Presidents, writes Lawrence Davidson in his piece, followed the messianism of Woodrow Wilson, who was himself an ardent pro-Zionist and who was easily persuaded back in 1916 by Chief Justice Louis Brandeis, who was himself of Jewish origin, to support the Balfour Declaration. Subsequent American presidents held a romanticized picture of the future state of Israel, a country which they viewed as their own spiritual homeland. In early postmodernity, their task was facilitated in so far as they could rely upon the millions of American evangelists, mostly residing in the American Bible belt, and whose behavior was often more Jewish than that of American Jews themselves. Once upon a time, during the Cold War, it was the "evil" communists who were damned by the American political class. At the beginning of the third millennium, under the guise of abstract notions like "war against terror" and "fight for democracy," America began waging endless wars against the real or alleged enemies of Israel. The high priest of this new Biblical fundamentalism in foreign policy, as Lawrence Davidson calls him, is American President George W. Bush. "American Manifest Destiny and Christian Zionist delusions now pave the road down which we all walk. It runs through Palestine and leads to hell."[183]

As many European journalists noted, the uniqueness of American Bible-inspired unilateralism has become in postmodernity a dangerous factor in world politics. But has it ever been different? The behavior of American President George W. Bush during the invasion of Iraq in 2003 was quite in line with the behavior of his precursors. "Bush's government is forced back to the doctrines of Puritanism as a historical necessity. If we are to understand what it is up to, we must look not to the 1930s, but to the 1630s."[184] And this new version of Bible-inspired American policy does not only apply to President Bush, but to all U.S. presidents since the American Declaration of Independence.

America's unconditional support of Israel resembles a belated form of White House Christian-inspired medieval neurosis. Fear of being called an anti-Semite prevents American politicians and a great number of American academics from openly criticizing Israel. When some sparse critical voices are heard, they usually leave out the founding myths of the Biblical narrative, and focus, instead, on dry facts relating to the influence of Jewish lobbies in America. In typical American "expertise" fashion, American academics who happen to be critical of Israel use one set of arguments while neglecting other scholarly approaches. In their analysis of the holy alliance between postmodern Israel and America, American scholars tend to forget that the Old Testament ties between these two counties had already predestined America to nurture special and privileged ties to the state of Israel.

Clearly, America has little, if any, geopolitical benefit from supporting Israel. Israel is more of a liability than an asset for America. Also, from the geopolitical perspective, Israel is a nuisance for America given that as a small country the size of Rhode Island, it is surrounded by a host of hostile cultures, religions, and neighbors, both outside and within its borders.

Although America, due to its unique insular position, has been able to avoid troublesome neighbors and their tribal problems, it has willingly accepted on its own soil the balkanized issue of the Middle East. America's special friend, Israel, acts in a similar way as ancient Prussia; in order to survive it must grow at the expense of its neighbors—or its must perish.[185] But America's special filial-fatherly links to Israel must prevent this from happening. Metaphysically speaking, Israel is a spot of the spiritual origin of the American divine world mission and the incarnation of American ideology itself. Only within the context of a strange filial relationship with Jewishness and Israel can one understand why America accepts with equanimity its own deliberate decline into a world-wide morass in the early 21st century. America's foreign policy actions stand in sharp contrast to the originally proclaimed goals of America's founding fathers.

Unfortunately, the fear of being called an anti-Semite prevents intelligent Americans from openly discussing the explosive issue of American-Israeli entanglement. Unlike previous geopolitical evaluations that had some sound basis behind American foreign policy decision-making, the role of Israel and the Jewish lobby in America are the two major elements that formulate overall American foreign policy. The imagery of Israel and "God's chosen people," represents the framework of America's commitments, not only toward the Middle East but also regarding other foreign policy issues. In the meantime "any aspiring policymaker is encouraged to become an overt supporter of Israel, which is why public critics of Israeli policy have become an endangered species in the foreign policy establishment."[186] These words were written in 2005 by two prominent American scholars whose essay was relayed by major media outlets around the USA and Europe, which in turn prompted Jewish lobbies in America to cry foul and raise the proverbial specter of "anti-Semitism." What John Mearsheimer and Stephen Walt write, however, is nothing new to knowledgeable individuals. Similar critical views of Israel were voiced earlier by many American authors, and these views also reflect, both in private and officially, those of many European scholars and politicians. But when such observations are uttered by scholars from respectable academic establishments they leave a different after-effect on the entire American political scene. This explains the reason for worry among American Jews and Israelis.

The extensive essay by John Mearsheimer and Stephen Walt is a well documented survey depicting the staggering amount of financial aid that America gives to Israel. The essay also depicts America's persistent ignorance of the root causes of Islamic fundamentalism. The authors detail both the awesome amount of help provided by American taxpayers to Israel that the cowed Congress is always ready to approve at any whim of American Jewish lobbies, and the irrelevance of Israel for the long term security of America. The Jewish American Lobby has its supporters among Christian Gentiles who often wish to show in public that they are more Jewish than the Jews themselves. This trait of political mimicry is widespread among American intellectuals and politicians who also wish to prove that they are more Zionist than Zionist Jews. In hindsight, their behavior resembles that of former communist apparatchiks in the old Soviet run Eastern block who, during the reign of communism, pledged their ideological allegiance to the Kremlin by putting on display surplus strength of their mimicked, albeit feigned, communist orthodoxy. After the end of the Cold War it was only a matter of days before they switched to the gospel of Americanism.

These authors note how the American Jewish lobby controls the research of major think-tanks and influences the decision making process in American foreign policy. The Jewish Lobby is also described as a modern thought police that monitors any critical inquiry about Israel by American professors. "The Lobby also monitors what professors write and teach; and it encouraged students to report remarks or behaviour that might be considered hostile to Israel"(...) Similar views to those expressed by these two American authors are privately shared by a large number of American academics, but for reasons described earlier they cannot be uttered freely in public. However, most critics of this unhealthy relationship between Israel and America seldom take into account the metaphysical relationship between Americanism and Jewishness. As a country deeply grounded in the monotheistic message of the Bible and in the philosophy of ontological chosenness, America must continue to support Israel even if Israeli policy takes America down the path to its own destruction. *Homo americanus* must trust the chosen country of God and his birth place in Israel.

A wide-spread sense of civic duty to provide service for the greater good does not prevent America's political elites from using violent methods in foreign policy. The deeply-rooted idea of chosenness is further legitimized by the belief in a democratic mission which, consequently, ignores or minimizes the truth or destiny of the "Other." Regardless of what the odds are, *Homo americanus* will always have a good conscience in his foreign military adventures. Being a new form of political theology, Americanism, as a derivative form of Puritanism, must remain resilient to foreign criticism. The compulsive political drive to lecture Europeans, Arabs, or the Japanese on the virtues of democracy, the urge to preach and pontificate, to "re-educate" heretics—all of these efforts were already tested out by America's elites during and after World War II. By moralizing every aspect of their political life, America's elites have attempted to extricate America from the tragic and from any form of power politics.

This brings us again to an earlier point mentioned in this book, i.e. that America, while rejecting any political ideology, embraces its own para-biblical political theology which it calls American democracy.[187] The question, however, needs to be raised as to how long this Biblical discourse will make up the major political and theological leitmotiv of American foreign policy. The brutal reality of the ever changing global environment has its own historical dynamics that refuse to be directed or wished away by "good or bad" analyses. Furthermore, America, just like any other country on earth, is also constrained by objective geopolitical factors and the ever changing constellation of smaller and larger powers. America's incredible luck and fortune in the twentieth century may not repeat itself in the 21st century. Its over-extended military position in the world does not mean that America must be forever a "major global player," as Brzezinski rightly notes. Brzezinski was himself one of the important men in shaping the theoretical foundations of Post-Cold War American foreign policy. He rightly adds that "America is not only the true superpower but probably also the last one."[188] Its sole advantage so far has been that a newcomer could become an American, or *Homo americanus* by choice — in contrast to other states in the world where nationality and citizenship are largely conferred by blood lineage.

Most importantly, as Brzezinski notes, given that America has become an increasingly multicultural and multiracial society, with different ethnic and cultural allegiances, "it will be more and more difficult to reach consensus concerning foreign policy issues."[189] This is a theme which few American politicians openly wish to address. What may be desirable tomorrow for American Jews regarding America's relationship to Israel may be seen as contrary to Arab American interests. What may be considered a priority for European Americans tomorrow may be viewed as a hostile act by Asian Americans or Mexican Americans. Short of a major crisis, such as a common security threat which can bring about consensus among all American ethnicities and racial groups, there will be less and less support among Americans for future foreign military adventures. After the terrorist bombing of the Twin Towers in New York in 2001 the common subject of anti-Islamism brought together, momentarily, Americans of different racial backgrounds and of all walks of life. Islamism became suddenly a new catalyst of evil, vindicating earlier predictions by the author Samuel Huntington about the clash between the Christian and Islamic civilizations. At the beginning of the 21st century, Islamism is seen in America as a seedbed of radicalism and a motor of world disruption and a no lesser evil than previously-defeated Fascism. "This is the only civilization which has threatened on two occasions the very existence of the West," writes Huntington.[190]

Although Huntington must be commended for his realistic views about the disruptive nature of multiculturalism in America, the scope of his analyses and predictions about Americanism are far behind the probity of the German jurist Carl Schmitt or the expert on geopolitics Karl Haushofer. They both described a long time ago American expansion as a history of 'longitudinal dynamics' transforming itself into "latitudinal dynamics."[191] Haushofer, who was a sharp critic of Americanism and American economic expansion, had some influence on the views held by National Socialist Germany. In his numerous articles and books he views American economic imperialism irreconcilable with the notion of Germany's self-sufficient large spaces (*Grossraum*), i.e. an international regime best suited for co-existence with different states and cultures.[192] In contrast to Haushofer, the American conservative author Huntington is enamored with the concept of the "West," and notes "that whenever Americans look for their cultural roots then they find them in Europe."[193] However, Huntington also points out that during the last two hundred years America has been at war with almost every European power and had as a sole interest to "prevent Europe or Asia from being dominated by a single power."[194] Like most American conservatives from the establishment, Huntington uses the concept "West" as a synonym for both Europe and America, although European conservative thinkers, including Haushofer, use the term "West" solely when depicting America.

How can America safeguard Americanized Europe in the future, given that since its incipience America has been at war with practically every European state, notably England, Spain, and lastly Germany? Huntington's obsession with the specter of Islam is typical for American mainstream conservatives and many right-wingers at the beginning of the 21st century. The difference in bellicosity and fundamentalism between Americanism and Islamism appears, however, marginal. Both aim for a global civilization, albeit by using a different set of value systems. Both are eager to convert unbelievers to their cause exclusively. Which side will win this historical contest only time will tell. Until now, the main ingredient of Americanism has consisted in the opposition to the creation of an ethnic and racial cohesiveness among European-Americans and the rejection of a common cultural identity for the European-American population. The social fabric of America has traditionally been atomized, yet with the influx of non-European immigrants American society runs the risk of becoming thoroughly Balkanized. Inter-racial clashes and the subsequent break-up of the country into smaller entities seem to be a looming American reality.

Chapter VI

Post-America and Postmodernity

The employment of general political terminology by American political and media elites has been an efficient way to cover up America's dark side of postmodernity, both at home and abroad. The general nature of expressions, such as "human rights," "struggle for peace," "democracy," has entered all social and political spheres of public discourse. The accompanying rise of the term postmodernity reflects an intellectual climate in which preceding political paradigms are meant to be discarded on the grounds of their allegedly outdated nature. Pretentious diction and flowery language that was in vogue during the preceding modernity has now received a trove of new vocabulary. During the Cold War it was common for the Americans to lambast dictatorships, notably Communism, which became for a while part of a negative model in the liberal vernacular. But despite the arrival of a new age of postmodernity the political diction has not changed much, except that it has adopted "softer" qualifiers. What strikes the eye of an observer is the constant usage of the negative referent "fascism" and the avoidance of the referent "communism." The word "fascism" has figured prominently in the prose and rhetoric of all theorists of modernity—ever since 1945, and especially since the end of Soviet communism. Possibly, a hundred years down the road, the word fascism will be studied as a symbol of America's negative legitimacy, as something that had to be used to describe the dark side of humanity in order to profile the bright and good side of American modernity. In most cases, postmodern authors do not even bother studying in detail the intellectual origins of fascism because in most cases it is considered to be an infectious element in the field of demonology. It is the incredible plasticity of the word *fascism*, containing two easy syllables which have given this word such negative popularity. Its constant use by various theorists of modernity and postmodernity accounts also for its constant demand in scholarly analyses, despite the world-wide claim by postmodernists that old paradigms need to be deconstructed. By contrast, the word communism, despite its legacy of the Gulag, contains some positive intonations. In fact, its verbal derivatives, such as "communalism," "communitarian," and "community," convey positive and humanitarian messages that will likely continue to attract the masses.

The same negative referent surrounds the word "Nazism," a word often derogatorily used as a synonym for fascism. However, the word "National Socialism," is carefully avoided. Although the word "Nazism" was never officially in use in the Third Reich, postmodern critics consider this word more appropriate in denouncing their enemy as a symbol of ultimate evil. By contrast, the noun "socialism," when coupled with the adjective "national," has something unnerving for leftist and liberal proponents of postmodernity and is carefully avoided. How can somebody be a socialist and a "Nazi" at the same time? Socialism is something that the American intelligentsia has been identifying with since the late 19th century. It cannot be a privilege of the Nazis.

If one studies the intellectual pedigree of theorists of modernity and postmodernity one notices a host of former Freudo-Marxian intellectuals and activists. Now, in postmodernity, and with the so-called end of all truths and the end of all grand ideological narratives, their new social experiment in American neo-liberalism is meant to be a more successful alternative. New linguistic constructs are used, and juggling with new concepts has replaced the former psycho-babble which was once typical of the American left.

Postmodernity seems to be a trend in the intellectual life of America and Europe since the etymology of the word implies that there cannot be any political paradigm after the occurrence of the modern Jewish Holocaust. Intellectual history has finally come to an end and everything must be replaced by micro-histories and consensual truth from all parts of the world, including all life styles imaginable.

Christian Ruby makes the distinction between postmodernity and neo-modernity, the latter being more convivial and more egalitarian in its sources, having its philosophical root in the philosophy of Kant and universal reason. By contrast, the first one has its inspiration in nihilist and pro-fascist philosophers, Nietzsche and Heidegger. Can there be, after postmodernity, any standard norm of inquiry into anything?[195]

Despite allowing a free field for questioning all aspects of modern political thought and political action, postmodern language has not moved an inch from its entrenched dogmas of the Enlightenment, that is, from its belief in egalitarianism and the myth in boundless economic progress. One can, therefore, argue that postmodernity is a historical oxymoron, a buzzword which neatly covers up intellectual mendacity. It is certainly not an accident that the new religion of political correctness, and all that political correctness entails in terms of judicial constraints, follows in the footsteps of postmodernity. Although being once enamored with the Marxist dogma, theorists of postmodernity use as their founding fathers paleo-fascist and fascist critics of modernity, such as Martin Heidegger and Friedrich Nietzsche. On the one hand they abhor every aspect of fascism yet, on the other, their theories are inconceivable without the extrapolation of Nietzsche's and Heidegger's prose. One must commend their effort in retrieving these two giant anti-egalitarian and antidemocratic thinkers, although one cannot expect them to do the same with hundreds of European-American eugenicists, anthropologists and legal scholars and their criticism of liberal and communist modernity.

Theorists of postmodernity usually delve into the intellectual heritage of paleo-fascist European and American thinkers only when these thinkers meet their methodological standards. A possible retrieval of their anti-egalitarian, elitist, racialist and antidemocratic substance is never welcome. The same can be said about the repetitive usage of the concept and negative referent, "totalitarian," a term poorly defined and which in postmodernity is more in use than during its documented historical occurrence. In postmodernity, the word totalitarianism is used more as a social scarecrow than as a political noun for some real past or present police state. In his seminal essay, *"Politics and the English Language,"* George Orwell, shortly after the end of the Second World War, noted how politicians, semi-intellectuals and would-be opinion-makers in the victorious West liked to envelope their prose and rhetoric with double-meaning words. With the birth of the word and concept "postmodernity" not much has changed either. In academe and in public fora one can hear and read clumsy dangling sentences and propositions teeming with adjectives glorifying multiculturalism and racial diversity; one can encounter a whole verbal arsenal full with messages gloating over multiracial postmodernity. The same flowery language is used and extra care is taken to avoid vocables that may in any way be offensive to members of racial minorities or to different lifestyles. Even when a postmodern topic revolves around an apolitical issue, a person who disagrees runs the risk of being smeared with the all-encompassing referent, "fascism."

Real and Hyperreal America

An important phenomenon has occurred in the relationship between the American power elites and the media elites. At the beginning of the 21st century America, unlike other European countries, openly boasts of total freedom of speech. Yet the American media hardly dares tackle the topics that are viewed as contrary to the postmodern spirit of Americanism. In fact, the postmodern American *mediacracy* operates more and more in common with the executive power of the ruling class. This cohabitation occurs in a corrective fashion, whereby one party sets ethical standards for the other, and vice versa. Major TV networks and newspapers in America such as *CNN, The New York Times,* or *The Washington Post* toe the line of politicians and vice versa, or for that matter both set the standards for general political behavior. Among American citizens the idea is wide-spread that the media represents a counter-power to the system and that by its vocation it must be hostile to the decision making of power elites. But in reality, the American media has always been an extended spokesman and the inspirer of executive power, albeit in an anonymous fashion, never citing the names of its governmental leaks. Ever since the First World War the American media has had a decisive influence in creating a psychological ambiance for American foreign policy, particularly when hectoring American politicians into large-scale firebombing of European cities during World War II. The same strategy, although reduced in scope, was partly extolled by the American media during the American military engagement in Iraq in 2003.

In its choice of words the American ruling class and its transition belt in the media opinion-making industry no longer function in a disjointed and mutually exclusive manner; they operate jointly, in a same pedagogical effort to "spread democracy and tolerance" word-wide. "Regardless whether it has or has not administrative sponsorship over the media," writes Régis Debray," it is the media which is the master of the state. The state has to negotiate its survival with opinion makers."[196] Debray, a prominent theorist of postmodernity, does not reveal anything new, except that in postmodern "video-politics," as he calls it, which is distilled by the modern electronic media, the lying of the politician appears more digestible than ever before. In other words, the presidential palace no longer has a decisive political importance; it is the TV tower that is now in charge of high politics. All major political narratives no longer make up the *"graphosphere"*; they enter the domain of the emerging *"videosphere."* In practice this means that it is no longer important what nonsense the politician thinks or says, but how well presentable and likeable he and his nonsensical comments are on the TV screen. There may be minor differences as to how the media and the American ruling class formulate their message, or how their corrective efforts supplement each other, but the substance of their message must always have the same tune.

Have the TV and visual media changed the picture of the objective world? Or can the reality of the objective world be grasped when first aired by the media? Remarks by academics and politicians deemed contrary to the canons of media-fabricated truths immediately encounter a wall of silence. Rebel sources and information, critical of the dogma of democracy and human rights, are usually kept outside the TV limelight. This is particularly true regarding those authors who question the essence of American democracy and who challenge the legitimacy of the free market.

Modern American politicians resort more and more to verbal referents that are veiled in a hermetic meta-language and that are meant to give an aura of respectability to their authors. Postmodern politicians, including university professors, increasingly resort to bombastic words of exotic origin, and their jargon is often hidden behind a phraseology that they themselves seldom understand. With the rapid onslaught of postmodern meta-discourse at the beginning of the 21st century the unwritten rule has become that the reader or the viewer, and no longer the author, should be the sole interpreter of political truth. From now on, the political lexicon is allowed to have multi-faceted meanings. But this, of course, does not apply to the dogma of the free market or to modern historiography which must forever remain in a static state. Postmodern discourse enables a politician or an opinion maker to feign political innocence. Thus he is free to plead ignorance in case his political decisions go wrong. This, however, must not apply to his tentative wish to deconstruct the proverbial signifier "fascism" which is meant to remain a referent for supreme evil.

In his above mentioned essay, published in 1946, a year after the total defeat of National Socialism, Orwell noted how the word "fascism" had lost much of its original meaning; "it has now no meaning except in so far as it signifies something not desirable."(...) The same can be said for a vast array of postmodern referents, including the polymorphous word, "totalitarianism," which back in the early twenties of the preceding century when it first appeared, did not have a negative connotation. And who says it always should if one assumes that the proverbial American system, in case of emergency, will likely have to use totalitarian tools in order to guarantee its survival? If America was to face a major racial disruption (the massive racial division that arose after the devastation of New Orleans by Hurricane Katrina in 2005 can be seen as a warm-up), it will more than likely have to adopt classical disciplinary measures—that is, police repression and martial law. Arguably, most postmodern theorists would then not object to the implementation of such measures, although the word "totalitarian" would be wisely skipped. A long time ago, Carl Schmitt, who has already been mentioned, realized an age old truth; namely, political concepts acquire their true meanings only when the chief political actor, i.e. the state and its ruling class, find themselves in a sudden and unpredictable state of emergency. Then all former interpretations of "self-evident" truths become obsolete. One could witness that after the terrorist attack of 9/11 in America—an event that was never fully elucidated—the ruling class in America used that opportunity to redefine the legal meaning of the expressions "human rights" and "freedom of speech." After all, is not the best way to curb real civic rights the adoption of abstract incantations, such as "human rights" and "democracy"? Seemingly, with the possible declaration of a large-scale political emergency in the future, America will finally be able to assign true meanings to its current political vocabulary. For the time being, however, postmodernity in America can be depicted as a passing semantic and artistic fad, best suited for academic and political surveillance, under the guise of one word: democracy.

Unlike the word, the concept of postmodernity denotes a political or social event that, according to diverse circumstances, means anything and, therefore, nothing. Postmodernity is both a break with modernity and its logical continuation in its bloated form. But as noted, in terms of the egalitarian dogma of multiculturalism as well as the religion of progress, postmodern discourse remains unchanged. A French theorist of postmodernity, Gilles Lipovetsky, uses the term "hypermodernity" when describing postmodernity. Postmodernity is hypermodernity in so far as the means of communication render all political signs disfigured and out of proportion. Henceforth, something considered hypermodern must also be hyperreal or surreal, a fact exemplified by the indefinite proliferation of mini-discourses; from those eulogizing tribal historical memories to those honoring mass commemorations of the war dead. New signs and logos emerge representing the diverse nature of the Americanized world system. Lipovetsky notes that "very soon there will not be a single activity, no object, no location that does not have the honor of a museum institution. From the pancake museum to the sardine museum, from the Elvis Presley museum to that of the Beatles."[197] In multicultural postmodernity everything is the object of surreal remembrance and no tribe or a lifestyle must be left out of the loop. Jews have already secured themselves a privileged position of being globally memorialized; now it is the turn of a myriad of other tribes, lifestyles, and of different marginal groups in search of their piece of the of global memory pie.

Officially, in multicultural America there are no races and no racial differences. Yet affirmative action quotas and the scarecrow of racism constantly bring the word "race" to the fore. For something that is repeatedly rejected by the postmodern establishment in America, it surely is obsessed over and about incessantly. Racial minorities call for more equal human rights and advocate the need for social diversity; yet, in terms of their own demands they never shy away from pointing to their own stylish "otherness" and their own racial uniqueness.

If their demands are not met, authorities run the risk of being accused of "insensitivity." So why not then, from now on, use the word hyper-racial hyper-America? The important thing is that the reader grasps what those terms mean in view of the fact that postmodernity, according to circumstances, can have contradictory meanings.

America is as modern a country as it has always claimed to be. Modernity and the religion of progress are part of its historical process. At the same time, however, metastatic elements of postmodernity, particularly the famous American overkill in media representation, have become present everywhere. Postmodernity has its traps. In order to avoid them its spokesmen use approaches to modern discourse by resorting to apolitical and less loaded qualifiers. In the postmodern world, writes Lipovetsky, "one notices the predominance of the individual sphere over the universal sphere, the psychological over the ideological, communication over politicization, diversity over homogeneity, the permissive over the coercive."[198] Similarly, social and political issues surface into the limelights that were totally ignored and unheard of in the last decades of the twentieth century. The sexual impotence of a presidential candidate is considered a prime time political event—more so than his handling of an important domestic crime issue. A death of an infant in war ravaged Africa is considered a case of national emergency. Even the most ardent supporter of multiculturalism could have hardly imagined the phenomenal changes in pan-racial discourse among American elites. Even the most optimistic consumer-prone progressivist in America could have never imagined such a mass display of linguistic permissiveness, including an explosion of millions of signs of sexual seduction. Everything turns into a softer form of a new ideology; from the ideology of sex to the new religion of football—all the way to the ideological crusade against real or purported terrorism.

Mass culture in neo-postmodernity, as Ruby writes, facilitates extreme individualism to the extent that every tiny spot in human existence must be henceforth viewed as a perishable or a hygienic commodity. "Someone's personality is gauged by his white teeth and no spots of sweat under his armpits, as well as the absence of all emotion."[199] Even the word culture in the English language has been subject to semantic changes. Now this word stands for different lifestyles and has nothing in common with its original meaning. Therefore, one might just as well call postmodern America a "hypermodern" America, a description which suggests that in the years to come there will be more hyper-narratives all around hyper-America and the hyper-Americanized world.

And what comes after postmodernity? "Everything appears," writes Lipovetsky, "as if we had moved from an age of "post" to an age of "hyper;" a new society of modernity is resurfacing. No longer does one wish to leave the world of tradition in order to accede to rational modernity, but to modernize the modernity, to rationale the rationalization..."[200] It is the attempt to always add more progress, more economic growth, more TV special effects that is thought to fuel the existence of hyperreal America. The surplus of American symbolism must continue to attract disillusioned ones from all races and all lifestyles, and from all corners of the world. A TV image or a theater story serves henceforth as a normative value for its global emulation—not the other way around. First comes the American virtual icon, most likely by means of a movie, a TV show, or a computer game; then the masses start using this imagery in the implementation of their own local reality. It is the media projection of hyper-real America which serves from now on as the best propaganda weapon for the American dream.

A typical example of American hyperreality occurs when the American political class assumes that every error in its multicultural universe and each flaw in its gigantic judiciary can be repaired by bringing in more foreign immigrants, by adding more racial quotas, or by further liberalizing its already liberal laws. In other words, the haunting fear of the balkanization of the country is thought to be best curable by infusing more racial diversity and by bringing in more non-European immigrants. Likewise, flaws in the free market, which are becoming more and more visible everywhere in America, are thought to be solvable not by setting curbs on market competition but by allowing more competition, by espousing more privatization, by encouraging more economic deregulation, etc. This trait of postmodern "overkill" is the main ingredient of the American ideology which seems to have found its accelerated momentum in early postmodernity. It never crosses the mind of America's elites that social consensus in multiracial America cannot be reached by decree. However, resorting to policies contrary to these hyperrealist endeavors already in place could mean the end of postmodern America.

Already at the end of the 20th century, America started showing signs of social obesity. It is the irrational nature of belief in progress which has grown in a metastatic fashion and which will eventually spell America's end. Lasch noted, quite some time ago, how back in the late twentieth century, the American narcissus savored sensual pleasures and indulged in all forms of self-gratification. Having fun has always been part of American ideology. But the postmodern American fun seeking narcissus, as Lipovetsky calls it, has different worries now. His cult of body and his love of himself have yielded to panic attacks and mass anxiety: "Obsession with oneself manifests itself less in the joy fever, but more in fear, illness, and old age, in the "medicalisation" of life."[201] In hyperrational America everything needs to be explained away by rational formulas, regardless whether the issue is a person's sexual impotence or the US president's political impotence. The unpredictable nature of life represents the biggest danger for *Homo americanus* because it does not offer him a rational formula as to how to avoid death, therefore defying the very nature of Americanism. Everything frightens American man today; from terrorism to his receding pension plan; from uncontrolled mass immigration to his possible job loss. It would be a waste of time to provide figures and numbers on American social ills at the beginning of the third millennium, such as child abuse, drug abuse, violent crime, etc., but the number of these abnormalities will climb exponentially with the progressive march of America's postmodernity.

Each postmodernist uses his own meta-language and gives his own interpretation to historical meanings. If one accepts the definition of postmodernity by the French theorist Baudrillard, then everything in postmodern America is a grotesque copy of realty. America has functioned since 1945 as a giant Xerox copy of meta-reality; not America as it is but America as it should be for the entire globe. The only difference is that by the 21st century the once gentle pace of history has shifted all the way upward into fifth gear. Events reel by in no historical sequence and pile headlong onward towards all-out chaos. According to Baudrillard, who is surely one of the best European observers of Americanism, America's hyperreality has devoured America's reality. Therefore, the question needs to be asked: in order to achieve the American dream, are not present and future Americans supposed to live in a projected dreamland? Is not America a pretense, a fiction, a meta-reality? Is there any substance to America—given that Americanism, at least in the eyes of its non-American imitators, functions solely as a make-believe system, i.e. as a hyper-copy of its own projected and embellished self? In a postmodern virtual world of the internet and computers, the enactment of real events in America already has its preceding ready-made reenactment plan that is supposed to serve as a pedagogical tool for different contingency plans. For instance, the American military elites have all possible formulas for any case of emergency, and in any spot on earth. One can, therefore, safely bet that a scenario in at least one formula will match with a real event on the ground. Briefly, argues Baudrillard, in a country of millions of fractal events, however overrepresented and overplayed they are, everything turns into a non-event. Postmodernity brings about the trivialization of all values, even those it holds dear to its own political survival.

America and its ruling class may some day disappear, or America may break up into smaller American entities, but American hyperreality will continue to seduce the masses world wide. Postmodern America must remain the land of seduction, albeit its seduction designed more for the non-European masses and less for white Americans who privately dream about going to other undiscovered Americas. In a country such as America, writes Baudrillard, "where the energy of the public sphere, the energy which creates social myths and dogmas is gradually disappearing, the social arena turns obese and monstrous; it grows like a mammal and a glandular corpse. Once it was illustrated by its heroes; today it refers to its handicapped, its weirdos, its degenerates, its asocial persons—and all of this in a gigantic effort of therapeutic maternity."[202] Social outcasts and marginal types have become role models in America's postmodernity. Political truth has already become an issue of the private and emotional sphere, whereby a member of a religious sect or a spokesman of some lifestyle exercises at will his nebulous political judgments. A crank has as much liberty in publicly voicing his political opinion as a university professor. A serial killer becomes a TV superstar, both before and after his killing spree. In fact, as the quest for diversity forever widens, new social groups and with them new social demands endlessly emerge. The therapeutic state of post-America, as Gottfried calls it, is the ideal system for studying all pathological behaviors.

As much as postmodernists at the beginning of the 21st century like to urge everybody to question all paradigms and all political myths, they do, however, cherish their own petty verities; notably those of an ethnic and gender nature. They continue to advocate affirmative action programs that are meant to give visibility to non-European life styles and that espouse different anti-white narratives. Diversity has become the magic word of postmodernists—albeit diversity based on negative legitimacy, that is, diversity which rejects European diversity by emphasizing the alleged nefarious nature of the white man's interpretation of history.

However much postmodernists attempt to deconstruct modernity by using Friedrich Nietzsche as their main guide, they basically uphold their own micro-ideological and infra-political racial and diverse lifestyle agendas. They reject other interpretations of reality, especially if these clash with the all pervasive-myth of Americanism. The intellectual approach regarding their micro-verities and micro-myths must not be criticized under any circumstance. Their narratives remain the sacrosanct foundation of *their* postmodernity. Essentially, each tribe's or each group's narrative appears as a big lie carried out in a horizontal fashion, whereby each lie cancels out the validity of another competing lie. A proponent of some bizarre lifestyle in America knows that his narrative is a falsehood; yet he must pretend to be telling the truth. Essentially, the discourse of postmodernity is a grand discourse in meta-mendacity.

If one adopts the logic of permissive postmodernity and the hyperreal micro-narrative of a religious zealot or a postmodern tribesman, regardless whether he aspires to be a TV talk show host, a porn star, or a would-be guerilla spokesman, then one might just as well accept the idea of "post-democracy," "post liberalism," "post-Holocaust," and "post-humans" in post-America. Since all the grand narratives of dying modernity are allowed to be questioned freely, one can find ample reason to question and discard the grand narrative surrounding American democracy. By the same token, one could resurrect thinkers, authors, and scientists in America, who since the end of the antebellum South and particularly since the end of the Second World War in Europe, have been pushed into oblivion, or who are denounced as racists, bigots, and fascists in the endless fauna of political exclusion. But postmodern authors prudently avoid the field of taboo themes. They realize that in the "freest of all societies" antifascist anti-anti-Semitic myths must continue to thrive.

U.S Calling: A Revocable Nostalgia

One must be cautious with comments regarding the alleged irrational resentments by many European and American authors against the American creed. Ironically, the most cynical remarks about Americanism and *Homo americanus* do not originate among European critics but are voiced by isolated yet well-known American writers. One of these is the American novelist Henry Miller, better known in Europe for his erotic prose than by his insights into the European and American mind. He is one of those rare urban Americans who once visited Europe, not for tourist purposes, but to live there for an extended period of time in various capacities; as an artist, as a bum, a beggar and an adventurer. Only after his lengthy stay in Europe and upon his return to America, prior to the outbreak of World War II in Europe, did the rediscovery of true America enable him to become aware of its hidden mystic parts which he had earlier been unaware of. In his novel, *The Air-Conditioned Nightmare*, a book now almost ignored in America and Europe, Miller describes America's obsession with the idea of progress and the resulting uglification of the country. Even today, his visionary views seem to be a rare privilege of only a few American individuals, in so far as their stay in Europe helps them to critically assess their own country of birth and their new spiritual homeland of choice. Miller seems to be aware of the new American subspecie he encounters in large cities: "Some other breed of man has won out. This world which is in the making fills me with dread. I have seen it germinate...It is a world suited for monomaniacs obsessed with the idea of progress."[203] Strangely, Miller seems to be rediscovering true America only in the mystical Deep South, in the bayous of Louisiana, and the deserts of Arizona. Miller's novel and his own life demonstrate that in order to understand and love true America, one must have a strong will to power, an exemplary Promethean spirit of cultural curiosity, and intellectual ability to constantly put oneself in diverse socio-political and esthetical perspectives.

Other than the already mentioned authors critical of Americanism, there is also an "un-American" writer and American journalist, H.L. Mencken, who needs to be mentioned here given that he is viewed by many dissenting conservative Americans as the best American stylist. To him, America is a country of third-rate half-wits. He calls the American species *"boobus americanus,"* a specie who only knows how to indulge in petty sensual gratifications. "The only thing that made life difficult for him," writes Mencken, "was his congenital dunderheadedness"; "a nation of senescent Europeans," "Anglo-Saxon immigrants," "the botched and unfit...," "Scandinavians run to all bone and no brain, Jews too incompetent to swindle even the barbarous peasants of Russia and Poland." In short, early Americans, the offspring of European immigrants were, according to Mencken, "weary peasants eager only for the comfortable security of a pig in a sty."[204] It is hardly conceivable that prose as acerbic as Mencken's could be published during the heyday of American postmodernity, i.e. at the end of the 20th century.

Mencken was a master of the English language, similar to his contemporary, the "un-American" poet and writer Ezra Pound. Pound is also critical of the psychology of *Homo americanus* and the ruling class in Washington D.C. It must be pointed out, however, that in comparison to Pound, Mencken savages the American system and the lifestyle of his compatriots in a pamphleteering fashion, playing with words, thereby rendering his prose a good piece of social satire. This is not the case with a more radical Pound who, similar to right-wing European and American critics of Americanism, looks in detail at the biological and political substructure of Americanism, always probing into the tragic and deadly elements behind America's belief in progress. Pound's prose, similar to Francis P. Yockey's, is reminiscent of the revolutionary conservative European critics of Americanism and still has considerable popularity and readership in Europe.

Pound is a case in point in view of his post World War II troubles with the American military judiciary. His American anti-Americanism may remind one of a handful of Russian anti-Soviet dissidents, such as Alexander Solzhenitsyn and Alexander Zinoviev who both hated the communist system yet refused to trade off their anticommunist beliefs for the love of plutocratic liberalism.

Pound complains about an inveterate American inability to put things in perspective; "the lack in America of *any* habit of connecting and correlating *any* act or thought to *any* main principle, whatsoever..."²⁰⁵ However, Pound's eulogy for a founding father of America, Thomas Jefferson, leaves one perplexed and confronts the reader with a puzzling dilemma of the meaning of postmodernity. The heritage of Jefferson, according to Pound, is "Here and Now, in the Italian peninsula and the beginning of the fascist second decennia, not in Massachusetts or Delaware."²⁰⁶ These words by a fascist author sound too laudatory for somebody who is viewed by liberals and leftists as an icon of American democracy.

Who can now give a proper definition of Americanism in light of Pound's eulogy of egalitarian and liberal American founding father, Thomas Jefferson? Naturally, at the beginning of the 21ˢᵗ century, judgment will be made by those who are in charge of defining postmodern discourse and the meaning of the so-called self-evident truths of our times, American lies and truths notwithstanding.

Pound left the USA after his releases from an insane asylum. On April 18, 1958, upon his arrival at Naples, Italy, Pound told the crowd of Italian journalists: "I left for good a psychiatric asylum of 180 million people."²⁰⁷ He probably wanted to show that a true American patriot shines best only when he quits America's shores for good.

Is it only after the departure from America that a good observer can discover America's hidden attractions? This was the case with Miller and other uprooted American-born and European artists and thinkers who may be described as double returnees, suffering from double nostalgia. Miller rightly takes to his heart the rooted America teeming with the mystical character in places which had been spared the steamroller of Americanization. These areas still exist in the Deep South. In understanding Miller's Ulysses-like love and hate of America one must, therefore, decide to be a constant voyager, forever ready to live between two different worlds and in both of them at the same time. One could cite the insightful Jewish-French philosopher of cultural pessimism, Vladimir Jankélévitch, who depicts the phenomenology of nostalgia as an ingredient of "pathetic geography," a long forgotten memory of locations whose immemorial traces spur reminiscence and evoke all kinds of imagination. "The nostalgic person is at the same time here and there, neither here nor there; he is present and absent, two times present and two times absent."[208] This is in particular true for the Jewish people, constantly on the run, constantly on the road, having no desire to mix with others, or to cast permanent geographic roots anywhere in the world. Hence the reason Jews find the uprooted American system as the most appealing system of all.

But nomadic Americanism must be distinguished from the traditional and rooted Americanism of the South which still exerts attraction from many European artists and thinkers who are resentful of both here and there, i.e. of both their host country and their native country, yet who secretly yearn for a static moment of spiritual or intellectual bliss in both locations. Nostalgia enables them to keep that moment frozen in the past; a moment to be kept secret and used as mental nourishment in times of national or personal distress. After a lengthy absence from America, a returnee is bound to discover riveting spots that his eyes could never have spotted before. He may remember nostalgically his once-upon-a-time cigarette in some American cheap motel, his cup of coffee on Santa Monica beach, or the unexpected help by an unknown "hick" in Tennessee who helped him fix his flat tire. Or he may savor retroactively his uplifting moments of mobile solitude on a large highway, with nobody in the back seat to breath down his neck.

These fleeting moments of the American dream may turn someone's life upside down; they may become the centerpiece of the meaning of life. But these moments may also acquire a different meaning after physical absence elsewhere on the globe. The other side of the nostalgia-come true can result in ugly disappointment. The much romanticized homeland, rediscovered after decades of painful absence, may have become in the meantime a wretched reality replete with different peoples of different lifestyles. The return to a long searched homeland may become a nightmare, as it did for Ulysses, who upon his much cherished return to his wife in Ithaca, spends his time cleaning up anarchy in his household. The ugly side of nostalgia retrieved is stored away, side by side with dark spots of unpleasant souvenirs. Subconsciously, every disappointed returnee, be he an American or European, is forced time and again to ponder about a new departure. Jankélévitch remarks well that "each departure holding each return in suspense is the best means to revive our nostalgia."[209] Is not the dream of having another geographic alternative at hand the only way to make human life bearable?

Nostalgia is the reaction to the irreversible; it is the essence of the will to live; it is the memory of static times. America is the perfect embodiment of irretrievable times in retrievable space. In its vast and protean geography lies a spell both charming and dreadful.

It can be said that just as somebody can be a good American patriot by living outside postmodern America's jurisdiction, so can a person turn into a travesty of American man by living and mimicking Americanism in America itself. In this sense, a true American heretic does not differ much from an anti-European or an anticommunist heretic who, once upon a time was forced to leave his country of birth, yet who refused to become an emulator of the political system of his adoptive homeland.

One must conclude that reactionary, traditionalist or racialist anti-Americanism, is a sign of refusal of the American political experiment and its ideology of progress, as well as the rejection of the founding myths of the Enlightenment. European authors, who critically write about Americanism, do that more for political or esthetical reasons, while secretly dreaming about the spatial advantages that only America offers. Many of them are aware of the claustrophobic nature of political life in Europe which cannot expand in a small area of so many crowded national narratives. The origin of this claustrophobic European spirit lies in the extreme compartmentalization of European languages and cultures, and along with them the always looming possibility of civil strife. European historical memories, whatever sweet dreams they provoke, have their share of nasty side-effects—as they have had for every European since the Stone Age.

American and European traditionalists and racialists make a mistake when advocating Sameness as a precondition for their ethnic and cultural survival. Often it is the Otherness in its geographic or racial expression that helps a person discover his own national and racial uniqueness. No traditionalist, no white spokesman of his in-group identity can ever deny the fact that in his life time he has more than once been victimized by his fellow tribesman and in his old homeland. Sometimes, meeting a distant alien or moving to a far away country becomes the only solace.

Nostalgia often brings about romantic thoughts and compels many American traditionalists to dwell in the past. But nostalgia has also its demonic side, however limited, apolitical and individualistic it may appear. The lack of large space and urban density, such as is the case in Europe, provokes a different perception of reality. Brooding over European traditionalism does not only bring back sweet memories; those memories may resurrect a painful detail harking back to an unpleasant event or a haunting souvenir of someone's ugly face. It is often the imagery of a past in-group tribal quarrel that makes life a nightmare in Europe and which is less to be encountered in America. Subconsciously, many Europeans who once decided to move to America wished to rid themselves of the layers of unpleasant memories or substitute them for new referents, new imagery, while embracing the new notion of large space. The kingdom of forgetfulness makes life bearable, whatever European traditionalists and postmodern racialists may say to the contrary.

And why not admit that the much vaunted trade mark of "historical memory" which Europeans often brag about can have its dark side? Just because the vast majority of Russians were victims of *Homo sovieticus* syndrome does not mean that the whole of Russia was synonymous with communism. By the same token, being critical of *Homo americanus* or rejecting the American political experiment does not mean that there cannot be another America—which still waits to be discovered.

Chapter VII

E Pluribus Dissensus: Exit European Americans

There is one advantage to postmodernity: it is self-destructive. Given that postmodernity offers a myriad of conceptual frameworks, the future of Americanism can, from now on, be studied from a myriad of post-American viewpoints. It can be studied from a traditionalist, nativist, or racialist American perspective. The plethora of literature on eugenics and racialism and extensive revisionist literature stretching from the antebellum South to critical analysis of the Second World War, could also be used as a tool in bringing about changes in postmodern America. Surely, books can always be banned, but truth seems to be alive and well online on the Internet. Traditionalist Americans could resurrect their values and truths and make them look more palatable for the masses. The antebellum South and an anti-egalitarian America could be revived and explained in a cogent and convincing fashion. After all, according to the theorists of postmodernity, truth is a matter of consensus.

With the end of the antebellum South an important chunk of American history has been lost to Americanism—a pattern which was to be repeated a hundred years later in Europe. However, the lost Southern legacy could be extrapolated and post-modernized in a new context, while retaining its principles that are officially rejected as reactionary and un-American. And this means primarily attacking the ideology of progress that has been the centerpiece of Americanism and the Americanized world at large, particularly since 1945. Furthermore, postmodernity can be a launching pad for diverse forms of Euro-American-nationalism, including the rebirth of a new European-inspired American political elite. In the years to come, nobody can rule out the prospect of racial segregation and the balkanization of America into different ethnic and racial entities. No one can rule out that European-Americans will cordon themselves off into their own well-guarded racial reserves. At this moment this may sound preposterous, but it should not be viewed as improbable. In these hypothetical cases, postmodern America will have to resort to different myths that will have a bad or good side—depending on the judgment of the future leaders in power. Postmodernity can provide spiritual material for the revival of old American antebellum customs that are long gone and that stand in sharp contrast to the American ideology of progress.

Postmodernity means the come-back of anti-modernity and the return of old American traditions which lay dormant in present day America. Why not conceive of an American system that, while rejecting the egalitarian version of postmodernity, can recuperate ideas and thoughts of American pre-Enlightenment and anti-Puritan thinkers? Moreover, Nietzsche should not just be left out as a leftist tool for postmodern theorizing. With his radical rejection of egalitarian dogmas, Nietzsche can be a major locomotive for the European-American revival and their spiritual reawakening from the Puritan dogma of hypermoralism.

The term postmodern has a disadvantage of being equivocal, although the same can be said about the term *Homo americanus*, which has been used in this book to describe a species and a by-product of American ideology. But *Homo americanus*, within a different historical context and with a different value system, could be seen as a positive species, i.e., as a prototype for a new Promethean man whose anti-mercantile, anti-capitalist and anti-egalitarian values differ from those he once displayed when disembarking from the Mayflower and which ended up with his progeny on Wall Street. If America should be a pluralistic and heterogeneous entity, as postmodernists argue, i.e., a land consisting of millions of multicultural narratives, then one must also accept the heritage of eugenics and racialism in its fold, and above all, the incorporation of traditional European cultures. According to this definition, America could combine traditionalism with hyper-modernism; it could become a repository for both traditional and postmodern European values. This is important to consider as the legacy of the anti-egalitarian, eugenic, and polytheistic thought has been purposely ignored and demonized by the modern interpreters of historical meaning.

The present meaning of postmodernity is partly due to the legacy of World War II. Having succumbed to the process of cultural brainwashing, more often by their own will than as a result of the American system, critics of Americanism have failed to use other tools in order to capture cultural hegemony. All what they have done so far has consisted in displaying derision for American decadence and American politics on the one hand, or sending servile signs of love to American elites on the other. And even that servility on the part of European critics has been managed and hypocritical, since post-war America has been able to exert influence on its foes and friends alike. In the eyes of many European critics, America has been reduced to the imagery of Hollywood and East Coast money sharks, with no nuanced description in between. The pristine and honorable America as depicted by Ambrose Bierce, or the heroism shown in early black & white cowboy movies, no longer exists—however limited it may be in scope and number. Other notions of Americanism are possible, but those notions need to be based on anti-modern and postmodern values and opposed to the dogma of the Enlightenment. Ironically, the medieval man of Europe, with his traditional values of chivalry and self-sacrifice, has been better preserved in America than in Europe. The author Christopher Lasch, a Euro-American author was one of those rare observers who spotted the vestiges of rudimentary and honorable Americanism, while realizing that the ideology of American progress and its mutation into liberalism, "turns out to be its greatest weakness; its rejection of a heroic conception of life."[210] Essentially, the ideology of progress, according to Lasch, was designed as a liberal antidote to the Southern culture of despair.

The ideology of Americanism and it carrier *Homo americanus* are showing fissures in their respective edifices. Memory of past America, with its frozen times, provokes nostalgia and a desire for future static times. Nostalgia for the past has the advantage of being immobile and not subject to accidents; it evolves around imagery that is not subject to historical disruptions. It is paradoxical that with all the yearning for progress and all that progress brings, most Americans, probably more than Europeans in Europe, suffer from a deep seated nostalgia. And this nostalgia, within a static America, as seen in previous chapters, was once revolving around the first America of the South West—an America that still resides in the memory of many of its citizens. "Progress implied nostalgia as its mirror image," recalls Lasch.[211] "Americans were notoriously given to recurrent fits of melancholy evoked by suggestions that some primal innocence... had been lost in the headlong rush for gold."[212] Indeed, a foreign observer, who understands the spirit of European Americans and all the nuances of the American language, can see a curious sense of "Weltschmerz" among the majority of white Americans, regardless of their educational level. These Americans often display a truly primeval European character trait. In his own pessimistic tone, as much as he wishes to hide it, Lasch reflects this nostalgia for a primeval American time and his deep pessimism about the culture of progress. The fact that he often quotes Georges Sorel, a French author and a critic of liberal progress and a thinker who influenced intellectual fascism, indicates what Lasch himself thinks about the future of Americanism. He and his kindred hardly fit into the category of "*Homo americanus.*"

Southern Comfort: White Man's Discomfort

The metaphysical roots of traditional America are largely ignored in Europe and even in postmodern America. This should not come as a surprise, in view of the fact that the cultural heritage of the antebellum South has been deliberately suppressed by the mainstream media and educational elites. Although America was a military and political winner of the Second World War, it also had to undergo a white man's atonement process and its own soul-searching homework, similar to vanquished Germany and its allies. As a result, anti-egalitarian and anti-liberal American authors and ideas, which had sporadically thrived until the early 30s in America, were simply relegated to oblivion. Hence the additional perception among European authors that America has nothing to offer other than fast food and fast death.

Unlike Europe at the beginning of the 21st century, America can boast a number of rebellious thinkers who in many ways surpass their European colleagues with cultural achievements. Amidst thousands of bizarre sects, clans, and religious denominations in America, one can encounter individuals of great probity and intellectual innovation. Their only problem is that in atomized and postmodern America their message cannot result in the creation of mass movements. Modern American conservatism falls short of a historical oxymoron, and one wonders what is left to conserve in America in the first place? Americanism, by its definition, is an ideology of progress that rejects any notion of a European-based traditional society and state. Therefore, American conservatism is a semantic anachronism. Different theories about American conservatism versus modernity and postmodernity appear often as a misnomer since all brands of conservatism in postmodern America carry a strong resentment against state and social welfarism. Therefore, American conservatives stand in radical opposition to traditional European conservatives who are usually respectful of a strong socially-oriented state. To make things even more confusing, many former disillusioned Jewish American intellectuals, who were once sympathetic to Marxism, began to label themselves in the early eighties of the previous century with the term "neo-conservatives," a term that added more semantic misery to an already bloated neo-post-modern American discourse. In postmodern America, the so-called American neo-conservatives play a crucial role in the American opinion-making industry.[213]

In the early twentieth century, America made unique scientific breakthroughs in the fields of eugenics and later in sociobiology, two fields that could be used as a paradigm for racialist in postmodernity. In the first half of the twentieth century, eugenics was an important field of academic study with far reaching implementations in the judicial system of America. But the grand egalitarian narrative of Americanism, having the subject of race as the great scarecrow, prevents the study of eugenics from entering the public forum. Eugenics and racialism, although usually associated with the radical right and traditionalism, are also the product of the Enlightenment and the ideology of progress. The study of human genes and genetic differences among humans is by no means the prerogatives of the so-called modern American racialists or National Socialists of the Third Reich. Research in eugenics had considerable popularity among early theorists of socialism such as Marx and Engels, and their later successors in the early Soviet Union. At some point in recent history, eugenics matched with the communist and liberal ideas of progress.[214] It was in the interest of early American capitalists to improve biological performance of their workers, less for the reasons of their racial beauty and more for the reasons of their own capitalist profit. Modern American racialists often forget that the goal of early eugenicists was not so much racial betterment of Americans for some allegedly cultural or spiritual purposes, but a crass attempt by an ultra-rationalist capitalist society to equip itself with healthy robots and happy consumers. Hypothetically speaking, if an all-white racialist America was ever to become a political reality, and if that society was founded on the values of economism, adhering only to the theology of the free market, it would be an equally ugly system, not much better than present multiracial America.

Many American conservative and, especially, racialist authors and writers, while observing with concern the changing racial profile of America, tend to downplay or leave out cultural factors in their analyses of decaying America. There is a lack of positive cultural, scientific, and social achievement that could go beyond their simplistic all-white-America propaganda rhetoric. Most so-called white nationalist groups in postmodern America, or those who label themselves as such, cannot cooperate with other conservative and traditionalists factions on a larger political scale. Often, they are ridden by bizarre quarrels and factional infighting and are hardly able to conceive of a theory that would lay down the principles of a society that would even remotely resemble the kind they dream about. Most American racialists, irrespective of their commendable sense of sacrifice and idealism, display outdated political romanticism grounded often in Biblical hypermoralism.

Also, the problem with American racialists, traditionalists, but also many paleo-conservatives, is their fixation on genetic determinism in explaining social problems in America. In their journals and conferences they tirelessly focus on the role of the I.Q., the human phenotype, the genotype of different races, and the high crime rate of non-European racial minorities, including the propensity of different ethnic groups to different illnesses. They use race as the only field of study in order to explain all of America's social ills, while forgetting other approaches, such as art, culture and languages. This reductionism, so typical of Americanism, is no less harmful than the economic reductionism of modern liberals and Marxists, who argue that the problems of mankind can be solved through permanent economic growth. Furthermore, American racialism, which boasts some intelligent writers, hardly squares with Biblical fundamentalism, which continues to be the trade mark of most American traditionalists and racialists. As long as traditionalist Americans continue to lug about their monotheistic deities, they will be in a permanent position of political contradiction. Their neurotic behavior, i.e. the acceptance of Christian ecumenism on the one hand and the tacit approval of racial segregation on the other, cannot be a weapon for cultural success. These two social phenomena exclude each other. Similar parallels could be drawn with post-Christian Europeans who in a similar fashion lament the changing racial demographics of Europe and the withering of white Europeans. In private, millions of them complain about the influx of foreign immigrants while at the same time they continue to adhere to Christian beliefs of universalism, which by their very essence posit social and racial mixture.

In hindsight and by using the causal approach method, one may realize how events in Europe after the Second World War bear strange parallels to the events of the post-bellum American South. The psychological effects that the end of the Civil War had left on Americans in the late 19th century had similarities with the effects of Americanism on the European population after World War II. Attempts by American authors in the early 20th century to historically contextualize America in light of the antebellum South, and with different traditionalist values, remain meager at home and unheard of in Europe. At best these descriptions resemble exercises in forgotten memories, however much these memories may have a romantic spell for European traditionalists. The efforts to re-examine the legacy of the antebellum South can be dubbed as "revisionism," a term usually associated with a different interpretation of history than the one officially accepted. What would have happened if the South had been able to secede and if its way of life had been preserved? This now appears as a futile attempt in guesswork.

The destructive nature of progress, inherent in modernism and postmodernism and their political offshoots in post-liberalism and post-communism, was well described in the early 30s by American traditionalist authors, known as the Southern Agrarians. In many instances their prose is reminiscent of European revolutionary conservatives of the same epoch, whose echo one comes across among postmodern European nationalist thinkers. These Southern critics of the new post-Civil War American system resemble the authors of the same caliber in Europe as they both carry a touch of literary and poetic verve in their metapolitical prose. These Southern authors need to be commended for their background which was not limited to political science only, but which encompassed other fields of social science, including literature and art. This needs to be stressed, as there is a custom among American thinkers and academics, quite in line with the hyper-rationalization of postmodernity, and going back to the period of early scientism during the Enlightenment, to compartmentalize their field of study and make a small niche for their own specialization. The Germans have a nice word for such a hyper-analytical American approach, which is also a trade mark of postmodernity: *"Fachidiotismus"*. It is a scholarly obsession among American academics to excel in one field, while ignoring and rejecting other fields. And this is not just the sign of left-leaning and liberal authors, but also of so-called racialist and right-wing authors. Hence the problem we encountered earlier in this book: American conservatives and traditionalists have a big problem putting things in perspective, precisely because they miss the wider social framework for thinking in different time zones and from distinct and contradictory cultural and historical viewpoints. They are masters in one field; a field which in turn needs to be broken down into other smaller fields.

This hyperanalytical approach is typical of American eugenicists, racialist authors, and other prominent traditionalists. Individually, they all provide analyses of astounding scholarship, but fail to examine their subject of study within other fields of analysis. Similarly, American historical revisionists, who critically deal with some aspects of modern history often produce well-documented books on the topic of their research, but fail to introduce other perspectives into their study. Other scholars will devote their entire life to the critical study of egalitarianism, but will fail to give a historical, cultural, or racial context to their analyses. In America, there is a standard lack of an interdisciplinary approach to any subject matter under consideration. This inorganic approach proves that "*Homo americanus*" in academia is also a byproduct of an atomized and hyperreal system that hates a holistic approach to human science. How, then, can American traditionalists or racialists, or whatever they may be called in the coming decades, come close to capturing cultural hegemony?

Postmodern Agrarians

The Manifesto of the Southern Agrarians, "I'll Take My Stand" is a valuable literary document that helps us understand the other would-have-been organic America. It was written by scholars who had a good sense of literary metaphor and who were not victims of academic overspecialization. In terms of substance, their essays appear in hindsight as a gloomy foreboding of what was to happen not just in America, but also in Europe after 1945—not just in the political arena, but also in the realm of the spirit. These authors seem to have well understood what one calls today "the crisis of modernity," in so far as they saw in Roosevelt's New Deal capitalism, not the foe of early Soviet communism, but its twin brother preaching the same ugly goals, albeit by vulgar mercantile methods. Both systems were founded on egalitarianism, multiculturalism, and the religion of progress. One can argue that the Southern Agrarians were—if one were to use postmodern vernacular—a very un-American lot. They conceived of a true rebirth of American man, not as of "*Homo economicus*," i.e. a happy consumer waiting in line for cheap thrills in the shopping mall, but first and foremost as a man with spiritual needs that American industrialists and New Dealers had mercilessly ground into dust. By reading their nostalgic prose a reader gets a different taste of what the South was meant to be and what the whole of America could have become under different historical circumstances. Probably now, in the open field of postmodernity, some of their traditionalist Southern legacy could be restored and used as a weapon in future culture wars.

One wonders in hindsight how it was possible that America, and later Europe, succumbed to the Almighty Dollar whose architects have neatly covered their rhetoric behind the slogans of globalism and human rights? The South, after the Civil War, underwent a process of forcible re-education— similar to the re-education and overhaul of the European mind by the Americans after 1945. One of those Southern Agrarians writes: "The rising generation read Northern literature, shot through with the New England tradition. Northern textbooks were used in Southern schools; Northern histories, despite the frantic protest of local patriotic organizations, were almost universally taught in Southern high schools and colleges..."[215] The Puritan mindset from the North invaded the South so that Southerners gradually began to believe that their ancestors were Pilgrim fathers like in New England. Similar psychological changes occurred in Europe after the Second World War, notably when the American educators introduced into European places of higher learning the curricula consisting of Puritan derived hypermoralism, mixed with atheistic Catholic-bashing Freudo-Marxian scholasticism, and carried out by Frankfurt School theoreticians.

The South was forced to deny its history, just as a century later Europe (particularly Eastern Europe) was forced to deny and rewrite its own. Any form of revisionism in Southern literature, let alone revisionism in historical writing, was banned. Ordinary criminals, following the Civil War, turned into heroes like the maniac serial killer John Brown. A hundred years later, under the auspices of American opinion-makers, former Marxist terrorist sympathizers achieved similar prominent places in the pantheon of Western thought. At the end of the Cold War, despite the breakdown of communism and the end of the so-called Cold War, these ex-revolutionaries retained their influential perks.

The North did not just defeat the South in a military conflict; it also managed to win the war of intellectual and spiritual conquest and in "this conquest the North fixed upon the South the stigma of war guilt, of slave guilt, of treason..."[216]

The parallel with silenced European thinkers in a defeated Europe after 1945 again becomes glaring, although by that time the complex of guilty feelings had spread to all Gentile nations, regardless whether they were on the fascist side or on the victorious anti-fascist side.

The end of the antebellum South can serve as a laboratory for studying the guilty feelings that European peoples have been subject to in early postmodernity. The social malady consisting in self-hate started in America after the Civil War, only to be re-enacted a hundred years later all over Europe and postmodern America. In early postmodernity, Europe and America participated in the same joint guilt trip that can only be atoned by financial gifts and excuses to non-Europeans. One could speculate what America could have become if the South had managed to retain its autonomy. The South was not just a geographic slice of North America; it was a separate civilization. A reader, when judging and evaluating those past events in the South, and in the light of new postmodern values, must come to entirely different conclusions from those officially foisted upon him by the ruling class and the media.

Every opposing viewpoint was labeled by the liberal North as "hostile to freedom," similar to the smear campaign of modern Northern successors against authors who criticize globalism and Americanism. A Norwegian Nobel prize winner, author, novelists and later a sympathizer of National Socialism, as well as a good observer of America, Knut Hamsun, noted that the Civil War in America was not a war for the liberation of blacks; this was a war of annihilation of the aristocracy of the South. "The war was a war against the aristocracy and was fought with democratic people's raging hate against the Southern plantation Noblesse."[217]

The term "agrarian," used to describe America's Southern anti-liberal racialist authors prior to the Second World War, is not suitable for postmodern and post-democratic discourse. One could probably substitute it with a more appropriate word such as "organic," because what those Southern authors had in mind was a community-oriented and traditional America not based on economism and egalitarianism but on racial communitarianism. Nor should one limit the usage of the term "South" to the description of those states that made up the former Confederacy. The South was a peculiar mentality that, although now rare and sporadic, can still be detected scattered around some layers of American society. It would be false, however, to extrapolate the legacy of the antebellum South or what is known as the "Deep South," into postmodernity and make of it yet another romantic myth. After all, the Deep South is also the most fanatical Bible-prone area known in the 21st century with its rabid Christian Zionists and their strong influence on the general conduct of the American political machinery. These Bible-thumping Americans in early postmodernity surpass with their Biblical zeal even the earlier proselytizing efforts of their Northern ex-enemies from New England. In the eyes of Europeans, the nostalgic and pristine America of valor and cowboy courage exists in the movies only; the so-called conservative Deep South with its Biblical mindset hardly offers a model or an answer to the challenges of America's future. So far, all efforts in America on the conservative cultural level have been conducted by splinter groups of atomized individuals, either in academia or among political currents of a very sectarian nature. One wonders, indeed, whether postmodern America can have any alternative and where will this putative new America search for moral and cultural guidance?

For America's Agrarians, American man was not designed to return to the trees or solely live by ploughing the land. He was primarily destined to realize his spiritual values, to show sacrifice and safeguard his racial and ethnic roots, and place them all above the fleeting materialistic values of American hyper-capitalism. Regarding this point, most American traditionalists are in agreement, although their own differences do not provide much hope for a radical social change in post-America.

Lyle Lanier and other Southern Agrarians seem to have well grasped the scope of the incoming postmodernist liberal propaganda, much earlier than many of his future postmodern contemporaries, especially when he criticizes the ideology of American progress. He realized that so-called industrialism stood for big business and plutocracy. In postmodern discourse, his premonitions will find manifestations in neo-liberal economic growth without substance, including the birth of abstract words like "downsizing," "outsourcing," etc.[218] Lanier attacks the founding father of modern American education, Dewey, and argues that "man is not *tabula rasa* on which arbitrary patterns of conduct may be inscribed without regard to his natural propensities."[219] Man has his genetic and historical endowments and his cultural diversity needs to be respected. His words aimed at the heart of liberal propaganda and its offshoot *Homo americanus,* a new-born American species who during this time began to display traits of fake historical optimism and belief in economic progress.

The problems these Southern authors encountered and which their postmodern disillusioned successors are also confronted with, lies in the nature of the American system and its anomic character. In Twenty-First Century America it is impossible to find a dozen cultivated conservatives, traditionalists and racialists capable of staging a solid meta-political campaign for their cause. One rarely encounters in postmodern America a traditionalist Gentile thinker who, outside his narrow field of expertise, shows signs of Renaissance learning. Serious university professors or politicians with anti-liberal and traditionalist bent have no political significance. If they do, they are quickly silenced or framed by educational authorities on some trumped up charges, as was the case with the gifted writer and racialist Dr. David Duke, or to some extent with ex-presidential candidate and Catholic author Patrick Buchanan. Political attempts by less visible traditionalist politicians or scholars remain unnoticed in America, as powerful opinion making elites, including all-powerful Jewish lobbies, realize that in postmodern America the best way to silence critics is to ignore them.

One often encounters conservative thinkers and scholars in America whose erudition has no parallel in Europe. But the inorganic nature of American society makes them often appear like archival species who hardly know how to use the public platform and launch a credible cultural counter-offensive. Their professorial or research role is decoupled from the grass roots level; their teaching profession is just another economic branch in the giant free market. A number of American traditionalist writers and thinkers have anachronistic value with no meta-political significance. Under such circumstances, they can never have an impact on the mainstream opinion making industry.

However, there is some hope with the rapid rise of the Internet, which has already helped heretic American thinkers enter the media limelight to the great distress of official American opinion-makers. Despite its atomizing character, postmodernity can offer opportunities for intellectual battles and can provide an environment for spreading different versions of the truth. Thus far, a journalist or a TV anchorman in America has had more of an impact on the consciousness building of Americans than dozens of professors in the humanities taken together. But now, the virtual world of electronic media offers everybody a weapon to become his own political *impressario*. If this impressario is competent and cultivated enough, he might have some success—provided that he can distinguish between friend and foe. So far, the inability to think with an "opponent's mind" has been one of the biggest failures of traditionalists in America and has resulted in their repetitive failure to conceptualize the outside world. Their provincialism continues to create serious problems in their own communications, as well as with their own self-perception.

There is also a problem with historical and political referents for most American traditionalists and racialists. America was founded during the period of the Enlightenment, a prime example of modernity. Hence, most American critics of hyper-Americanism, even when they strive to give America a different conservative cultural or ideological veneer, inevitably resort to the dated concepts of the 18th century, or circle around a limited field of political options. By contrast, European traditionalist thinkers can pick out from a vast panoply of political ideas in case their present political system becomes tiresome or runs afoul. Europeans can chose from the heritage of socialism, syndicalism, anarchism, from different brands of monarchism, diverse types of nationalisms, or fascisms. It must be the supreme irony of history that it was Europe that gave birth to Americanism and Sovietism, i.e. to *Homo americanus* and *Homo sovieticus*, yet which has always been critical of both. For historical reasons these two ideologies remain alien to Europe, although the European ruling classes have had to ape them in order to stay politically correct, that is, politically alive.

An additional problem regarding sound alternatives to the present American system is that most of its critics, including the Southern Agrarians, dwell too often on America's extrapolated past with no coordinated follow-up on the postmodern level with media militancy. This explains why insightful authors such as Ezra Pound, Francis Yockey, or later, the left-leaning Christopher Lasch, were rapidly neutralized or used only in narrow intellectual and political circles. Undoubtedly, the twelve Southern Agrarians were impressive intellectuals, surpassing even their likes in Europe, and who, if born in Europe, would have certainly left their marks and provided a good intellectual tool for the struggle against modernity. Nothing of this ever happened, other than the standard regurgitation in academia about their works and loads of scholarly pieces by like-minded scholars about their conservative revolutionary heritage, having no impact at a grass-root level. Scores of their modern sympathizers in America remain isolated, known only in tight networks and playing no important role in the opinion making process in postmodern America. This is the big tragedy of America, all the more so as America has the rare advantage of having a compact and strong white European constituency, which although dwindling in number, is not torn apart by intra-European tribal conflict. American traditionalists still have a chance to achieve their vision in postmodernity, in so far as they have better technical tools to grab cultural hegemony. However, the nature of American traditionalism, mixed with a high dose of moralism, needs to be abandoned first. Moreover, the pervasive concept of democracy and equality must be revised.

Richard Weaver, a Southern Agrarian disciple, analyzed the pathology of democratism in America. His prose seems to be a carbon copy of European revolutionary conservative thinkers from the first half of the 20th century. His essays are similar to those of the European sociologist of elitism, Vilfredo Pareto, the jurist Carl Schmitt, and scores of European thinkers who were removed after World War II from "the grand narratives" and who still remain ignored by American academic and political circles. Weaver's problem, similar to the problems of other radical conservative American thinkers, seems to have been a lack of a political follow-up. Weaver demolishes the democratic mystique in America and calls for a true spiritual aristocracy based on meritocracy and fraternity, that is, on the elements that make up an organic and traditional society. But how is this possible in a system where everything is reduced to the veneration of material commodities and where the rules of the market discard any spiritual value as a perishable commodity? Weaver dissects with precision, similar to his Southern predecessors, the nefarious dynamics of liberalism and its associated value of egalitarianism as a system which creates "a reservoir of poisonous envy."[220] All these points had been earlier analyzed by European revolutionary conservative authors in their own descriptions of the American system. Weaver's words, however, attack the core of Americanism and the belief in progress, since any egalitarian society, such as America, "if it promises equality of condition, it promises injustice, because one law for the ox and the lion is tyranny."[221] The paradox of liberal democracy lies in the fact that it constantly resorts to double standards in order to sustain its legal functioning. The author exemplifies this by noting that in America "an election is after all a highly undemocratic proceeding; the very term means discrimination. How is it possible to choose the best man when by definition there is no best?"[222] The same paradox of American democracy was earlier well grasped by the sharp

French observer De Tocqueville, who had spotted in the American system an incipient danger of majority terror.

It is unusual that American and European critics of the American system are not more aware of the Southern author and scholar George Fitzhugh, who could be safely called a postmodernist racial traditionalist. Why postmodern? Because his ideas of an organic society could serve as a model for postmodern racialists in America. In light of present historical quarrels and ideological debates about the future of multiracial America, Fitzhugh stands out as a special, albeit lone man, not the least because he was aware of the semantic distortions of the English language by American politicians. But he is also intriguing in so far as he had a foreboding of the forthcoming Civil War in America and by extension of what was to be the destiny of Europe a hundred years later. His racialist successors, including linguists, should read him, but so should all critics of modernity, including those who study the spirit of democratism. Fitzhugh, who was a lawyer by education and a good judge of the English and Latin languages, and also of ancient Roman thought and Roman law, had a peculiar sense for linguistic and political nuances. He understood that words like "freedom," "free trade," and "justice" could serve as a hide-out for new barbarians. Conversely, and in a reversed Orwellian twist, he sounds like a spokesman for slavery, not the least as he understood that each honorable person in a given social circumstance must be a slave to higher ethical goals. A slave does not only mean a physical slave, subject to physical torments on the part of his master; it could be a highly cultivated person or a leader who decides to become a slave to his Promethean self-ascribed intellectual goals. The negative value judgment ascribed to the word "slave" must be rejected, as this word is bound to acquire different meanings in diverse social and historical circumstances. A soldier, a general, a statesman—each man who takes up the duty of fighting for a higher cause, forfeits his "state of nature," and becomes a slave.

Black slavery was to Fitzhugh a matter of fact; a social bond necessary for black Americans, who due to their incapacity to equally participate in free trade and cut throat competition, are far better off in farm bondage in the South, supervised by a paternalistic white farmer, than working for a Northern white crook who pontificates about human rights and strips them of human dignity. In what sense are 21st century blacks in America better off than their predecessors? Once left to themselves, as demanded by northern abolitionists, they end up destitute and adrift in large cities at the mercy of capitalist sharks who brag about free trade and lecture on about human rights. The widely proclaimed American equality becomes then a bitter pill because sooner or later everybody must conclude that in some human fields he or she will always lag behind. And this applies not just to American blacks, but to other races and individuals who do not have the stamina nor the genes to compete in the free market, or whose talents are not in demand. Heidegger, who was quoted at the beginning of this book, summarized this point when he denounced America as a place for a boxing career, but not a place for a career in philosophy.

Fitzhugh attacks the icon of American democracy, Thomas Jefferson, a founding father of America and the main author of the Declaration of Independence, whose words he views as "abstractions." Fitzhugh sounds postmodern in so far as he understands the mendacious nature of egalitarian and democratic meta-narratives. The flashy words of the Declaration of Independence were bound to open up the floodgates to incessant and never ending economic demands which had to lead to the capitalist war of all against all. The verbal tricks such as "we hold these truths to be self-evident that all men are created equal, are bottomless pits out of which torrents of modern new demands keep arising: It is, we believe, conceded on all hands, that men are not born physically, morally or intellectually equal—some are males, some females, some from birth large, strong, and healthy, others weak, small and sickly—some are naturally amiable, others prone to all kinds of wickedness—some brave others timid. Their natural inequalities beget inequalities of rights."[223] Is it also not self-evident that all people are equal; a cripple dreams about being a strong man, just as an ugly man desires to become beautiful, or a moron wishes to become intelligent. "Bestowing upon men equality of rights is but giving license to the strong to oppress the weak. It begets the grossest inequality of condition."[224]

Again, one can observe how the dogma of the free market, which found its ideal terrain in America, resulted in the worst form of racial discrimination, something readily apparent from the legal status of "freed" slaves in the abolitionist and democratic North. Fitzhugh was aware that this was going to happen, although similar views, in a more veiled language, will be later heard by modern eugenicists. Verbal constructs, suggesting that people are equal must lead to the final historical conclusion of liberal dynamics: demand for a communist system. Therefore, only a true aristocratic society, where leaders are role models, can have lasting legitimacy. The leader, in this fashion, becomes a slave as soon as he decides to take the duty on himself and fight for the interests of his community. Fitzhugh's remarks sound very Platonic and remind us of the gold class in Plato's *Republic*. In this sense "the masters in free society or slave society, if they properly perform their duties, have more cares and less liberty than the slaves themselves."[225] His words appear also "self-evident," as historical examples show that great leaders or greet thinkers have always been slaves to higher ideas.

The Oddity of American Democracy

What do modern American traditionalists, agrarians, or racialists have in common and how do their ideas square with postmodernity and its inborn specie, *Homo sovieticus*? To continue to review American authors who fit into the lexical and political category of "un-American" thinkers, and whose vision of the American dream is different from its present hyperreal image, has little effect. Even if their ideas about the rebirth of a postmodern and traditionalist America received in coming years better media coverage, it is questionable whether these ideas could ever sway the masses. One could add that American democracy, by its nature, has always been a common denominator for egalitarian impulses, reaching their apex at the beginning of the third millennium. The compulsive mimicry by European and American leaders of this new brand of multicultural democracy must be traced to it prime source: Judeo-Christian monotheism and its secular version in the ideology of egalitarianism.

Many white conservative Americans and Europeans continue to nurse the illusion that democratic societies such as theirs are congenitally pacifist and that only anti-democratic nationalism of the European brand, as well as the radical white racialist heritage, lead to war and violence. They are wrong, as they confuse causes and consequences of racial and ethnic violence.

Why do American citizens, more than other citizens in the world, reject the idea of having a hierarchical society with a strong leader, and why is it that this political option is immediately rejected as contrary to American democracy? Why do Americans opt instead for a horizontal type of democratic control where the system of checks and balances inevitably transforms itself into the system of mutual surveillance? The French anti-egalitarian and postmodern author, Claude Polin, while raising this disturbing question, also provides some cogent answers. Similarly to De Tocqueville, Polin observes with concern the horizontal nature of the democratic process in America that furnishes the framework for "terror of all against all." "How is it possible," he asks, "that one fears a king exercising his power and why is it that one has less fear if the same power is conferred on millions of little kings?"[226] Surely, in a dispersed egalitarian system of power sharing, such as in Americanism and Communism, with both attempting to project their power worldwide and under the cover of global democracy, no citizen will ever dream about having absolute power. In the atomized system of Americanism, dispersed power inevitably leads to dispersed terror in which the line between the victim and the henchman is bound to disappear. Similar to Communism, Americanism was destined to morph into a meta-system in which the vast majority of citizens while complaining of being terrorized by other fellow citizens also terrorize fellow citizens in their turn. In America's early postmodernity, following the precepts of democracy, everybody is content, as was once laid out in the classical liberal social contract, to have a small fraction of power. Surely, everybody feels miserable for not having more power; yet everybody will try to retain sufficient power for himself at the expense of the *Other*. This leads to similar appetites among other citizens. Americanism has become, in a far better manner than communism, a world system resembling a giant state of nature in which an ongoing latent civil war can at any time degenerate into a full scale global civil war.

In a county that is rapidly losing its racial homogeneity and increasingly turning into a mega-system of diverse and contradictory ethnic, racial and economic interests with competing narratives, there is a distinct possibility of the country's break-up. An incipient civil war in America will become a reality when a state of emergency is declared, following some major racial riot or a catastrophic terrorist attack. This is the scenario American and pro-American elites in Europe fear most. At that moment American post-democracy, similar to the proverbial clothes-less emperor, will have difficulty trying to hide its nudity. "A democratic society is a society which contains no real principle of unity. It does not even merit the name of society. In democracy, there can be no citizens; there are only private citizens whose occasional civic behavior does not even indicate the will to be citizens," writes Polin.[227] In atomized postmodern America, the nature of the social contract makes everybody suspicious of everybody and always on guard against fellow citizens.

Furthermore, the dynamics of the omnipotent market forces have everybody trying to outsmart and deceive everybody. Led by an unquenchable desire that he must exclusively act on his physical environment and improve his earthly lot, *Homo americanus* must come to the conclusion that the only possible way to realize his happiness is by placing his material welfare and his individual well being above all other goals.[228] He is less and less prone to abide by common values of his racial or ethnic community. Instead, he focuses his attention on not being left out of the economic battle, always thinking of his fellow citizens and of the entire system as agents wishing to cheat and rob him. The famous German philosopher, Max Scheler, observed long ago the psychology of American man and remarked that he is a "person living in a society which gives him the 'right' to compare himself to everybody; yet, in reality, a society in which he can compare himself to nobody."[229]

It is fundamentally wrong to assume that in a so-called market democracy, American and Americanized citizens automatically develop an organic and fraternal relationship to each other. Communal relationship is feasible only in an ethnically and racially homogenous society or a sharply segregated society with each ethnic group pursuing its own destiny. There is not a single case of a multiracial egalitarian society in recent history that has survived over an extended period of time. Sooner or later it breaks up violently. Moreover, excessive individual gratification offered by the omnipotent American market strengthens the desire of citizens to act solely as free economic agents with no spiritual bonds to each other. A sense of the common good and the notion of historical community become devoid of any meaning.

We seem to be back at the beginning of the book. The egalitarian appetite, once observed in communist *Homo sovieticus*, is well under way and under a new name in America and in Americanized Europe. American ideology will gain more prominence in the future, as egalitarian dynamics and wide-spread advocacy of permanent economic progress gain momentum. Once, when inequality was considered something natural, as it was in the antebellum South, or prior to the American Revolution, then even the crassest sign of inequality did not offend the observer's eye. By contrast, when everybody is declared equal even the smallest dose of inequality becomes unbearable. "The desire for equality becomes more and more insatiable as equality increases," noted De Tocqueville.[230] Consequently, as the American system becomes more and more economically opulent, even the slightest economic crisis, resulting in a small drop in living standards is bound to cause social discord and political upheavals.

It remains to be seen how Americanism will pursue its odyssey in a society in which those who are successful in the economic arena live side by side with those who lag behind. American ideology prohibits the development of ethical and political values that justify hierarchical differences, such as they were sustained in medieval Europe. In the near future, Americanism, similar to the former system of communism, will only function as an elementary form of mass survivalism in which interracial wars will be the norm.

- Finis -

Notes

Foreword by Professor Kevin MacDonald

[1] http://www.vdare.com/macdonald/041027_immigration.htm

[2] http://news.bbc.co.uk/1/hi/education/4838498.stm

[3] Bettelheim, B., & Janowitz, M. 1950.

[4] Lipset & Raab 1970, 3.

[5] *Ibid.*, p. 6; italics in text.

[6] Gottfried 1998; Lasch 1991, 455ff.

[7] Lasch 1991, 455.

[8] MacDonald, 2004.

[9] See Svonkin (1997, 1) for an account of the Jewish role in the intergroup relations movement.

[10] Svonkin 1997, 10.

[11] Svonkin 1997, 5.

[12] Svonkin 1997, 30, 59.

[13] Svonkin 1997, 75.

[14] E. Fairbanks (2006). A hot paper muzzles academia. *Los Angeles Times,* May 14. http://www.latimes.com/news/printedition/opinion/la-op-fairbanks14may14,1,6447050.story?coll=la-news-comment

[15] English, B. (2006). Immorality play. *The American Conservative,* May 22, 12–13.

[16] Taylor, S. (2006). In Duke's case, a rogue's gallery. *National Journal,*

[17] Ceci, S. J., Willliams, W. M., & Mueller-Johnson, K. (2006). Is tenure justified? An experimental study of faculty beliefs about tenure, promotion, and academic freedom. *Behavioral and Brain Sciences,* in press.

[18] E. Fairbanks (2006). A hot paper muzzles academia. *Los Angeles Times,* May 14. http://www.latimes.com/news/

printedition/opinion/la-op-fairbanks14may14,1,6447050. story?coll=la-news-comment

[19] http://www.frontpagemag.com/Articles/Printable. asp?ID=22313

[20] A. M. Lindbergh 1980, 220-230; italics in text.

[21] A. M. Lindbergh 1980, 220-230; italics in text.

[22] See: Fischer, D. H. 1989. Albion's Seed: Four British Folkways in America. (NY: Oxford);   MacDonald, K. B. (1994/2002). Diaspora Peoples preface to the paperback edition of A People that Shall Dwell Alone: Judaism as a Group Evolutioanry Strategy. Lincoln, NE: iUniverse; Phillips, Kevin. 1999. The Cousins' Wars: Religion, Politics, and the Triumph of Anglo-America. New York, NY: Basic Books.

[23] Preface to the paperback edition of The Culture of Critique. K. MacDonald 2002; Bloomington, IN: AuthorHouse.

[24] Fischer 1989, 357

[25] Vaughn, A. T. (1997). The Puritan Tradition in America, 1620–1730, revised ed. Hanover and London: University Press of New England, p. 20.

[26] Phillips ibid., 477

[27] In Phillips ibid., 556

[28] Preface to the paperback edition of The Culture of Critique. K. MacDonald 2002; Bloomington, IN: AuthorHouse.

Chapter I

[29] Numerous essays by European traditionalists, conservatives, including the so-called revolutionary conservatives and anti-egalitarian novelists, essayists and poets express views critical of America and the American way of life. Among many: Aldous Huxley, America and the Future (Austin and New York: Jenkins Publishing Company, 1970); Robert Steuckers, "L'Ennemi américain," in the quarterly Synergies européennes (Brussels, 1996); Jean Cau, Discours de la décadence (Paris: Copernic, 1978); D.H Lawrence, "Europe vs. America," and "America, Listen to Your Own," in Phoenix; The Posthumous Papers (1936 London, New York: Penguin Books, 1978); pp. 87-

91; 117-118; Gottfried Benn, "Über den amerikanischen Geist,"
in *Gesammelte Werke 7, Vermischte Schriften* (Wiesbaden: Limes,
1963), where on page 1658, Benn writes: "Personally I am
against Americanism. I hold the opinion that the philosophy
of purely utilitarian thought, of optimism 'a tout prix' (at any
cost) (French in text, n.a) of "keep smiling" (English in text,
n.a.) with the everlasting smirk on the face, is not worthy
of the Occidental man and his History." Also the recently
deceased Serbian elitist anti-liberal author, Dragos Kalajic,
Americko zlo (Beograd: Izdavacki graficki zavod, 1993). Also
the Italian neo-pagan philosopher, Julius Evola's *"Civilta"*
Americana (American "Civilization"), first published in 1945,
and reprinted in 1983 by the Julius Evola Foundation in Rome.
See the link to Evola: http://www.feastofhateandfear.com/
archives/jevola3.html See also the speech and article by Jean
Cau, "Le triomphe de Mickey " in *Etats-Unis: Danger (Actes du
XXV colloques national du Grece* (Paris: Grece, 1992), p.8 where
Cau compares America to a "gigantic washing machine of
national memories." Also Pierre Krebs "Kulturkrieg: Gegen
den American Way of Life in *Das Thule Seminar* (Horn:
Burkhart Weecke Verlag, 1994), p. 39-46. Pierre Krebs,
Europe contre Occident (Burkhart Weecke Verlag: Horn, 1997),
especially the chapter "Americanopolis" p. 63-84. Also a Nobel
prize winner and Norwegian *völkisch* novelist Knut Hamsun,
who was quite critical of Americanism, and who similar to the
American rebel Ezra Pound fell into intellectual disrepute
after World War II - as a result of his sympathies to fascism.
See his *Fra det moderne Amerikas Aandsliv* (København/
Copenhagen: Aandsliv, P.G. Philipsens Forlag, 1889). On page
129, he writes: ".... And time passed, people came in huge
waves to the country, steam to ship them over the ocean was
invented, Boston was overflowed, New York was breached.
Day after day, day after day, a world's mass of people flooded
the prairie, people of every race and language, countless good
men, bankrupts and criminals, adventurers and insane, priests
and Negroes – all limbs of the pariah breed from the whole of

the earth. And no noble souls..." (I owe this quote and the English translation to my Norwegian friend and author Tord Morsund).

[30] Jean Baudrillard, *America* (translated by Chris Turner) (NY, London: Verso, 1988), p.94.

[31] Werner Sombart, *Warum gibt es in den Vereinigten Staaten keinen Sozialismus?* (1909 Darmstadt: Wissenschaftliche Buchgesellschaft, 1969), p. 17, and p.57.

[32] Peter Brimelow, *Alien Nation* (New York: Random House, 1995), p. 217.

[33] George Sunderland, "The End of History: Democracy of Chaos?," in *Will America Drown?*, ed. Humphrey Dalton (Washington: Scott Townsend, 1993), p. 91. Also about the "Mexicanization" of the USA, see George McDaniel and B.F. Long, *Metamorphosis* (Raleigh: Representative Government Press, 2003).

[34] Kevin MacDonald, *The Culture of Critique: An Evolutionary Analysis of Jewish Involvement in Twentieth Century Intellectual and Political Movement* (Bloomington: Autorhouse, 2002), Originally published by Praeger Publications, Westport CT, 1998), p. lxix.

[35] MacDonald, p.259.

[36] MacDonald, p.280.

[37] Alan McGregor, "The Double Nature of Prejudice," *The Mankind Quarterly*, Vol. XXXIII, No 4, (Summer 1993), pp.423-432.

[38] J. P. Rushton, "Ethnic nationalism, evolutionary psychology and genetic similarity theory," *Nations and Nationalism*, 11 (4) p.498.

[39] Yves Christen, *L'Heure de la sociobiologie* (Paris: Albin Michel, 1979), p. 97.

[40] Roger Pearson, prefaced by Arthur B. Jensen, *Shockley on Eugenics and Race* (Washington: Scott-Townsend Publishers, 1992), p.220.

[41] Jean Baudrillard, *America* (translated by Chris Turner) (NY, London: Verso, 1988), p.28.

42 Noam Chomsky, *Secrets Lies and Democracy* (Tucson: Ordonian Press) pp. 16-17.

43 Lawrence R. Brown, *The Might of the West* (Washington: Joseph J. Binns Publisher, 1963), p. 529 and passim. By contrast, Jefferson can often be monopolized by right-wing and nationalist Americans, such as the pro-fascist and "un-American" poet and author Ezra Pound, *Jefferson and/or Mussolini* (London: S. Nott, 1936). According to different interpretations the early founding fathers can be seen either as traitors or heroes.

44 Quoted in Rüdiger Safranski, *Martin Heidegger: Between Good And Evil* (Cambridge, London: Harvard University Press, 1998), p.289, See also M. Heidegger, *An Introduction to Metaphysics*, trans. by M. Mannheim, page 62. See also the erudite author associated with the conservative cultural revolution in Weimar Germany and close in many aspects to Heidegger, Ludwig Klages, *Sämtliche Werke,* Band 4, *Charakterkunde* I. (2. Auflage) (Bonn: Bouvier Verlag Herbert Grundmann, 1983). On page 408 Klages writes: "These 'free citizens' are, in fact, mere marionettes; their freedom is imaginary, and a brief glance at American work methods and leisure time entertainments is enough to prove conclusively that *l'homme machine* is not merely imminent: *it is already the American reality.*"

45 Joseph Goebbels, "Aus Gottes eigenem Land," *Das Eherne Herz: Reden und Aufsätze aus den Jahren 1941/1942* (München: Zentral Verlag der NSDAP, 1942), p. 421.

46 Ibid., p. 423.

47 Ibid., p. 426.

48 Charles Beard, *An Economic Interpretation of the Constitution of the United States* (New York: The Macmillan Co. 1946), p. 324 and passim.

49 Arthur Wallace Calhoun "Economic Factor in Eugenics," p.408 in *Eugenics in Race and State,* Volume II. (Scientific papers of the Second International Congress of Eugenics) (Baltimore: Williams and Wilkins Co., 1923).

[50] Ludwig Woltmann, *Politische Anthropologie* (Jena: Eugen Diederichs Verlag, 1903), p. 213. Also Ludwig Woltmann, *Die Darwinsche Theorie und der Sozialismus* (Düsseldorf: Hermann Michels Verlag, 1899). On page 326 Ludwig Woltmann writes: "Undoubtedly in an economic competitive battle occurs a selection so that under given circumstances people with technical and mercantile gift have the upper hand."

[51] Francis Parker Yockey, *Imperium* (1948 Washington: Noontide Press, 1962), p.497.

[52] Ibid., p.498.

[53] Alvin H. Rosenfeld, "Anti-Americanism and Anti-Semitism: A New Frontier of Bigotry" (New York: American Jewish Committee, 2003), p. 21.

[54] Joe Sobran, "For Fear of the Jews." Speech given at the IHR Conference, Los Angeles, June 21-23, 2002. www.sobran.com/fearofjews.shtml. The author talks about "guilt by association," notably when he was himself a victim of general and generic accusations of mingling with Holocaust deniers: "I note that my enemies have written a great deal about me, yet they rarely quote me directly."

[55] Josef Joffe, "Nations We Love to Hate: Israel, America and the New Anti-Semitism." (Speech delivered at the Centre for German Studies at Ben Gurion University, Spring 2004).

[56] A French expert on America, journalist Justin Vaïsse, in his essay "Des clichés qui font mal," *Le Figaro Magazine* (February 8, 2003), writes how American opinion makers and editors, sympathetic to Israel viewed the French refusal to support American foreign policy during the Iraqi crisis in 2003. Thus, American editorialists aligned six French sins: "intellectual arrogance, fundamental immorality of French diplomacy, venality, frivolity, anti-Semitism and cowardice. Is there something more reasonable to ad after such an ideological barrage?"

[57] Natan Sznaider, "America, du machst es besser," *Die Zeit* (Nr. 5), (January 23, 2003), p.29. The controversy about the US military involvement in Iraq provoked a flurry of

pro-American and pro-Jewish activities on the one hand, and a torrent of anti-American, anti-capitalist, and anti-Zionist literature on the other. Many leftist and communist activists in the West were also targeted by American and Jewish journalists and scholars for their alleged crypto anti-Americanism, i.e. anti-Semitism, because of their criticism of American capitalism. "One resorts to the truncheon of anti-Semitism in the hopes that any critique of (capitalist) machinations will be removed," in "Kommunisten on-line;" www.kommunisten-online.de

Chapter II

[58] Alain de Benoist, "L'Amérique," in *Critiques et Théoriques* (Lausanne: L'Age d'Homme, 2002), p.142.

[59] Julius Evola's article ""Civilta" Americana" (American "Civilization") was first published in 1945 and reprinted in 1983 by the Julius Evola Foundation in Rome. See the link: http://www.feastofhateandfear.com/archives/jevola3.html

[60] Augusto del Noce, "Le marxisme meurt à l'Est parce qu'il s'est réalisé à l'Ouest," *Krisis* (Paris), No. 6, October 1990, pp. 124-129.

[61] Alexander Zinoviev, *La suprasociété globale* (Lausanne: L'Age d'Homme, 2000), p.73.

[62] Alexander Zinoviev, *Homo sovieticus* (London: Victor Gollancz, LTD, 1985).

[63] Alexander Zinoviev, *The Reality of Communism* (London: Victor Gollancz, 1984) p.28 and passim.

[64] There is an extensive number of books dealing with the psychology of communism - more in France than in the USA. See my *Against Democracy and Equality: Tthe European New Right* (1990 Los Angeles: Noontide Press, 2004), pp. 186-200. Also "Zinoviev's Homo sovieticus," in *The World and I* (June, 1989). Also Claude Polin, *Le totalitarisme* (Paris: PUF, 1982), p. 89. See Alain Besançon, *Les Origines intellectuelles du léninisme* (Paris: Calmann Lévy, 1977), p.292.

[65] Zinoviev, *The Reality of Communism*, p.103-104 and passim.

[66] This analysis is an abridged version of my essay "America in the Eyes of Eastern Europe," *World and I* (November 2001).

[67] Claude Karnoouh, "Ex Occidente lux"! in *Outre Terre* (Paris) No 5, May, 2003, pp. 195-204. http://www.edition-eres.com/resultat.php?Id=1288

[68] Ibid.

[69] Claude Karnoouh, "De la chute du communisme à la tiers-mondisation," in *La grande braderie à l'Est,* edited by Claude Karnoouh et Bruno Drweski (Paris: Le Temps des cerises, 2005), p.131.

[70] Ibid., p.132.

[71] Ibid., p.146.

[72] Thomas Molnar, *L'Américanologie* (Lausanne: L'Age d'Homme, 1991), p.33-34.

[73] Bruno Drweski and Claude Karnoouh, "Les dirigeants des pays de l'Est 'ânes de Troie' des Etats-Unis," in *Utopie critique* (Paris, 2003), No. 26; pp.24 and passim.

[74] A. James Gregor, *Metascience and Politics* (1971 London: Transaction, 2004), p.318.

[75] Ibid p.309.

[76] Alan Charles Kors, "Thought Reform: The Orwellian Implications of Today's College Orientation," in *Reasononline*, (March 2000). See the link: http://reason.com/0003/fe.ak.thought.shtml

[77] Jean Baudrillard, *The Evil Demons of Images* (University of Sydney: The Power Inst. of Fine Arts, 1988), p.14.

[78] Ibid., p.24.

[79] Alain de Benoist, "Au delà des droits de l'homme," in the quarterly *Krisis* (Paris, 2004). On page 44 he writes: "The study of human biological nature, which has been endlessly moving ahead over the last past decades, shows that "Nature" is very little egalitarian," writes de Benoist. "Far from it that each individual makes the basis of each collectivity; rather it is the collectivity which constitutes his individual existence."

[80] George Fitzhugh, *Cannibals All or Slaves Without Masters* (Cambridge, Massachusetts: The Belknap Press of Harvard University Press, 1982), p.135.

[81] Aldous Huxley, *America and the Future* (Austin and New York: Jenkins publishing Company), pp.8-9.

[82] Aldous Huxley, *L'Eminence grise* (Paris: La Table ronde, 1941). Also *Brave New World Revisited* (New York: Harper & Row, 1958).

[83] Aldous Huxley, *America and the Future,* p.16.

[84] Thomas Molnar, *L'Américanologie* (Lausanne: L'Age d'Homme, 1991), p.29.

Chapter III

[85] Tomislav Sunic, *Titoism and Dissidence* (Frankfurt, NY: Peter Lang, 1995).

[86] Paul Gottfried, *The Strange Death of Marxism* (Columbia and London: University of Missouri Press, 2005), p.108.

[87] Caspar Schrenck Notzing, *Characterwäsche* (Stuttgart: Seewald Verlag, 1965), p.115.

[88] Caspar Schrenck Notzing, p.120.

[89] Manfred Heinemann and Ulrich Schneider, *Hochschuloffiziere und Wiederaufbau des Hochschulwesens in Westdeutschland, 1945-1952)* (Editon Bildung und Wissenschaft, 1990), pp. 2-3 and passim. Also, *Die Entnazifizierung in Baden 1945-1949* (Stuttgart: W Kohlhammer Verlag, 1991), regarding the process of purging German teachers and professors by French occupying forces in the occupied German province of Baden. Approximately 35 to 50 % of teachers in the American occupied parts of Germany were suspended and barred from teaching and other research activities. The percentage of suspension in the French occupied parts of Germany was between 12- 15%. See Hermann Josef Rupieper, *Die Wurzeln der westdeutschen Nachkriegsdemokratie* (Westdeutscher Verlag), p.137.

[90] Hermann Josef Rupieper, p.137.

[91] Ernst von Salomon, *Der Fragebogen* (1951 Hamburg: Rowohlt, 1999).

[92] Tomislav Sunic, "L'Art dans le IIIème Reich: 1933-45," *Ecrits de Paris* (July- August, 2002), pp.30-36. Women were quite active in the Third Reich. A famous German Olympic female athlete, the Olympics champion, Tilly Fleischer (1911-2005); two famous women pilots, Elly Beinhorn (1907) and Hanna Reitsch (1912-1979); a Head of the League of National Socialist Woman Gertrud Scholtz-Klink (1902-1999), etc.

[93] Caspar Schrenck Notzing, p.11.

[94] Patrick Buchanan, *The Death of the West* (New York: St Martin's Press, 2002), pp.82-83.

[95] Serge Thion, *Historische Wahrheit oder politische Wahrheit?* (Berlin: Verlag der Freunde, 1994). The book discusses the fate of the French professor of literature, Robert Faurisson, who has been since 1977 in social and academic disgrace due to his skeptical accounts regarding the number of Holocaust victims.

[96] In the age of electronic media and due to anti-revisionist laws, prominent European and American historians, but also some racialists, resort to the use of different web sites.

[97] Caspar Schrenck Notzing, p.140.

[98] Josef Schüsslburner, *Demokratie-Sonderweg Bundesrepublik* (Lindenblatt Media Verlag. Künzell, 2004), p.631.

[99] Schüsslburner, p.233.

[100] Günther Maschke, *Das bewaffnete Wort* ("Die Verschwörung der Flakhelfer") (Wien und Lepzig: Karolinger Verlag, 1997) p. 74.

[101] Schüsslburner, p.591.

[102] Marc Perelman, "Europe Seen Cracking Down on Holocaust Revisionists," in *Forward*, November 25, 2005.

[103] Alain Finkielkraut, "Résister au discours de la dénonciation" in *Journal du Sida*, April 1995. Also "What sort of Frenchmen are They?" interview with Alain Finkielkraut in *Haaretz*, November 17, 2005. As was to be expected, there was an outcry in leftist journals in France following his interview. In his subsequent interview in *Le Monde*, under the title

"J'assume," of November 26, 2005, Finkielkraut resorts to new wordings and disclaimers in order to justify his earlier critical remarks about the Arab youth rioting in France.

[104] Alain de Benoist, "Die Methoden der Neuen Inquisition," in *Schöne vernetzte Welt* (Tübingen: Hohenrain Verlag, 2001), pp.190-205.

[105] Quoted in Dominique Venner, *Histoire de la Collaboration* (Paris: Pygmalion, 2000), p.512.

[106] See the anti-Semitic satire, wrongly labeled a "pamphlet," and banned in France, by the French novelist, Louis Ferdinand Céline, *Bagatelles pour un massacre* (Paris: Denoël, 1938), in which the author after his return from the Soviet Union describes the mores of communized citizens and the role of Jews.

[107] Dominique Venner, pp.515-516.

[108] Marcel Aymé "L'Epuration et le délit d'opinion," prefaced by Lucien Rebatet (Liège: Edition Dynamo, 1968), p.13.

[109] Ibid, p.17

[110] Eric Delcroix, *La Police de la pensée: du jugement de Nuremberg à la loi Fabius-Gayssot,* 1994. See http://www.codoh.com/inter/intpensee.html

[111] Delcroix, Ibid.

[112] Gottfried, p.82-94.

[113] G. Maschke, p.82.

[114] Speech by the German Reichsminister Dr. Joseph Goebbels, "Weltgefahr des Bolschewismus" (The Global Threat of Bolshevism) given at the Nuremberg NSDAP Congress on September 10, 1936. From *Dokumente der Deutschen Politik* (Berlin: Hochschule für Politik, 1937), Vol. 4, p.53. Goebbels goes on: "... because the Soviet Union cannot stand the truth regarding its internal situation, especially regarding an enlightened Western Europe. As flattering and tantalizing as the poison of Bolshevik theory may be, so frightful and gruesome is the Bolshevik practice."

[115] Germar Rudolf, *Diktatur Deutschland* (Hastings, UK: Castle Hill Publishers, 2005), p.35.

[116] U.S. Court of Appeals/ Petitioner Germar Scherer/ Nos. 04-16231 & 05-11303; Board of Immigration Appeals No A 78-660-016 (April 13th, 2006).

[117] G. Rudolf, *Diktatur Deutschland*, p.54.

[118] Text of Address by Alexander Solzhenitsyn at Harvard Class Day Afternoon Exercises, Thursday, June 8, 1978.

Chapter IV

[119] Christopher Hill, *The World Turned Upside Down* (London: Penguin books, 1972). See, Knut Hamsun, *Cultural life of Modern America* (Copenhagen: Philipsens forlag, 1889), who on page 110 writes: "Americans are ardent church goers. The majority of them are of course women, but quite a few men are political enough to go there. It is mandatory for a Yankee if he wants to move up in the world, to be on good terms with the Churches; indifference to the Church and her superior and lower life; in effect the heavenly and mundane affairs – this indifference will most certainly be punished.

[120] Roger Garaudy, *Les Etats-Unis, avant-garde de la décadence* (Paris: Editons Vent du Large, 1997), p.72.

[121] Roger Garaudy, p.202.

[122] Dieter Kronzucker, "Kirchen und Kulte" in *Der amerikanische Alptraum* (München: Wilhelm Heyne Verlag, 1992), p.170.

[123] Robert de Herte and Hans Jürgen Nigra, "Il était une fois l'Amérique," in *Nouvelle Ecole* (No. 27/28), fall-winter, 1975, pp 50-60 and passim. This whole volume of *Nouvelle Ecole* is crucial to understanding the European conservative view of American civilization and European "anti-Americanism."

[124] Arnold Gehlen, *Moral und Hypermoral* (Frankfurt: Vittorio Klostermann GmbH, 2004), p.78. Also on "hypertrophe" of the ethics pp.141-165.

[125] Louis Rougier, *La mystique démocratique* (Paris: Albatros, 1983), p.220.

[126] Adams, James Truslow, *The Founding of New England* (New York: Atlantic Monthly Press, 1921), p.80.

[127] Ibid., p.82.

[128] Oswald Spengler, *Der Untergangs des Abendlandes*, Vol II (1923 München: Beck'sche Verlagsbuchhandlung, 1976), p. 933-934.

[129] Ibid., p.934.

[130] Alain de Benoist, "L'Amérique" in *Critiques - Théoriques* (Lausanne: L'Age d'Homme 2002), p.142.

[131] Alexis de Tocqueville, *De la démocratie en Amérique* (Paris: Calmann-Lévy, 1988), p.222. See also the critical description of America by Gerald Messadié, *Requiem pour superman* (Paris: Robert Laffont, 1988) and by the former French foreign minister Michel Jobert, *Les Américains* (Paris: Albin Michel,1987).

[132] Emma Goldman, "Anarchism and Other Essays" (Second Revived Edition) (New York and London: Mother Earth Publishing Associations, 1911), pp.173-182.

[133] Werner Sombart, *The Jews and Modern Capitalism*, translated with notes by M. Epstein, (New York: Burt Franklin, 1969). Originally published in London 1913), p.43-44.

[134] Ibid., p.38.

[135] Ibid., p.249.

[136] "American Life in the 1840s" Bode, Carl (ed.). (New York: Doubleday & Company, 1967), p.315.

[137] Hervé Ryssen, *Les espérances planétaires* (Paris: éd. Baskerville, 2005), p. 333.

[138] Ibid., p.274.

[139] Jacques Attali, *Les Juifs, le monde et l'argent* (Paris: Fayard; 2002), p. 419 and passim.

[140] Hervé Ryssen, *Les espérances planétaires,* p. 415.

[141] For the Jewish role in the Soviet Union and America respectively, see detailed accounts published in the series "Judaica," in National Socialist Germany. Rudolf Kommos, *Juden Hinter Stalin* (first published by Niebelung Verlag in 1944, reprinted by Buchkreis Faksimile Verlag: Bremen, 1989). On page 70 Kommoss writes: "The name of the Cheka, the GPU, and the NKVD is linked to Jewishness for all times." Regarding the role of Jews in America, see in the same series,

Walter Freund, *B'nai B'rith- Judentum und Weltpolitik* (first published by Essener Verlag 1942, reprinted by Buchkreis Faksimile Verlag: Bremen, 1990). Freund writes on page 226, "Regarding the Jewish influence in the history of the USA, Margulis names in the first place the Bible which set up the temple of democracy."

[142] Yuri Slezkine, *The Jewish Century* (Princeton: Princeton University Press, 2004), p.152.

[143] Ibid., p.369.

[144] Ibid., p.209.

[145] Kevin MacDonald, *The Culture of Critique: An Evolutionary Analysis of Jewish Involvement in Twentieth-Century Intellectual and Political Movements* (Bloomington: Autorhouse, 2002), Originally published by Praeger Publications, Westport CT, 1998), p.304.

[146] Alain de Benoist, *Comment peut-on être païen?* (Paris: Albin Michel, 1981), p.168.

[147] Ibid., p.169.

[148] Ibid., p.170.

[149] Ibid., p.171.

[150] Milton Konvitz, *Judaism and the American Idea* (Ithaca: Cornell UP, 1978), p. 71. Also, Jerol S. Auerbach, "Liberalism and the Hebrew Prophets," in *Commentary* 84:2 (1987): 58. Compare this with Ben Zion Bokser in "Democratic Aspirations in Talmudic Judaism," in *Judaism and Human Rights,* ed. Milton Konvitz (New York: Norton, 1972): "The Talmud ordained with great emphasis that every person charged with the violation of some law be given a fair trial and before the law all were to be scrupulously equal, whether a king or a pauper" (146). Ernst Troeltsch, *Die Soziallehren der christlichen Kirchen and Gruppen* (1922; Aalen: Scientia Verlag, 1965), 768; also the passage "Naturrechtlicher and liberaler Character des freikirchlichen Neucalvinismus," pp.762-72. Compare this with Georg Jellinek, *Die Erklärung der Menschen-und Bürgerrechte* (Leipzig: Duncker und Humblot, 1904).

[151] Wilmot Robertson, *The Dispossessed Majority* (Cape Canaveral, FL: Howard Allen, 1972), p.180.

[152] Ibid., p.180.
[153] Oswald Spengler, *Der Untergang des Abendlandes,* Vol II (1923 Beck'sche Verlagsbuchhandlung: München 1976), p.941.
[154] See Deuteronomy XIII.
[155] Louis Rougier, *Du Paradis à l'Utopie* (Paris: Copernic, 1979), p. 249.
[156] Kevin MacDonald, p.312 and passim.
[157] Alain de Benoist, *Eléments,* July 1997.

Chapter V

[158] Carl Schmitt, *Der Nomos der Erde* (Berlin: Duncker und Humblot, 1950), p. 265 and passim.
[159] Zbigniew Brzezinski, *Die einzige Weltmacht* (Frankfurt: Fischer Taschenbuch Verlag, 1999), p. 44
[160] Carl Schmitt, *Ex Captivitate Salus* (Köln: Greven Verlag, 1950), especially p. 58.
[161] Jean-Claude Valla, *France sous les bombes américaines,* 1942-1945 (Paris: Librairie nationale). Over 70.000 civilians in France perished during the Anglo-American firebombing during World War II.
[162] James Bacque, *Other Losses* (Toronto: Stoddart, 1989). Also Alfred M. de Zayas, *Die Anglo-Amerikaner und die Vertreibung der Deutschen* (1977 Frankfurt: Ullstein 1996). See also James L Payne's article "Did the United States Create Democracy in Germany?," *The Independent Review,* v XI. n. 2, Fall 2006. The author, a known figure in the US media and academic establishment, writes about the subject that all honest scholars have always known about, but have been afraid to speak about it in public. On page 211, Payne writes: "Modern writers' first mistake is to assume that the goal of the American occupation in Germany was to make the country a democracy... Building democracy was *not* the aim of occupation policy. Instead, policy makers aimed to punish Germany and to deny it any war-making potential."
[163] Jordis von Lohausen, *Les Empires et la puissance* (Paris: Labyrinthe, 1985), p. 23.

[164] Carl Schmitt: "Grand espace contre l'universalisme" in *Du Politique* (Paris: Pardès, 1990), p.129.

[165] Carl Schmitt, "Les formes de l'impérialisme en droit international," in *Du Politique* (Pardès: Paris, 1990), p.86.

[166] Ibid., p.88.

[167] Ibid., p.99.

[168] Georg Jellinek, *Die Erklärung der Menschen und Bürgerrechte* (Leipzig: Duncker und Humblot, 1904), who writes on page 46 that "the idea to establish legally the unalienable, inherent and sacred rights of individuals, is not of political, but of religious origins."

[169] Joe Lockard, "American Millennialists and the EU Satan," *Bad Subjects*, issue No. 72, February, 2005. See: http://bad. eserver.org/issues/2005/72/lockardamericanmillenialists.html

[170] Giselher Wirsing, *Der masslose Kontinent: Roosevelts Kampf um die Weltherrschaft* (Berlin, Wien: Eugen Diederichs Verlag, 1943), pp. 428-429. Wirsing was a well-known expert on the USA during National Socialist rule and has published numerous books and articles dealing with the American system and the American mindset. In the same book he uses the phrase "the species of Homo americanus" (*Spezies des Homo Americanus*), p. 55.

[171] Claes G. Ryn, "The Ideology of American Empire" (Foreign Policy Research Inst., published by Elsevier Sc. Ltd.), summer 2003, p. 385

[172] Ibid., p.387.

[173] M. E. Bradford, "Politics of Oliver Cromwell" *The Reactionary Imperative* (1990 Illinois, Sherwood Company), p.214.

[174] See Prof. Dr Helmut Schröcke, *Kriegsursachen, Kriegsschuld* (CZ-Ostrava: Verlag für ganzheitliche Forschung, 2000). This book was printed, like thousands of similar revisionist titles, by the author himself - which is often the case in Germany with books dealing with sensitive topics of German World War II losses. Also Gerd Honsik in his "Geheimnis des Westens," posted on his site, where he writes about 13, 5 million German

civilian and military fatalities during and after WWII. See
http://www.honsik.com/briefe/westen.html

[175] Freda Utley, *The High Cost of Vengeance* (Chicago: Henry
Regnery Co. 1949), p.183. See also, Ralph Franklin Keeling,
*Schreckliche Ernte; Der Nachkriegs-Krieg der Alliierten gegen das
deutsche Volk* (Long Beach: IHR, 1992). Translated from the
original *Gruesome Harvest* (Institute of American Economics,
1947).

[176] *Alliierte Kriegverbrechen und Verbrechen gegen die
Menschlichkeit* (Kiel: Arndt Verlag, 2001). The book represents
a compendium of documented crimes committed by American
soldiers in Germany after World War II.

[177] Utley, p.187 and passim.

[178] Schröcke, *Kriegsursachen, Kriegsschuld*, pp. 296-297.

[179] "Vergeltung statt Recht," by Franz W. Seidler, in the
German annual military journal, *Deutsche Militärzeitschrift*
(Kiel 2006): pp.118-123.

[180] John B. Judis, "The Author of Liberty: Religion and U.S.
Foreign Policy," in *Dissent* (fall 2005), pp.54-61. Also see the
link: http://www.dissentmagazine.org/article/?article=182
See also "One War is Enough," by Edgar L. Jones, *Atlantic
Monthly*, 1946.

[181] Louis Rougier, *Du Paradis a l'utopie* (Paris: Copernic, 1979),
p. 262.

[182] George Steiner, *A Reader* (Oxford University Press: New
York, 1984) p. 212.

[183] Lawrence Davidson, "Christian Zionism and American
Foreign Policy: Paving the Road to Hell in Palestine" in *Logos*
(winter 2005) http://www.logosjournal.com/issue_4.1/davidson.
htm

[184] George Monbiot, "Puritanism of the Rich: Bush's ideology
has its roots in 17th century preaching that the world exists to
be conquered," *The Guardian*, November 9, 2004.

[185] Jordis von Lohausen, p.266.

[186] John Mearsheimer and Stephen Walt, "The Israel Lobby"
London Review of Books, Vol. 28 No. 6 March 23, 2006. Also
published in an extended version by Harvard University, "The

Israel Lobby and U.S. Foreign Policy," by John J. Mearsheimer
and Stephen Walt; Working Paper Number: RWP06-011
Submitted: 13/03/2006.

[187] Carl Schmitt, *Politische Theologie* (München und Leipzig:
Verlag von Duncker und Humblot, 1934), p.80.

[188] Brzezinski, p.298.

[189] Brzezinski, p.301.

[190] Samuel Huntington, *Le choc des civilisations* (Paris: Odile
Jacob, 2000), p. 306-307.

[191] Karl Haushofer, "Les Dynamiques latitudinales et
longitudinales," in *Vouloir* (Bruxelles), No 9, Spring 1997. First
published in *Zeitschrift für Geopolitik*, Nr. 8, 1943. See also a
book by the prominent Swedish Tibet explorer and friend of
National Socialist Germany, Sven Hedin, *Amerika im Kampf
der Kontinente* (1943 Kiel: Arndt Verlag, 2006), especially pp.
179-180.

[192] See Frank Ebeling, *Geopolitik: Karl Haushofer und seine
Raumwissenschaft,* 1919-1945 (Berlin: Akademie Verlag, 1994),
pp.95-100. Haushofer's last letter immediately sent before the
end of the war to his wife is reprinted in the book on page 98,
where he compares the new world of the USA to a "handsome
alligator ... which first honoured the old world of Europe with
syphilis, and now with the Yankees."

[193] Samuel Huntington, pp.461-462

[194] Ibid., p.344.

Chapter VI

[195] See Christian Ruby, *Le Champ de bataille postmoderne, néo-
moderne* (Paris: Editions l' Harmattan, 1990).

[196] Régis Debray, *Cours de médiologie générale* (Paris. Gallimard,
1991), p.303.

[197] Gilles Lipovetsky, Sébastien Charles, *Les Temps
hypermodernes* (Paris: Grasset, 2004), p.124.

[198] Gilles Lipovetsky, *L'ère du vide* (Paris: Gallimard, 1983),
p.165.

[199] Ruby, p.59.

[200] Gilles Lipovetsky, Sébastien Charles, *Les Temps hypermodernes* (Paris: Grasset, 2004), p.78.

[201] Ibid., p.37.

[202] Jean Baudrillard, *Les stratégies fatales* (Paris: Grasset, 1983), p.79.

[203] Henry Miller, *The Air-Conditioned Nightmare* (London: Panther edition, 1965), p.19.

[204] H.L. Mencken, "On Being An American," in *Prejudices: A Selection* (New York: Vintage Books, 1955), pp.98-99 and passim.

[205] Ezra Pound, *Impact; Essay on Ignorance and the Decline of American Civilization* (Chicago: Henry Regnery Co., 1960), p.221.

[206] Ezra Pound, *Jefferson and/or Mussolini* (New York: Liveright, 1970), p.11.

[207] Quoted in Christophe Dolbeau, *Les Parias: Fascistes, pseudo-fascistes et mal-pensants* (Lyon: Edition Irminsul, 2001), p.264.

[208] Vladimir Jankélévitch *L'irréversible et la nostalgie* (Paris: Flammarion, 1974), p.281.

[209] Ibid. p.296.

Chapter VII

[210] Christopher Lasch, *The True and Only Heaven* (New York: WW Norton, 1991), p.78.

[211] Ibid., p.92.

[212] Ibid., p.93.

[213] Paul Gottfried, *The Conservative Movement* (New York: Twayne Publishers, 1993), especially pages 142-166.

[214] For a comprehensive introduction to the history of eugenics and its possible usage in postmodernity see the well documented book by John Glad, *Future Human Evolution: Eugenics in the Twenty-First Century* (Schuylkill Haven, PA; Hermitage Publishers, 2006). On page 73-74, he writes: "Vladimir Lenin himself derided the claim that people are equal in ability. Galton's chief pupil and the leader of Britain's eugenics movement, Karl Pearson, was a Fabian socialist, as

was Sidney Webb, who contributed an essay on eugenics to the influential 1890 Fabian Essays. Geneticists in the early Soviet state attempted, unsuccessfully, to model the socialist experiment along eugenic lines."

[215] Frank Lawrence Owsley, "The Irrepressible Conflict," *I'll take my Stand* (1930 New York: Harper and Row, 1962), p.64.

[216] Ibid., p.66.

[217] Knut Hamsun, *Cultural life of Modern America* (Copenhagen: PG. Philipsens forlag, 1889), p.119.

[218] "A Critique of the Philosophy of Progress," p.123.

[219] Ibid., p.142.

[220] Richard Weaver, *Ideas Have Consequences* (1948 Chicago: The University of Chicago Press, 1984), p.42.

[221] Ibid., p.44.

[222] Ibid., p.46.

[223] George Fitzhugh, *Sociology for the South, or the Failure of Free Society* (Richmond VA: A Morris Publisher, 1854), pp.177-178.

[224] Ibid., p.233.

[225] Ibid., p.86.

[226] Claude Polin "Pluralisme ou Guerre civile"? *Catholica* (winter, 2005-06), p.16.

[227] Ibid., p.18.

[228] Claude Polin, *Le libéralisme, espoir ou péril?* (Paris: Table ronde, 1984), p.211.

[229] Max Scheler, *Das Ressentiment im Aufbau der Moralen* (Abhandlungen and Aufsäzte) (Leipzig: Verlag der weissen Bücher, 1915), p.58.

[230] Alexis de Tocqueville, *De la démocratie en Amérique,* Vol. II (Paris: Gallimard, 1961), p.193.

Index of Names

CPSIA information can be obtained
at www.ICGtesting.com
Printed in the USA
FSHW022019061119
63845FS